Real World Windows 8 App Development with JavaScript

Create Great Windows Store Apps

Edward Moemeka

Elizabeth Moemeka

Real World Windows 8 App Development with JavaScript: Create Great Windows Store Apps

ISBN-13 (pbk): 978-1-4302-5080-7

ISBN-13 (electronic): 978-1-4302-5081-4

President and Publisher: Paul Manning
Lead Editor: Ben Renow-Clarke
Development Editor: Chris Nelson
Technical Reviewer: Damien Foggon
Editorial Board: Steve Anglin, Mark Beckner, Ewan Buckingham, Gary Cornell, Louise Corrigan, Morgan Ertel, Jonathan Gennick, Jonathan Hassell, Robert Hutchinson, Michelle Lowman, James Markham, Matthew Moodie, Jeff Olson, Jeffrey Pepper, Douglas Pundick, Ben Renow-Clarke, Dominic Shakeshaft, Gwenan Spearing, Matt Wade, Tom Welsh
Coordinating Editor: Anamika Panchoo
Copy Editor: Tiffany Taylor
Compositor: SPi Global
Indexer: SPi Global
Artist: SPi Global
Cover Designer: Anna Ishchenko

Distributed to the book trade worldwide by Springer Science+Business Media New York, 233 Spring Street, 6th Floor, New York, NY 10013. Phone 1-800-SPRINGER, fax (201) 348-4505, e-mail orders-ny@springer-sbm.com, or visit www.springeronline.com. Apress Media, LLC is a California LLC and the sole member (owner) is Springer Science + Business Media Finance Inc (SSBM Finance Inc). SSBM Finance Inc is a Delaware corporation.

For information on translations, please e-mail rights@apress.com, or visit www.apress.com.

Apress and friends of ED books may be purchased in bulk for academic, corporate, or promotional use. eBook versions and licenses are also available for most titles. For more information, reference our Special Bulk Sales–eBook Licensing web page at www.apress.com/bulk-sales.

Any source code or other supplementary materials referenced by the author in this text is available to readers at www.apress.com. For detailed information about how to locate your book's source code, go to www.apress.com/source-code/.

I dedicate this book to the four women without whose love and kindness I would be lost and altogether useless. In order of appearance: my mother, my sister, my wife, and my mother-in-law. Thank you for helping guide me into manhood and fatherhood. To my darling, beautiful boys Alex and Azuka, thank you for introducing me to the full capacity of life in all its crying, laughing, fighting, and hugging mystery. Finally, a special word to my darling wife, who has suffered through nine years with me and shows no signs of wavering (or, more than likely, hides it deftly). If words could match the feeling of gratitude and love I take with me every day that I leave your side and bring back when I return . . .

—Edward Moemeka

I dedicate this book to all my original partners in creative endeavors: Louis, Linda, and Alex. It was a joy exploring the world with you. Without that legacy, I would not have been led to my current partner in creation, exploration, and life.

—Elizabeth Moemeka

Contents at a Glance

Contents

About the Authors

Edward Moemeka is an enterprise architect with over 18 years of experience building, integrating, and delivering high-profile, large-scale applications for clients. He is currently a founding partner of XOCHL LLC, a product development boutique that focuses on using cloud-based technology to enable mobility in the enterprise. XOCHL LLC delivers mobile solutions within the Microsoft product line, specifically Windows Phone, Windows 8, and Windows Azure. Follow Edward at Twitter handle @moemeka.

Elizabeth Moemeka's background spans project management and writing. She is a regular contributor to various newspapers and magazines. She blogs on technology and other subjects of personal interest. She has spent time in many parts of the United States and currently resides with her husband, two sons, and cat in West Hartford, Connecticut.

About the Technical Reviewer

Damien Foggon is a developer, writer, and technical reviewer in cutting-edge technologies and has contributed to more than 50 books on .NET, C#, Visual Basic, and ASP.NET. He is the co-founder of the Newcastle-based user group NEBytes (online at www.nebytes.net), is a multiple MCPD in .NET 2.0 and .NET 3.5, and can be found online at http://blog.fasm.co.uk.

Acknowledgments

We would like to thank Richard and Priscilla Cote for watching their boisterous grandsons whenever uninterrupted hours were needed to dedicate to the writing of this book. We would like to thank Ben Renow-Clarke for reaching out to us with the opportunity, Anamika Panchoo for keeping us on our toes with deadlines, and Damien Foggon and Chris Nelson for reading through our manuscript with a fine-toothed comb.

Introduction

Welcome to *Real World App Development for Windows 8 with JavaScript*. From a technical side, this book provides a step-by-step process for creating Windows 8 apps using JavaScript. From a functional side, this book seeks to inform you about the guidelines, process, and interfaces specific to the Windows 8 OS. Through this book, we hope you'll learn everything you seek for creating as well as publishing your own Windows 8 apps.

Who This Book Is For

You've already picked up the book; so, like us, you've got a passion for cutting-edge technology. We didn't choose to write this book simply based on subject-matter knowledge. We're excited about application development as well as the newest Microsoft user interface, Windows 8—and we're excited about the possibilities, expansion, and impact inherent in both these technological movements.

We should clarify that this is not a beginner's book. To grasp the knowledge and information in this book, you should possess basic skills and a sound understanding of HTML and JavaScript. If you would like to put these skills to work by learning how to program in Windows 8, then this book is for you. In the following chapters, we systematically lay out the tools and tricks of the trade so you can forge ahead with your very own one-of-a-kind app concept and turn it into something real, usable, and out there in the Windows Store—and, more to the point, on peoples' devices, integrated into their lives.

This book's topic is something new and exciting in technology, and you get to be part of this expedition. Microsoft is deeply integrated into the daily lives of millions of individuals and businesses. Windows 8 specifically is Windows reimagined, liberated from the desktop analogy and rooted in the concept of interfacing in a dedicated fashion with whatever the user may be doing. Because of this reimagined concept of Windows, there is a breadth of new information to learn, and there are new ways of looking at the possibilities. In this book, we hope to expand and enrich the opportunities for your own creative and professional endeavors.

What This Book Covers

As the title implies, we use JavaScript and HTML for the development of Windows 8 applications. We rely heavily on samples and examples in this book. The purpose of this approach is to take you by the hand with concrete showing-not-telling instruction.

This book doesn't begin and end with the development of applications. Being a successful app developer goes far beyond a good idea and the ability to develop and write code. This is why we spend significant time on the ins and outs of what it takes to create a final product. We guide you through the process of getting your app into the Windows Store, with instructions on topics such as claiming and naming your app, passing certification, making sure your app meets the technological and appropriateness guidelines, and how to get set up to be a Microsoft vendor.

This book will work for you whether you read it through and learn incrementally, or use it as a reference volume. With clearly laid out chapters and topics, you should feel comfortable turning to this book as a guide along the way as you create your Windows 8 app.

We encourage you to explore the information in this book and to use it as a catalyst toward the success of your own unique great app idea!

■ ■ ■

CHAPTER 1

The Windows 8 Ethos and Environment

Welcome to the brave new world of Windows 8. In this introductory chapter, you take a walk through the new, drastically different UI. You grab a glimpse into the meaning of "Windows reimagined." You begin the exploration of what it means to a Windows app developer when you take away the iconic desktop concept and replace it with full application integration. Technological and social impacts are considered as you, the developer, prep through explanations, examples, and an examination of where the technology melds with the business of life.

Presently, Windows 8 is essentially the only OS out there that can run on anything from a phone all the way up to a personal computer with the diverse reach of languages that are supported natively for Windows 8 development. This book is about one such language—JavaScript—and how you, as a JavaScript developer, can use your knowledge of the language (and of HTML and CSS as a UI layout engine) to build Windows 8 applications that feel to the user as real as applications using .NET or even native C++.

A Not-So-Brief Introduction

To begin, allow us to shed some light on who we are so that you, dear reader, might understand the unique perspective of this book. This is not a book by Microsoft fan-boys, but rather by commonsense, get-the-job-done technology lovers. We also love an opportunity to make money while doing something cool, cutting edge, and meaningful, so when we say that Windows 8 is the most significant opportunity for developers since ... well, ever, take notice. Although this might sound like regurgitated MS marketing spin, we've been on the front API lines, and we boldly claim that everything in Windows 8 *is* reimagined from the ground up, examined, and innovated upon.

Before diving in, it's important to provide an introduction to Windows 8 from a developer's perspective, specifically focusing on how applications work and are managed by the system. The discussion isn't exhaustive, because the subject could probably span multiple books, but it should provide you with a baseline of information in order to understand the basics of Windows 8 and Windows 8 app development using the Windows Runtime.

For the purpose of explanation, let's walk through the Windows 8 UI artifacts—not because you don't already understand how Windows works, but for those of you who may not yet have access to the operating system.

The Windows 8 shell is a sort of digital reverse mullet: party time in the front, and good old-fashioned business behind that. At a first glimpse of Windows 8, you're immediately struck by the party component of the analogy: the Windows 8 Start screen shown in Figure 1-1.

Figure 1-1. *Windows 8 Start screen*

The Windows 8 Start screen is the new—or rather, reimagined—Launchpad for applications. It replaces the Windows Start menu. *This means there is no Start menu on Windows 8*. So don't expect to find some registry hack or setting that will enable it: there is none.

■ **Note**　There are some third-party applications that can be purchased to enhance the Windows 8 experience with a Start menu: Start8 from Stardock, for example.

A lot has been made of the omission of the standard Windows Start menu from Windows 8. The truth is that this is just a semantic removal. If people would calm down, they would realize that *every* feature you've come to love about the Start menu exists in the Start screen, with one difference: the old Start menu doesn't take up the whole screen. In every sense of the word, the new Start screen is a superset and natural evolution of its predecessor, and once people start using it, they quickly recognize this.

■ **Note**　Microsoft published a comprehensive blog outlining the details or the rationale behind many of the Windows 8 features. One such blog posts highlights the complex research that led Microsoft to using the Start screen in Windows 8 in favor of the old Start menu. If you would like to find out more about this, head to the Building Windows 8 blog at `http://blogs.msdn.com/b/b8/`. The specific blog post that walks through the evolution of the Windows Start Screen can be found at `http://blogs.msdn.com/b/b8/archive/2011/10/03/evolving-the-start-menu.aspx`.

In Figure 1-1, the colored rectangles with images in them are a sort of combo launch-point for applications. These magical rectangular surfaces are commonly referred to as *live tiles* and combine the application shortcut (particularly the version of the shortcut you might find on your Windows desktop), the representation of the running state of your application typically found on the taskbar (when your app is running), and the representation of the notification mechanism of your applications found in the system tray area. Figure 1-2 shows two states of the Calendar application live tile. The image to the left is the default state; when a meeting is approaching, the tile takes on a different appearance (right).

Figure 1-2. *A Windows 8 app tile*

An application like Windows Essentials (Windows Live for those of you who still have the earlier version of the application) may have a system tray icon that changes appearance when the application switches from online to offline; it may have a large, beautiful shortcut on the Windows desktop and flash yellow (on Windows 7) when an instant message is sent your way when the application isn't an active window. The Windows 8 live tile encapsulates those three functions in one. Through the live tile, you can of course launch the application; but as shown in Figure 1-2, tiles can also display notifications based on things happening in the application or even on things happening while the application isn't running.

Note that not all tiles on the Start screen are live tiles. Legacy applications such as Visual Studio, Microsoft Word, and Adobe Photoshop can also appear on the Start screen as tiles, but these tiles aren't "live"—they don't possess the ability to present dynamic content on their surface. Legacy Windows application tiles function more or less like the application icons of old (we say "more or less" because Windows 8 exposes some shortcut features to these sorts of tiles that follow patterns similar to their live alternatives, such as being able to launch in administrator mode). Applications built using the new paradigm, which can express themselves through live tiles, are referred to by Microsoft as *Windows 8 apps*. For the remainder of this book, we use this terminology to refer to them. Figure 1-3 shows how a launched Windows 8 modern application looks.

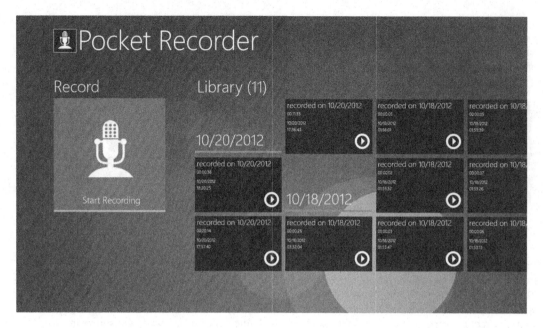

Figure 1-3. *A Windows 8 app*

Notice something missing? It's the ubiquitous *close, minimize, and maximize/restore* buttons. Windows 8 apps take up the entire screen at all times. There is no exception to this rule: even if the plan is to build a simple utility window, you as the developer must consider how you intend to lay things out in a manner that reduces negative space. It's a tough problem, compounded by the variety of screen resolutions your application must support. Later chapters delve more into this as we start to talk about style guidelines and how to pass certification.

Another question that might arise while looking at a launched application is, how do you close it? Traditional Windows development typically delegated application lifecycle management to the user, meaning the user had to explicitly click the close button at upper right. If they didn't, the application continued running. Applications such as Windows Essentials rely on this. Because the system provides no mechanism for automatically closing an application that is no longer in use (or has not been in use for some time), applications like Windows Essentials and Skype can treat a user's *close* request as a *hide* request and continue to run with an invisible window in the background. This wouldn't be a problem if everyone acted with honor and compassion, but it does create security concerns as well as consume system resources—if not unnecessarily, then at least without the user's consent.

Windows 8 strives to *reimagine* this situation by introducing an application lifecycle management model that takes both the user and system resources into account (see Figure 1-4).

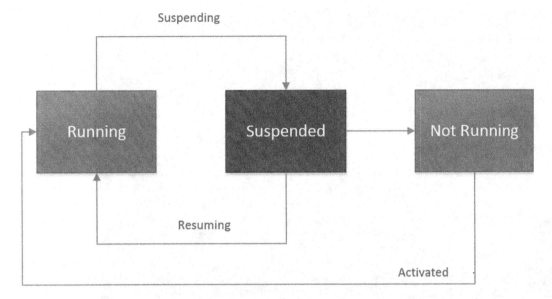

Figure 1-4. *A Windows 8 app's lifecycle*

In Windows 8's "party side," only the presently running application and, potentially, an application that has been chosen by the user to run in the background are active at any given time. All other applications are *suspended*, meaning their memory is intact and in the specified order, but no active threads are running that are owned by the applications. As with a saved file, a suspended application is intact just as it was left. And also like a saved file, which can be opened at any time and continues right where it left off, switching back to a Windows 8 app (or launching it again from the Start screen) takes you right back into it. Between those two states, the Windows 8 system also provides for closing an application if it determines the app needs to be closed. Future chapters talk more about the Windows 8 app lifecycle.

■ **Note**   You might have seen this in a demo of Windows 8 (or in a tutorial that we hope is included in a future version), but a modern application can be forcibly closed by dragging from the top of the application screen to the bottom of the screen ("throwing it away") or by using Alt+F4. An advanced user can also use good old Control Panel to stop a modern app.

One more thing missing from the application—something that is perhaps not as ubiquitous as the close and minimize/maximize buttons, but certainly a well-known Windows application feature—is the *menu bar*. Given that the application takes up the full screen, how commands are represented is probably a concern to any developer. The obvious choice is to put it onscreen, and to be sure, many applications do just that. But this pattern is against the style guidelines prescribed by Microsoft for Windows 8 apps. Instead, the Windows 8 system provides two areas, the *bottom app bar* and the *top app bar*, from which application commands can be launched.

Figure 1-5 shows how applications can use the app bar concept to segregate command functionality in a central location within the application. From here, an end user can launch searches, group recordings by category, clear their entire library, or pin the activity of starting a recording directly to the Windows Start screen. (Pinning and the concept of secondary tiles are discussed in more details in Chapter 6.)

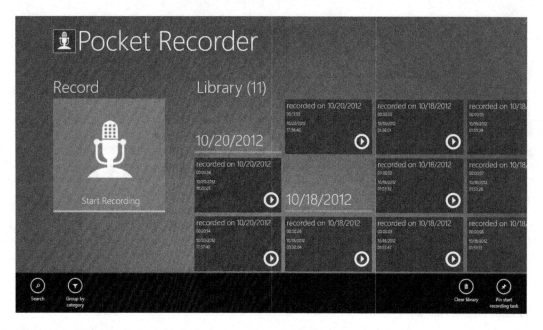

Figure 1-5. *Windows 8 app with the bottom app bar enabled*

In any Windows 8 app, the bottom/top app bar can be activated (made visible) by swiping from either the bottom or the top of the device screen upward or downward, respectively, if touch is enabled.

■ **Note**   Not all Windows 8 devices come touch enabled—or have a mouse, for that matter—so it was important that legacy devices continue to be usable when they upgrade to Windows 8. For this reason, Windows 8 provides mouse and keyboard support for all touch-related functions. To activate the app bar of any application using the mouse, right-click in the application. Using the keyboard, press Windows logo key + Z.

Regardless of the direction from which you swipe, both application bars are displayed. In all cases, the top and bottom of the device screen (and right-clicking, if you're using a mouse and keyboard) belong to the application. The left and right of the screen belong to Windows.

Swiping from the left (Windows logo key + Tab) gives the user access to suspended applications that currently aren't being viewed. Swiping from the right (Windows logo key + C) reveals the *charms*. In Figure 1-6, you can see the Windows 8 charms revealed. Note the information box to the left of the screen, which displays date-time information as well as network and battery status.

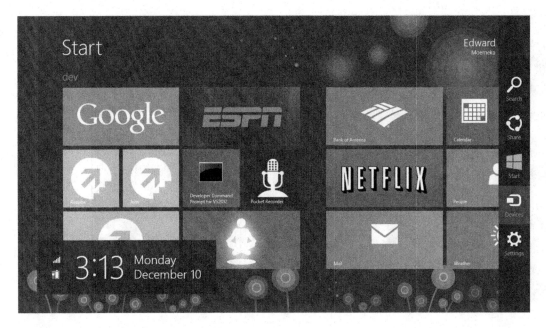

Figure 1-6. *Windows 8 charms displayed. Displaying charms also reveals the date-time, wifi signal status, and battery status in a block at lower left onscreen*

The Windows charms feature is an extremely important innovation. It provides users with the ability to search across all applications on the system (and even within them), share data between applications easily, access devices, and manage settings. Each charm has an exposed programming interface that you, as the Windows 8 developer, can use.

In addition, a developer building modern Windows 8 apps must contend with various system environment changes that applications developed using older frameworks simply don't have to worry about. This is because applications built using the Windows 8 APIs have a level of connectivity to the native OS that hasn't previously existed by default.

One instance of this is with the application *view state*. On devices that support rotation, Windows 8 apps can query the current layout of the system and adjust their UI accordingly. This way, an application can use vertical space that might not be available in landscape mode and horizontal space that might not be available in portrait mode. Examine the Netflix application shown in Figure 1-7 while running on a system where the view is locked in landscape mode.

Figure 1-7. *Netflix app in landscape mode*

The same application on the same system, with the only change being a shift from landscape to portrait mode, alters the UI as shown in Figure 1-8.

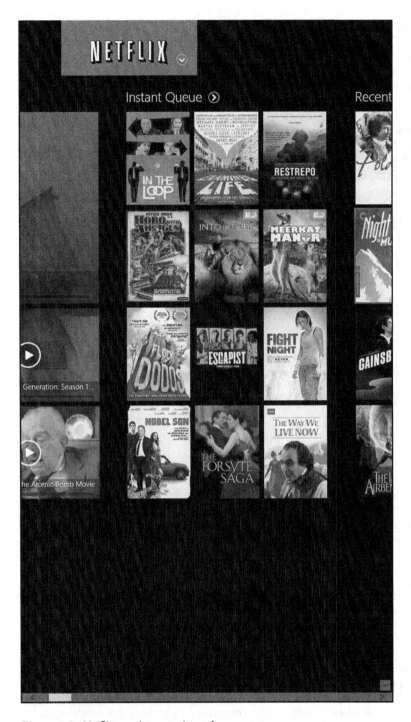

Figure 1-8. *Netflix app in portrait mode*

Building Windows 8 Apps

Windows 8 apps can be built using HTML/JavaScript, .NET languages (C# and VB), or native C/C++ through an extension of C++ called C++/Cx. Regardless of the technology used to develop the application, the Windows team has done a good job of providing a core set of APIs that are projected into each of the target languages. Figure 1-9 provides a layered view of the Windows 8 modern application programming interface.

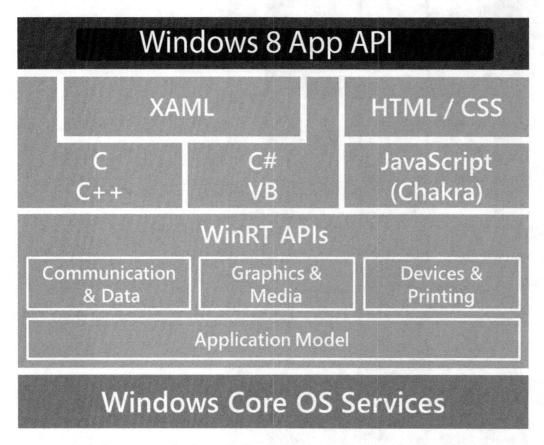

Figure 1-9. *Window 8 app API landscape*

Have you seen another platform that provides this kind power to its developers with that much flexibility? We don't think so. Applications built using these projected APIs end up in a package containing an application's code (in binary or text format); resources; libraries; and a *manifest* that describes the app (names, logos, and so on), its *capabilities* (such as areas of the file system or specific devices like cameras), and everything else that's needed to make the app work (such as *file associations*, declaration of *background tasks*, and so forth). The manifest describes the application to the Windows Store and also to potential Windows clients that download it from the store. The exact workings of the app manifest (as it relates to publishing your application and setting up its permissions) are discussed in Chapter 2.

So far we've discussed Windows 8 and the applications you can build with it in general terms. And to this point, the functionality, process, and partitioning are essentially the same regardless of your choice of development environment. Native development and .NET are great platforms for building Windows applications and do offer some distinct advantages for building Windows 8 apps. Most notable is access to a subset of legacy Win32 APIs. For those who might not be aware, *Win32* is the previous programming platform for building Windows applications. Programs like Adobe Photoshop, Microsoft Word, and Internet Explorer 10 are built using this technology, and it's still available for building Windows 8 apps that run on the desktop (the business side) view of Windows 8.

Windows 8 vs. Win32

The focus of this book is the use of HTML to develop Windows 8 apps, so it's prudent that we highlight some differences between the technologies at this point.

First, it's important to note that both .NET-based and native C++/Cx applications are compiled at build time. *Compilation* is a process to convert the code portion of a given program into an intermediate format that can be easily read by a machine's processor. C++/Cx is compiled directly into processor-specific native code. (This means that choosing to build an application using this technology requires the developer to compile a version for every platform they intend to support. Windows 8 presently supports 64-bit (x64), 32-bit (x86), and ARM-based processors.) .NET compiles the code into a sort of pseudo-binary format referred to as *bytecode*. Bytecode is an intermediate state that allows the application code to be far more portable than native code. This is because the bytecode is processor-architecture agnostic, so the same bytecode can be used on x64, x86, and ARM processors without issue. (Bytecode can accomplish this because it's compiled into native code on the fly at runtime on the target platform in which it's run.)

Windows 8 apps built using JavaScript follow a pattern similar to those built using .NET, but without the intermediate step. The HTML, CSS, and JavaScript code in a Windows 8 JavaScript application is always parsed, compiled, and rendered at runtime, so your application code is always transported in its entirety to every client it runs on. Furthermore, because these file types aren't directly executable, the Windows system must provide a hosting process in which to run them (similar to how these file types are usually run in the context of a web browser).

Because of this distinction between the two (native/.NET and JavaScript), and because the designers wanted to build a Windows developer experience for the targeted platforms that is as real and natural to the given platform developer as any other activities they might do in that space, many of the APIs and controls you're exposed to as a JavaScript developer building Windows 8 apps are provided through a complementary library tailored specifically to JavaScript development: the *Windows Library for JavaScript* (*WinJS*). For example, developers using C# or C++/Cx lay out their UIs and build or access system controls using a technology called Extensible Application Markup Language (XAML) as shown in Listing 1-1.

Listing 1-1. XAML Markup

```
<Page x:Class="AllLearnings.Samples.ApplicationBars.AppBarSamples"
    xmlns="http://schemas.microsoft.com/winfx/2006/xaml/presentation"
    xmlns:x="http://schemas.microsoft.com/winfx/2006/xaml"
    xmlns:d="http://schemas.microsoft.com/expression/blend/2008"
    xmlns:mc="http://schemas.openxmlformats.org/markup-compatibility/2006"
    mc:Ignorable="d"
    >
    <Page.BottomAppBar>
        <AppBar x:Name="appbar_bottom" VerticalAlignment="Bottom" Height="100"  >

            <Grid>
                <Button x:Name="btn_bottomone" Visibility="Visible" Content="+" ↵
                    AutomationProperties.Name="Add"  HorizontalAlignment="Right" ↵
                    VerticalAlignment="Top" Style="{StaticResource AppBarButtonStyle}"
                />
            </Grid>
        </AppBar>
    </Page.BottomAppBar>
    <Grid x:Name="LayoutRoot"  >
```

```
        <TextBlock>This sample tests the app bar functionality, right click or swipe from ↵
                the bottom to open the bottom app bar.</TextBlock>
    </Grid>
</Page>
```

On the other hand, you, as a HTML/JavaScript developer, can use HTML/CSS as the layout engine to design your UI and JavaScript to manipulate it in the same manner you would a web application (see Listing 1-2)!

Listing 1-2. HTML Markup

```
<!DOCTYPE html>
<html>
<head>
        <meta charset="utf-8" />
        <title>TestAppBars</title>

        <!-- WinJS references -->
        <link href="//Microsoft.WinJS.1.0/css/ui-dark.css" rel="stylesheet" />
        <script src="//Microsoft.WinJS.1.0/js/base.js"></script>
        <script src="//Microsoft.WinJS.1.0/js/ui.js"></script>
        <link href="TestAppBars.css" rel="stylesheet" />
        <script src="TestAppBars.js"></script>
</head>
<body>

  <section aria-label="Main content" role="main" style="margin-left: 100px;">
    <p>This sample tests the app bar functionality, right click or ↵
      swipe from the bottom to open the bottom app bar.</p>
  </section>
        <div data-win-control="WinJS.UI.AppBar" >
        <button id="btn_bottomone" data-win-control="WinJS.UI.AppBarCommand" ↵
                data-win-options="{id:'cmdAdd',label:'Add',icon:'add', ↵
                        section:'global',tooltip:'Add item'}">
        </button>
        </div>
</body>
</html>
```

Additionally, you as the developer are free to use whatever third-party modules you want (again in the same manner as is customary to an HTML CSS/ JavaScript developer). The example in Listing 1-3 selects and colorizes a specified class of element using the ever-popular and near-ubiquitous jQuery.

Listing 1-3. Using jQuery with HTML in a Web Application

```
<!DOCTYPE html>
<html xmlns="http://www.w3.org/1999/xhtml">
<head>
    <title></title>
    <script type="text/javascript" src="/Scripts/jquery-1.7.2.js"></script>
    <script type="text/javascript">
        $(document).ready(function ()
```

```
        {
            $("#btn_clickme")
            .mouseenter(function (e)
            {
                $(this).css("background-color", "lightblue");
            })

            .mouseout(function (e)
            {
                $(this).css("background-color", "slategray");
            })

            .click(function (e)
            {
                var txt_alerttext = document.getElementById("txt_alerttext");
                if (txt_alerttext != null)
                {
                    alert(txt_alerttext.value);
                }
            });
        });
    </script>
    <style>
        * {
            font-family: 'Segoe UI';
        }

        .canvas {
            width: 100%;
            height: 100%;
            position: absolute;
            left: 0px;
            top: 0px;
            background-color: white;
        }

        .dtable {
            display: table;
            margin: 200px auto 0px auto;
            width: 800px;
            background-color: ghostwhite;
            height: 300px;
            padding-left: 40px;
            padding-top: 10px;
        }

        .drow {
            display: table-row;
        }
```

```
        .dcell {
            display: table-cell;
            vertical-align: top;
            margin-left: auto;
            margin-right: auto;
        }

        #btn_clickme {
            background-color: slategray;
            border: none;
            width: 100px;
            height: 30px;
        }
    </style>
</head>
<body>
    <div class="canvas">
        <div class="dtable">
            <div class="drow">
                <div class="dcell">
                </div>
                <div class="dcell">
                    <div style="font-size: 24pt; font-family: Calibri">
                        Sample Application running on the web
                    </div>
                    <div style="height: 10px"></div>
                    <div>
                        <input id="txt_alerttext" type="text" style="height: 25px" />
                        <button id="btn_clickme">Click Me</button>
                    </div>
                </div>
            </div>
        </div>
    </div>
</body>
</html>
```

The example uses jQuery to select items on a web page's document structure and react to events within it. It also shows the use of CSS to control the layout of a very simple page. Running this application in a web browser should produce a layout like the one shown in Figure 1-10.

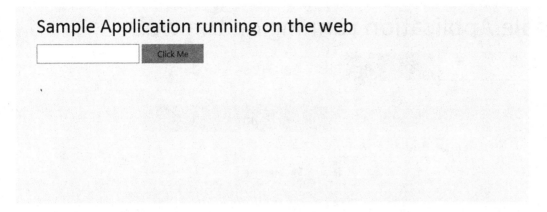

Figure 1-10. *Simple web application layout*

Notice that if you place your mouse over the Click Me button, the button changes colors. This is enabled by the jQuery instructions in Listing 1-4.

Listing 1-4. jQuery Handling Events on Elements That It Selects

```
.mouseenter(function (e)
{
    $(this).css("background-color", "lightblue");
})

.mouseout(function (e)
{
    $(this).css("background-color", "slategray");
})
```

jQuery simply listens for the user's mouse to enter the bounds of the target element, in this case the button with the identifier #btn_clickme. When the mouse has entered, the button's background color changes to lightblue; when the mouse exits, the color changes back to slategray. The jQuery code also listens for the button to be clicked and, when it is, presents a dialog box with the text entered in the text box. Figure 1-11 shows how the UI looks when this happens.

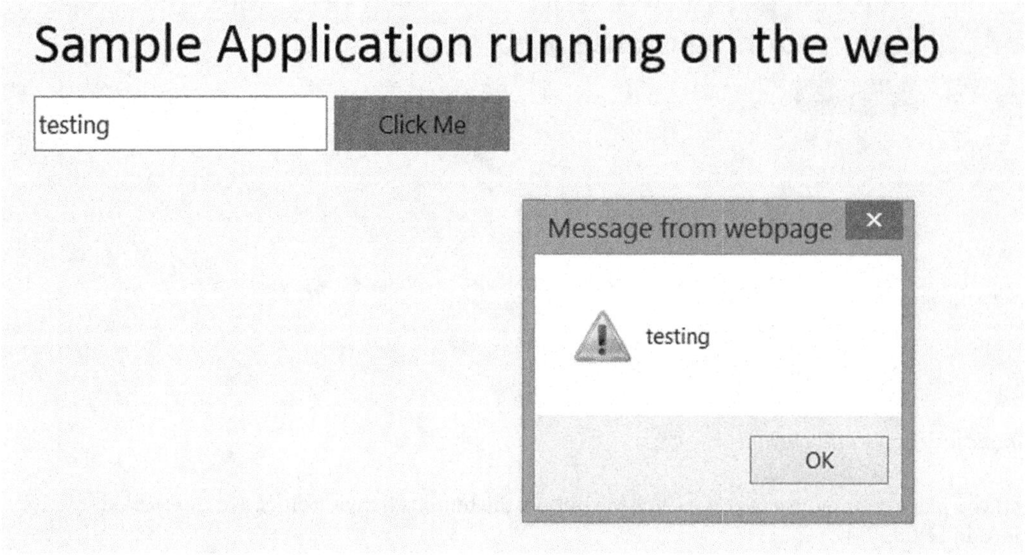

Sample Application running on the web

testing   Click Me

Message from webpage   ✕

⚠ testing

OK

Figure 1-11. *Result of a simple web application button click*

The code in Listing 1-3 can be copied verbatim (for the most part) into a Windows 8 app that targets JavaScript and, with very few changes, made to work. Listing 1-5 illustrates this, with bolded text indicating areas where changes have been made.

Listing 1-5. Windows 8 App Using jQuery

```
<!DOCTYPE html>
<html xmlns="http://www.w3.org/1999/xhtml">
<head>
    <title></title>
    <script type="text/javascript" src="/Scripts/jquery-1.7.2.js"></script>
    <script type="text/javascript">
        $(document).ready(function ()
        {
            $("#btn_clickme")
            .mouseenter(function (e)
            {
                $(this).css("background-color", "lightblue");
            })

            .mouseout(function (e)
            {
                $(this).css("background-color", "slategray");
            })

            .click(function (e)
            {
                var txt_alerttext = document.getElementById("txt_alerttext");
                if (txt_alerttext != null)
```

```
                {
                    //alert(txt_alerttext.value);
                    var v = new Windows.UI.Popups.MessageDialog(txt_alerttext.value);
                    v.showAsync();
                }
            });
        });
    </script>
    <style>
        * {
            font-family: 'Segoe UI';
        }

        .canvas {
            width: 100%;
            height: 100%;
            position: absolute;
            left: 0px;
            top: 0px;
            background-color: white;
        }

        .dtable {
            display: table;
            margin: 200px auto 0px auto;
            width: 800px;
            background-color: ghostwhite;
            height: 300px;
            padding-left: 40px;
            padding-top: 10px;
        }

        .drow {
            display: table-row;
        }

        .dcell {
            display: table-cell;
            vertical-align: top;
            margin-left: auto;
            margin-right: auto;
        }

        #btn_clickme {
            background-color: slategray;
            border: none;
            width: 100px;
            height: 30px;
        }
    </style>
```

```
</head>
<body>
    <div class="canvas">
        <div class="dtable">
            <div class="drow">
                <div class="dcell">
                </div>
                <div class="dcell">
                    <div style="font-size: 24pt; font-family: Calibri;">
                        Sample Application running on Windows 8
                    </div>
                    <div style="height: 10px"></div>
                    <div>
                        <input id="txt_alerttext" type="text" style="height: 25px" />
                        <button id="btn_clickme">Click Me</button>
                    </div>
                </div>
            </div>
        </div>
    </div>
</body>
</html>
```

From the example, you can see that there are very few items you need to change in order to get the code running. You explicitly set the background color of the application title (and change the text). Also, because the Windows 8 APIs don't support the HTML alert feature, you have to comment out that line and instead use a similar API designed specifically for Windows 8. Running this sample produces the behavior in Figures 1-12 and 1-13. The two figures represent an application before (Figure 1-12) and after (Figure 1-13) the Click Me button is clicked.

Figure 1-12. *Windows 8 app using jQuery*

As you can see in Listing 1-5, you include the jQuery libraries in the same manner in both scenarios, and you call and use them the same way. They produce the same result even though one is a web application and the other a Windows 8 app.

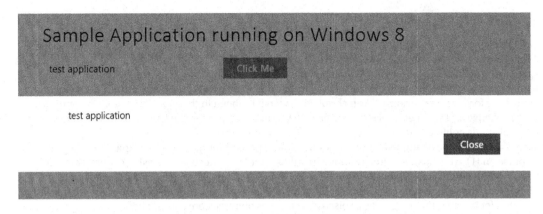

Figure 1-13. *Windows 8 app using a jQuery* `MessageDialog` *alert*

Developing for Windows 8 Apps

Now that you have a basic introduction to Windows 8, what Windows 8 apps look like, what technologies are out there to build Windows 8 apps, and where JavaScript fits into the equation, you're ready to start building samples and getting on your way to being the next Instagram.

Setting Up Your Environment

Before you begin, you need a couple of things. First, to build Windows applications and work through the samples in this book, you need a copy of Windows 8. You also need the Windows 8 SDK and, at the very least, a copy of Visual Studio Express 2012. The download links for the required tools are listed in Table 1-1. Please note that installing Visual Studio Express installs everything you need (including the necessary jQuery libraries). The other items are included in the table in case you ever need a specific component.

Table 1-1. *Windows 8 Development Environment Setup*

Tool	Location
JQuery	http://jquery.com/download/
Windows 8	http://windows.microsoft.com/en-US/windows-8/release-preview
Visual Studio Express	www.microsoft.com/visualstudio/eng/products/visual-studio-express-products
Windows 8 SDK	http://msdn.microsoft.com/en-us/windows/hardware/hh852363.aspx

Of course, because this is JavaScript development, much of the layout and functionality can potentially be achieved without any of this. If you have a simple text editor and web browser, you can follow along to a certain extent. This changes when you get to working with controls and integrating with the Windows system, so we recommend downloading the bits and using the SDK in those scenarios.

Getting Started with HTML

We have no doubt that many of you reading this book have some working knowledge of HTML, CSS, and JavaScript coming into Windows 8 app development. This is a primary reason for JavaScript being included as one of the development paradigms on which Windows 8 apps can be built. HTML/CSS and JavaScript are simply too popular at this point, with too many proponents and day-to-day users, for them to be ignored anymore as they have been by major players in the platform game previously. As technologists who have been in this game for years, we continue to be amazed by the resilience and sheer elegance of JavaScript. If you asked anyone in the late 1990s if JavaScript would be the king of the hill at this point, the answer would have been a resounding no.

Working knowledge and preexisting skill notwithstanding, it's important for the sake of completeness to present a brief refresher course on HTML/CSS here. Already know the subject and don't need the refresher? Great: you can skip ahead two sections to "Extending HTML5 for Windows 8" and continue reading. For the rest of you, welcome!

HTML5 is a general umbrella term that describes a set of related technologies used to make modern, rich web content. These technologies are numerous, but this discussion focuses on three core components:

- HTML5 itself, which defines the actual elements used to markup content

- Cascading Style Sheets 3 (CSS 3.0), which allows for discrete control of the appearance of marked-up elements

- JavaScript, which serves as a programming interface with which to build interactivity and program logic into an HTML document

HTML allows for the application of markup of some sort to content. In this definition, *markup* is typically an element (we go into what an element is shortly), and *content* can be text. You've already seen two examples of HTML in the previous section. The excerpt from Listing 1-3 shown in Listing 1-6 illustrates the basic features of a simple HTML document.

Listing 1-6. Two HTML Elements

```
<input id="txt_alerttext" type="text" style="height: 25px" />
<button id="btn_clickme">Click Me</button>
<title class="site-heading">Sample Document Title</title>
```

Elements in HTML have three primary parts: the start tag, the content, and the end tag. As is evident from this example, the start tag always begins with the less-than angle bracket followed by the element name. (See Listing 1-7 for the start tag on its own. You can find a list of element names at www.w3.org/TR/html-markup/elements.html.) The end tag begins the same as the start tag but has a forward slash before the tag name (see Listing 1-8). In the first line of Listing 1-6, input is an empty HTML element type, so it has no end tag. Such HTML elements end with a forward slash and the greater-than sign.

Listing 1-7. Start Tag for an HTML Element

```
<title class="site-heading">
```

Listing 1-8. End Tag for an HTML Element

```
</title>
```

Elements help you as the developer semantically describe content in a platform-agnostic way. Consequently, each element has an associated meaning. In the example, using the title tag to wrap the content indicates to any reader, human or otherwise, that the content contained within the element is a document title. A web browser might read this and render the text "Sample Document Title" in bold. A search engine bot might index the page based on the terms *Sample, Document, Title,* and *Sample Document Title,* so that if you typed **Sample Document Title** into, say, Google, the example page would appear. Some common elements and their meanings are listed in Table 1-2.

Table 1-2. *Elements and Their Meanings*

Element Name	Description
html	Outermost tag indicating that text is HTML
head	Provides information about the document
title	Provides the title of the document
script	Inline script ensuring upward compatibility
style	Style information ensuring upward compatibility
body	Document body containing the contents of the document
input	Generates buttons, input fields, and check boxes
a	Anchor tag for hypertext documents
hr	Draws horizontal rules across the browser window

Elements can be *void* (meaning the tag doesn't need to be closed). A perfect example is the hr tag, which can be used to represent a horizontal line the width of its container. These days, many developers write void elements as self-closing empty elements. So, <hr> becomes <hr />. Closing void element tags allows HTML documents to be processed as XML documents (a superset of HTML) by XML parsers (a document type referred to as *XHTML*).

Elements can be further tailored by using attributes in the start tag to configure them. An *attribute* is essentially a name-value pair represented in a *name=value* syntax in an element's start tag. The input tag uses the type element to specify the kind of input expected. An input type of button draws a button, and an input type of text draws a text box. Listing 1-9 illustrates this point.

Listing 1-9. Changing the type Attribute of the input Element

```
<input type="text" value="input is text" />
<input type="button" value="input is button" />
```

Listing 1-9 presents two input elements, one with the type attribute set to text and the other with type set to button. If you run this in a browser or on Windows 8, the application displays as shown in Figure 1-14.

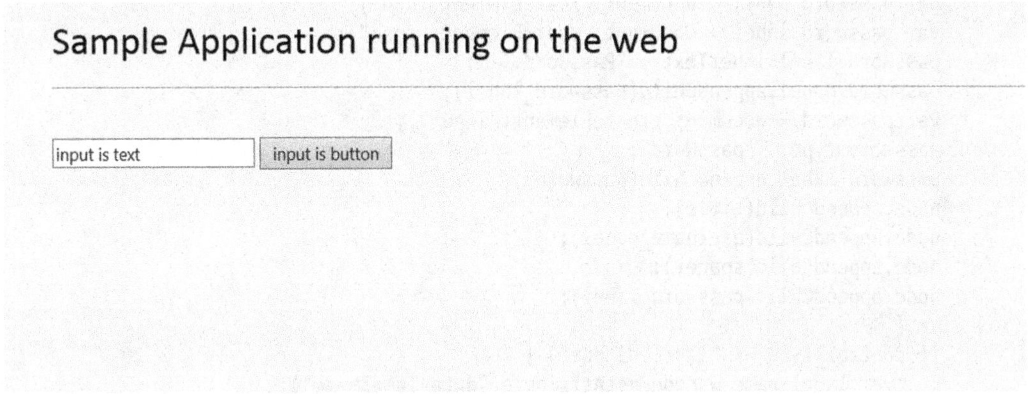

Sample Application running on the web

```
input is text        input is button
```

Figure 1-14. *Two input elements with different type attributes*

Provided the element supports them, you can add any number of attributes to achieve the desired effect. In general, attributes added to an element are of two varieties. *Global* attributes can be added to every element. These include the id attribute, the Style tag, and the Class tag. You saw all three of these global attribute types in Listing 1-3.

Elements may also define individual attributes that are specific to them. The image element, for instance, has the src attribute, which is used to indicate the location, relative to the root, of the image to be displayed (src can also point to an absolute location).

HTML also provides for the creation of author-defined attributes in scenarios where you would like to add more metadata to an element than is defined by the HTML standard. Author-defined attributes are ignored by the browser but serve as great waypoints for JavaScript injections because they're discoverable through the browser DOM. This technique is commonly used to inject HTML into the DOM at a specific place in the document. You can indicate that an attribute is author defined by prepending data- to it (see Listing 1-10).

Listing 1-10. Using Author-Defined Attributes as Placeholders for Controls

```
window.onload = function () {
    var list = document.getElementsByTagName("div");
    for(var i = 0; i < list.length; i++) {
        var node = list.item(i);
        if(node != null) {
            var islogincontrol = node.hasAttribute("data-controls");
            if(islogincontrol) {
                var control_type = node.getAttribute("data-controls");
                if(control_type == "logincontrol") {
                    var title_panel = document.createElement("div");
                    var title = document.createElement("span");
                    title_panel.appendChild(title);
                    var username_panel = document.createElement("div");
                    var username_label = document.createElement("span");
                    username_label.innerText = "Username: ";
                    username_panel.appendChild(username_label);
                    var username = document.createElement("input");
                    username.type = "text";
                    username_panel.appendChild(username);
                    var spacer = document.createElement("div");
                    spacer.style.height = "5px";
                    var password_panel = document.createElement("div");
                    var password_label = document.createElement("span");
                    password_label.innerText = "Password:   ";
                    password_panel.appendChild(password_label);
                    var password = document.createElement("input");
                    password.type = "password";
                    password_label.appendChild(password);
                    node.appendChild(title);
                    node.appendChild(username_panel);
                    node.appendChild(spacer);
                    node.appendChild(password_label);
                } else {
                    if(control_type == "labeledinput") {
                        var label_name = node.getAttribute("data-labelname");
                        var username_panel = document.createElement("div");
                        var username_label = document.createElement("span");
                        username_label.innerText = label_name;
```

```
                    username_panel.appendChild(username_label);
                    var username = document.createElement("input");
                    username.type = "text";
                    username_panel.appendChild(username);
                    node.appendChild(username_panel);
                }
            }
        }
    }
}
};
```

The pattern applied in Listing 1-10 is a simplified but common approach to using author-defined attributes to attach composite controls to an HTML page. Composite controls are wonderful tool for increasing development efficiency because they encapsulate multiple simple controls and associated canned behaviors into a single controllable entity that can configured through a centralized mechanism. For instance, if an application you're developing requires username and password text fields with identifying labels, you can instead create a Login control. This control can encapsulate all the necessary functionality for logging in to your site into one code base that can then be reused everywhere you need this functionality.

This is the power of controls, and *expando* controls enabled through the use of author-defined attributes allow JavaScript developers to do just this. The example in Listing 1-10 searches the DOM tree for div controls. The call to document.getElementsByTagName("div") does this and returns a list of each element that matches the tag name specified in the parameter (in this case div). Once returned, you simply loop through the list, querying each element to see if it defines the attribute data-controls. If that attribute is defined on the control, you read its value to determine which type of control to generate. When the control type is logincontrol, you generate a text box, a password box, and two spans—username and password—associated with them, respectively. When the control type is labeledinput you generate a text box and span combination. In the case of labeledinput, you expect another attribute to be defined, data-labelname, and you use its value as the innerText of the span that labels the text box. (Note that for the purpose of brevity, not all checks have been applied to the example code. In a real-world scenario, you would want to check to see if data-labelname is defined and not just expect it to be there.)

Listing 1-11 shows how the HTML for this application might look.

Listing 1-11. Using Author-Defined Attributes to Create Composite Controls

```html
<!DOCTYPE html>
<html xmlns="http://www.w3.org/1999/xhtml">
<head>
    <title></title>
    <script type="text/javascript" src="Scripts/ExpandoFile.js"></script>

    <style>
        * {
            font-family: 'Segoe UI';
        }

        .canvas {
            width: 100%;
            height: 100%;
            position: absolute;
            left: 0px;
            top: 0px;
            background-color: white;
        }
```

```
        .dtable {
            display: table;
            margin: 200px auto 0px auto;
            width: 800px;
            background-color: ghostwhite;
            height: 300px;
            padding-left: 40px;
            padding-top: 10px;
        }

        .drow {
            display: table-row;
        }

        .dcell {
            display: table-cell;
            vertical-align: top;
            margin-left: auto;
            margin-right: auto;
        }

    </style>
</head>
<body>
    <div class="canvas">
        <div class="dtable">

            <div class="drow">
                <div class="dcell">
                </div>
                <div class="dcell">
                    <div style="font-size: 24pt; font-family: Calibri">
                        Sample Application using custom controls
                    </div>
                    <div style="height: 10px"></div>
                    <hr />
                    <div data-controls="logincontrol" >
                    </div>
                    <div data-controls="labeledinput"  ↵
                        data-labelname="Some Information:"></div>
                </div>
            </div>
        </div>
    </div>
</body>
</html>
```

Run the code from Listing 1-11 in your browser, and you should see the page shown in Figure 1-15.

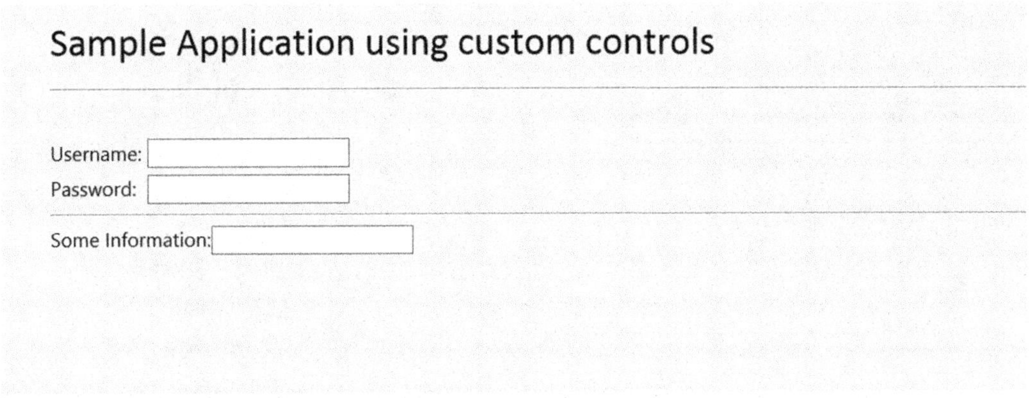

Sample Application using custom controls

Username: [   ]
Password: [   ]

Some Information: [   ]

Figure 1-15. *Custom controls injected onto a page dynamically*

Right-click the web page and open the source for this file, and you should notice something interesting: the source for this HTML document doesn't contain any of the elements or content that you see in the browser view. This is because that content is created dynamically and injected into the DOM.

Getting Started with CSS

One architectural philosophy on which HTML has prided itself since … maybe day two, is the separation of semantic markup from the appearance of that markup (with exceptions to that rule, of course). In the world of HTML, CSS provides you with the ability to perform this separation of semantic markup from the appearance of that markup initially or later. You've already seen what style sheets can do, as early as Listing 1-3 and as recently as Listing 1-11. If you remove the inline style sheet associated with the HTML page from Figure 1-15, it looks like Figure 1-16.

Sample Application using custom controls

Username: [   ]
Password: [   ]

Some Information: [   ]

Figure 1-16. *Application without styles*

This sample of what HTML looks like without styles only scratches the surface. Consider the site www.csszengarden.com/ (see Figures 1-17 and 1-18), and you begin to get a sense of how powerful CSS is and how much control it has over the layout of an HTML document (when you structure the HTML document such that it relinquishes layout and appearance concerns and focuses exclusively on semantic markup).

Figure 1-17. *CSS Zen garden default style*

Figure 1-18. *CSS Zen garden Under the Sea! template*

As you can see in the two figures, the same content in the Zen garden site can have a drastically different presentation simply by modifying the CSS styles associated with it. CSS is so broad a subject that this book can only give you a general understanding of the effects of its powers without overwhelming you. So, we suggest researching CSS through other means. There are more than a few sources available on the web that should do the trick, in addition books such as *Beginning HTML5 and CSS3: The Web Evolved* (Apress, 2012).

Extending HTML5 for Windows 8

Recall the discussion in the section "Getting Started with HTML" about author-created attributes. HTML5 hosts generally ignore attributes they don't understand, and this can be used as an insertion point for new content added to the DOM. In the example scenario, a login control and labeled text box were added to a div in a document based on searching the entire DOM tree for that special attribute and injecting the new HTML into any element that defined that attribute. As mentioned, this is an age-old technique for building UI functionality into HTML as custom controls.

Now, remember when we said that the HTML/CSS/JavaScript implementation of Windows 8 app development was designed specifically to tailor the development process to HTML/CSS/JavaScript developers? We talked about WinJS and how it's a natural bridge between JavaScript and the Windows Runtime (WinRT), injecting itself where necessary but only in a JavaScript-compliant way. This convergence of JavaScript and WinRT is never more evident than in the choice for implementing controls in the technology space.

In the HTML approach to Windows 8 development, extensions to the language used to support HTML development like the controls you built are implemented using author created attributes applied to preexisting controls like divs much like the example from Listing 1-11. This is achieved through two attributes: data-win-control, which indicates to the runtime what control you want expanded into the identified div area; and data-win-options, which lets you pass individual configuration parameters (much like attributes) into the selected control. More specifically, in the data-win-control attribute, you must specify the fully qualified name of a public constructor function that creates the actual control; and in the data-win-options attribute, you must specify a JSON string that can be used to configure that control object.

Additionally, in your actual JavaScript code you must call either WinJS.UI.process or WinJS.UI.processAll() to initiate the process of expanding the control into its container (in this case, a div). The Windows 8 app bar provides a basic yet clear example of using controls. Figure 1-5 showed the app bar for an application, and Listing 1-12 provides the HTML for creating one.

Listing 1-12. AppBar Control Added to the Bottom of the Page

```
<!DOCTYPE html>
<html>
<head>
    <meta charset="utf-8" />
    <title>TestAppBars</title>

    <!-- WinJS references -->
    <link href="//Microsoft.WinJS.1.0/css/ui-dark.css" rel="stylesheet" />
    <script src="//Microsoft.WinJS.1.0/js/base.js"></script>
    <script src="//Microsoft.WinJS.1.0/js/ui.js"></script>

    <link href="TestAppBars.css" rel="stylesheet" />
    <script src="TestAppBars.js"></script>
</head>
<body>

        <section aria-label="Main content" role="main" style="margin-left: 100px;">
                <p>This sample tests the app bar functionality</p>
        </section>
    <div data-win-control="WinJS.UI.AppBar" style="height:300px">
        <button id="btn_add" data-win-control="WinJS.UI.AppBarCommand" data-win- options= ↵
            "{id:'cmdAdd',label:'Add',icon:'add',section:'global',tooltip:'Add item'}">
        </button>
    </div>
</body>
</html>
```

Page/Navigation Model

The previous section talked about how the HTML used in Windows 8 development can be extended through author-generated attributes to include powerful new functionality that targets Windows 8. One of the primary (and most recognizable) features of HTML is the ability to link documents by using links in a given document or by having JavaScript call out to APIs that allow it to change the location the browser is currently pointing to. In web applications, application context is commonly managed on the server side, with the HTML/JavaScript presentation layer mainly as a thin stateless skin the user can use to initiate interaction. Windows 8 apps, at least their local parts, aren't server based. Rather, as stated earlier, all the display and code needed to execute and manage execution are downloaded and interpreted at runtime. This includes whatever state-management mechanism is baked into the code. Unlike our cousins on the .NET and native side, there is no sense of a consistent, in-memory, global application state inherently built into HTML. It collects variables, it renders views, and it computes values, but once you leave the current page and move to another, all that state, all content, and, worse yet, your entire script context are lost. The next page has to rebuild that context (even if it had previously already JITed it). Using some of the built-in features of Windows 8, like access to the file system or your application's settings container, you can create an IO bound version of that global context (from the standpoint of variables not context sharing). But that would be too complicated for the little bit of functionality it provides.

The Windows runtime for JavaScript introduces a new navigation paradigm to help resolve this issue. Using it, you're guaranteed the notion of a shared in-memory context across pages and a maintained visual fidelity as your application switches between views. The runtime achieves this by abandoning the notion of the full screen re-rendering in favor of *DOM injection*. If you recall, Listing 1-10 showed how new elements can be injected into a preexisting HTML document based at some insertion point determined by your function. The previous section showed how this is used to extend HTML with powerful new controls when running in Windows 8. Listing 1-13 illustrates how you can achieve navigation using the WinJS.Navigation object (it uses similar techniques under the hood).

Listing 1-13. Navigation Using Partial Documents

```
<!DOCTYPE html>
<html>
<head>
    <meta charset="utf-8" />
    <title>AllLearnings_html</title>

    <!-- WinJS references -->
    <link href="//Microsoft.WinJS.1.0/css/ui-dark.css" rel="stylesheet" />
    <script src="//Microsoft.WinJS.1.0/js/base.js"></script>
    <script src="//Microsoft.WinJS.1.0/js/ui.js"></script>

    <!-- AllLearnings_html references -->
    <link href="/css/default.css" rel="stylesheet" />
    <script src="/js/default.js"></script>
</head>
<body>
    <div class="TestAppBars fragment" style="height: 150px; background-color: #6E1313;">
        <div style="height: 50px;"></div>
        <header aria-label="Header content" role="banner" ↵
                style="margin-top: 0px; ↵
                vertical-align: bottom;">
            <h1 class="titlearea win-type-ellipsis" ↵
                style="margin-left: 100px;">
                <button id="btn_back"
                        class="win-backbutton" aria-label="Back" ↵
                        type="button" ↵
```

```
                  style="margin-left: 0px; margin-right: 20px; ↵
                      visibility: collapse;"></button>
              <span id="txt_title" class="pagetitle">Select a sample</span>
          </h1>
      </header>
  </div>
  <div id="frame" style="margin-top: 10px;">
  </div>
</body>
</html>
```

The first part of the example creates the general layout for the application. Notice the div with the id of frame. This is the target for the HTML injection you perform. Navigating with the WinJS Navigation class uses a callback model based on calls to the navigate command. Let's look at the JavaScript code for this in Listing 1-14.

Listing 1-14. Code-Behind for Navigation

```
(function ()
{
    "use strict";

    WinJS.Binding.optimizeBindingReferences = true;

    var app = WinJS.Application;
    var activation = Windows.ApplicationModel.Activation;
    var stack = new Stack();

    app.onactivated = function (args)
    {
        if (args.detail.kind === activation.ActivationKind.launch)
        {
            args.setPromise(WinJS.UI.processAll().then(function ()
            {
                WinJS.Navigation.navigate("samplelist.html");
            }));
        }

        var btn_back = document.getElementById("btn_back");
        btn_back.onclick = function ()
        {
            WinJS.Navigation.back();
        };
    };

    WinJS.Navigation.addEventListener("navigated", function (args)
    {
        //find the frame
        var frame = document.getElementById("frame");

        //clear the frame
        WinJS.Utilities.empty(frame);
```

```
        //stack.Push(args.detail.location);
        if (WinJS.Navigation.canGoBack)
            btn_back.style.visibility = "visible";
        else
            btn_back.style.visibility = "collapse";

        if (args.detail.state != null)
            txt_title.textContent = args.detail.state;

        //render the location onto the frame
        args.detail.setPromise(WinJS.UI.Pages.render(args.detail.location, frame, ↵
            args.detail.state));

    });

    app.start();
})();
```

There are two components to navigating between pages using the WinJS framework. First is the call to the navigate() function of the WinJS.Navigation class—passing in the name of the target page to which you want to navigated. This call is just one part of the equation, though. Before this call is made, the application should provide a handler for the navigated event. This handler lets your application receive any navigation requests and load the appropriate content onto the target div specified in listing 1-13. Another piece of the navigation puzzle is the WinJS. UI.Pages class. The Pages class has a render function that takes arbitrary HTML "pages" (essentially, loosely coupled HTML files) and inserts them into the DOM, giving the illusion of navigation. The process of executing the navigation is relatively straightforward:

1. Find the insertion point (in this case, the div name's frame).

2. Clear the insertion point of any child content from a previous navigation.

3. Pass the page name (through the args.detail.location property, which is retrieved from the event arguments passed into the navigated function), frame instance name, and any navigation state through the args.detail.state property. args.detail.state is accessed through the same event argument object, navigated. (Chapter 2 goes over navigation in greater detail.)

Listing 1-15 illustrates the pattern for handling navigation in JavaScript.

Listing 1-15. Handling Page Navigation

```
//find the frame
var frame = document.getElementById("frame");

 //clear the frame
WinJS.Utilities.empty(frame);

//navigate to the page
args.detail.setPromise(WinJS.UI.Pages.render(args.detail.location, frame, args.detail.state));
```

Promises and the New Asynchronous Programming Model

Traditionally, calling functions in JavaScript happens in a synchronous manner, meaning the caller waits while the called function completes before continuing. In scenarios where the called function is long-running—for instance, if it needs to download additional HTML to inject into the DOM from a server—the entire application may appear unresponsive. This is because JavaScript is single threaded, meaning, among other things, that the UI, UI events, and code share the same thread. If this thread is frozen while waiting for a response from some long-running function call, the user can't interact with any UI elements on the screen.

Callbacks are a popular approach to addressing this limitation. This approach is used across multiple applications to solve this very problem, and it works well. In fact, if technical implementation was the only concern, there would be no need to innovate further in this space.

The issue with callbacks is that they can drastically alter program flow because of the inherent non-deterministic nature of their execution. Examine the application in Listing 1-16. An asynchronous, long-running function is called, which accepts two callbacks. Each callback performs its own long-running operations as well.

Listing 1-16. Long-Running Asynchronous Process Test

```
function LongRunning(callback_one, callback_two)
{
    //perform long-running process
    var response = callback_one();
    callback_two(response);
}

//call method
LongRunning(function ()
{
    //do something async here
}, function (args)
{
    //then do something async here as well
});
```

Even if, as in the example, callback_one is called before callback_two, there is no guarantee what order the callbacks will be executed in, so there is no way to resynchronize the results in a serial manner. This is the fundamental problem with asynchrony: it must be programmed in a synchronous manner to maintain meaningfulness to the programmer, because it exists within a synchronous logic stream and programming construct. Callbacks disconnect the programmer from the synchronous constructs of the underlying language. In small cases it may have no impact, but once you start moving to scenarios where the asynchronicity must be synchronized (as in the example), you run into issues.

WinJS uses the concept of *promises* to reduce the complexity of asynchronous programing. Promises create a construct on which asynchronous callback execution can be synchronized in a sequential manner. Let's look at how the example from Listing 1-16 would work using promises. First, the LongRunning function must be changed to return a generic promise on completion rather than requiring all callbacks to be defined and passed in up front. See Listing 1-17.

Listing 1-17. Long-Running Function That Returns a Promise

```
function LongRunning()
{
    //perform long-running process

    //promise function does not exist but is used to denote the conceptual
```

```
    //return of a promise instance
    return promise();
}
```

Now that you no longer need to explicitly pass in the callbacks that execute when the LongRunning function is completed, you're free to chain as many of them as necessary to complete the task. Let's look at how this function is called in Listing 1-18.

Listing 1-18. Consuming a Long-Running Function That Returns a Promise

```
LongRunning().then(function (args)
{
    return (promise(callback_one()));
}).then(function (args)
{
    return (promise(callback_two(args)));
});
```

As you can see, the explicit definitions of the callbacks have been removed from the function argument. They're now executed only when the previous execution completes. In Listing 1-18 it's easy to see how sequentially oriented the code is. Not only is the code much easier to read and understand, but it also presents itself in a deterministic manner. The use of the then method attaches callbacks in a controlled way to the LongRunning function. When the function completes, the then callback is executed (with the results of the previous execution passed into it). This continues recursively until there are no more callbacks to execute. Using then guarantees several things:

- That you can specify a callback function to handle then when the target asynchronous operation completes

- That this callback provides in its parameter list a value that represents the result of the previously completed asynchronous operation

- That the then operation is also an asynchronous operation that returns a promise

Because then returns a promise that expects a callback containing the result of the previously executed then, you can chain dependent asynchronous calls by calling then on the result of any then call (as in the example). Needless to say nesting promises within each other returns everything to the old days, so you should avoid doing so if possible.

Here are a couple of operations for which you can use promises in certain situations:

- setPromise: You may find occasion to use promises within event handlers in your JavaScript code, particularly because many of the Microsoft APIs have been rewritten to be asynchronous in order to improve overall system performance. Due to the way the system treats event handlers, you need to tell it that your promise is still running. The WinJS implementation of system event handlers provides a function for doing this: setPromise. You saw an example in Listing 1-14. Chapter 2 dives further into the workings of this method.

- join: You may at some point need to synchronize across multiple promises. For instance, suppose you have two promise chains that are unrelated: one to retrieve user information and the other to read settings data from the file system. If you need to perform some action when both operations have completed, you can use the join operation to achieve this.

Summary

No doubt Windows 8 is a departure from anything you're used to. Developing for it is also somewhat so. The broad review of Windows 8 in this chapter should prepare you for the basics covered in the next chapter and give you the foundational knowledge you need for Windows 8 app development. You learned

- The traits, features, and properties of interacting with the Windows 8 UI

- How HTML is used in Windows 8 development

- The various technologies that can be used in Windows 8 development

■ ■ ■

CHAPTER 2

Getting the Basics Right

There are certain basic developer workflows to which you have to become accustomed if you intend to build Windows 8 apps, regardless of the technology stack you choose to use. At a fundamental level, having a good understanding of how to access the exposed file system is, if not critical, quite important to development in a given system. This chapter introduces you to these key areas by exposing you to the APIs used to work with them. Detailed examples are provided to help you work through how these APIs function. In this chapter you explore file-system access as well as some important elements of Windows 8 development new to the ecosystem. By the end of this chapter, you should understand how to do file access, how to interact with the lock screen, how to prompt the user with file dialogs, and how to use splash screens to keep the user engaged while the application continues to load in the background, and subsequently notify the user.

File I/O

Developers who have built server-side style code or even desktop clients are probably very familiar with the general patterns of file access. If you've been building HTML user experiences, you might be at a slight disadvantage, but only a minor one. The truth is, we've all worked with files while working with computers, and we all certainly understand their nature. They can be opened, edited, closed, deleted, listed, searched, copied, and moved.

Although logically similar (if not the same), this discussion is broken into three core areas. First, the chapter talks about storage locations (meaning the places where files are stored). This conversation is important because it has a huge impact on how your app is built, delivered, and ultimately deployed to the Windows Store. You then go into the nitty-gritty of actually working with files. This is done second because the approach to accessing files through the Windows Runtime for JavaScript requires you to understand the meaning of storage locations first. Without that core understanding, you'll most likely be pulling your hair out wondering why a given piece of functionality seems to be inexplicably failing with a completely useless and cryptic error.

Storage Folders

The StorageFolder class encompasses the general sense of a storage location. As stated earlier, a Windows 8 file can be resident in any number of places. An application you develop has access to these files either intrinsically or by declaring permissions in the application's manifest. Some storage locations to which your application has intrinsic access include the application's package-install location and isolated storage area. These storage locations are discussed in more detail in the following sections.

The Isolated Storage Area

An application's *isolated storage area* is an unpublished location on the Windows system where the application is installed. It serves as a cache for the application to read from and write to. Changes made to the isolated storage area through files being added or deleted, folders being created, and so on, are persisted across updates to your application. This is the principle difference between this and the package-install location discussed in the next section. Listing 2-1 shows how to create, edit, delete, and read files that are in an application's isolated store.

Listing 2-1. File Access from the Isolated Storage Area

```
//write the file to isolated storage
btn_createfile_iso.onclick = function ()
{

    if (txt_display.value.length > 0)
    {
Windows.Storage.ApplicationData.current.localFolder.createFileAsync("testfile.txt",↩
    Windows.Storage.CreationCollisionOption.replaceExisting).then(function (file)
        {
            Windows.Storage.FileIO.writeTextAsync(file,↩
                "The quick brown fox jumped over the lazy dog,↩
                and [" + txt_display.value + "]");
        });
    }
};


//read file
btn_readfile_iso.onclick = function ()
{
    Windows.Storage.ApplicationData.current.localFolder.↩
        getFileAsync("testfile.txt").then(function (file)
        {
            if (file == null)
            {
            } else
            {
                Windows.Storage.FileIO.readTextAsync(file)↩
                    .then(function (text)
                {
                    txt_display.value = text;
                });
            }
        });
};


//edit file
btn_editfile_iso.onclick = function ()
{
    Windows.Storage.ApplicationData.current.localFolder.↩
        getFileAsync("testfile.txt").then(function (file)
        {
            if (file == null)
            {

            } else
```

```
            {
                Windows.Storage.FileIO.writeTextAsync(file, txt_display.value);
            }
        });
};

//delete file
btn_deletefile_iso.onclick = function ()
{

    Windows.Storage.ApplicationData.current.localFolder.
        getFileAsync("testfile.txt").then(function (file)
        {
            if (file == null)
            {
                var v = new Windows.UI.Popups.MessageDialog("File was deleted");
                v.showAsync();
            } else
            {
                file.deleteAsync();
            }
        });
};
```

Listing 2-1 shows how to create a file in isolated storage using the
`Windows.Storage.ApplicationData.current.localFolder.createFileAsync` function. The version of this function
that you call expects two parameters: one that represents the file name (in this case `testfile.txt`), and one—called
`Windows.Storage.CreationCollisionOption`—that determines what to do when the file you want created has the same
name as a file already present in the target folder (in this case, the isolated storage folder). There are two versions of this
function: one expects a single parameter passed in (the file name), and the other also expects `CreationCollisionOption`
to be included. When you use the first version, the `failIfExists CreationCollisionOption` is automatically used.
Table 2-1 shows all the possible options of `Windows.Storage.CreationCollisionOption`.

Table 2-1. *Windows.Storage.CreationCollisionOption Members*

Member	Value	Description
generateUniqueName	0	Creates the new file or folder with the desired name, and automatically appends a number if a file or folder already exists with that name
replaceExisting	1	Creates the new file or folder with the desired name, and replaces any file or folder that already exists with that name
failIfExists	2	Creates the new file or folder with the desired name, or returns an error if a file or folder already exists with that name
openIfExists	3	Creates the new file or folder with the desired name, or returns an existing item if a file or folder already exists with that name

Continuing with the discussion of Listing 2-1, notice the use of the then promise discussed in Chapter 1. As stated, many of the Windows Library for JavaScript (WinJS) functions use an asynchronous programming model that requires the use of promises.

The rest of the example is straightforward. Listing 2-2 is a snippet of Listing 2-1 focusing in on the process of reading a file.

Listing 2-2. Reading a File from Isolated Storage

```
btn_readfile_iso.onclick = function ()
            {
               Windows.Storage.ApplicationData.current.localFolder.
                  getFileAsync("testfile.txt").then(function (file)
                  {
                     if (file == null)
                     {
                     } else
                     {
                        Windows.Storage.FileIO.readTextAsync(file).then(function (text)
                        {
                           txt_display.value = text;
                        });
                     }
                  });
            };
```

From Listing 2-2 you can see that file access is a two-step process. You first need to get the file, and then, once you have an object that represents the file you want to access (a StorageFile object), you can use that handle in subsequent calls (in this case, you use it as an argument in the readTextAsync function). You learn about StorageFile later in this chapter.

The Package-Install Location

Unlike files in the isolated storage location, modifications made to the application's package-install location, which you access using the Windows.ApplicationModel.Package class, are wiped away when a new update to your application is installed. Package contains a property, InstalledLocation, which returns a reference to a StorageFolder that represents the location on the end user's computer where the application was unpacked. As stated earlier, StorageFolder is the abstract container for storage locations and, specifically because it *is* an abstraction, you can use the same instance type to represent both locations (even if the underlying mechanisms for accessing the files are different). For instance, an application's installation location may be a folder on the user's system, but the isolated storage location may be a compressed and encrypted structure. The same programming interface will nonetheless work for both.

Let's rework the example in Listing 2-1 so it's generalized enough that any StorageFolder can work with it. First, let's create generalized versions of the create, read, edit, and delete functionality illustrated in Listing 2-1 (see Listing 2-3).

Listing 2-3. Generic Reading and Writing to a Storage Location

```
var createFileAsync = function (store, file_name, file_content) {

    return store.createFileAsync(file_name, ↵
        Windows.Storage.CreationCollisionOption.replaceExisting)
```

```
            .then(function (file) {
                Windows.Storage.FileIO.writeTextAsync(file, file_content);
            });

    };

    //write the file to isolated storage
    var readFileAsync = function (store, file_name, completeFunction) {
        return store.getFileAsync(file_name)↵
                .then(function (file) {
                    if (file != null) {
                        Windows.Storage.FileIO.readTextAsync(file).then(function (text) {
                            if(completeFunction != null)
                                completeFunction(text);
                        });
                    }
                });
    };

    var editFileAsync = function (store, file_name, new_content) {
        return store.getFileAsync(file_name)↵
                .then(function (file) {
                    if (file != null) {
                        Windows.Storage.FileIO.writeTextAsync(file, new_content);
                    }
                });
    };

    var deleteFileAsync = function (store, file_name) {
        return store.getFileAsync(file_name)↵
                .then(function (file) {
                    if (file != null) {
                        file.deleteAsync();
                    }
                });
    };
```

The preceding example generalizes the activity of manipulating files in a target storage location. You allow the user to pass in the storage location, file name, and, in the case of editing or creating the file, the content they want added to the file. You create four private functions: createFileAsync, editFileAsync, readFileAsync, and deleteFileAsync. (Notice the use of Async in the function names. You do this because each of these functions returns the promise returned by its internal file-access method call. Asynchronous functions like this don't need to have Async in their names, but it helps developers downstream quickly identify which functions are async and which ones aren't.) The file-access pattern in each of the button click events is encapsulated into these four functions and generalized so that any storage location can be passed in as an argument and the behavior will remain the same (provided the application has access to that storage location).

Assuming a user interface with buttons for creating, reading, editing, and deleting a file, Listing 2-4 shows how you can use the buttons' click handlers to manipulate files in the application's package-install location.

Listing 2-4. File Access Using the Application's Install Location

```
//read file in package

            btn_readfile_iso.onclick = function () {
                readFileAsync(Windows.ApplicationModel.Package.current.↵
                    installedLocation, "testfile.txt", function (text)
                {
                    txt_diplay.value = text;
                });
            };
```

The takeaway is that regardless of the underlying implementation, you can program against StorageFolder in the same manner. Because of this, the chapter doesn't focus on any more examples and instead gives an overview of the various locations available to you as a developer and which properties on which classes expose them.

More on Storage: the ApplicationData Class

Accessing an application's package-install location is great if you want a read-only cache of data to load and read from. But because it's so volatile (it's deleted when the application is updated), you should probably never write to it (or at least you should expect whatever is written there to be gone after each application update). The better solution, shown earlier in Listing 2-1, is to work with the classes in the Windows.Storage namespace, specifically the ApplicationData class. ApplicationData provides direct access to your application's virtual file stores. It can be used to access storage locations that are local, roaming, or temporary. Table 2-2 provides a view of the notable ApplicationData class members.

Table 2-2. *ApplicationData Notable Members*

Property	Description
current	Provides access to the app data store associated with the app's package. This is static and the only way to get access to an instance of the current ApplicationData object.
localFolder	Gets the root folder in the local app data store.
localSettings	Gets the application settings container in the local app data store.
roamingFolder	Gets the root folder in the roaming app data store.
roamingSettings	Gets the application settings container in the roaming app data store.
roamingStorageQuota	Gets the maximum size of the data that can be synchronized to the cloud from the roaming app data store.
temporaryFolder	Gets the root folder in the temporary app data store.

If you want to create and manage files and folders that are tied to the currently logged-on user and not a specific machine the user is on, then the roamingFolder property is the appropriate choice. Roaming folders are synced across all devices the user is logged in to. (Note that there are restrictions on the total storage quota that can be roamed and also on the naming convention used for files in order for them to roam.) The great thing about this approach is that it allows users of your app to flow seamlessly across devices without needing to explicitly synchronize back to a server. Store content in the folder, and let Windows 8 take care of the rest.

The temporary store for your application is even more volatile than package storage. Items stored in this location are only guaranteed to last as long as the currently running session of the app. Files here can be deleted by the system at any time and may even be manually removed by the user using the Disk Cleanup tool. Hence, the ideal usage of this location is as an in-application session cache.

The User's Known Folders

Your application isn't limited to working with files in the application's isolated data store, package-install location, or local/roaming/temporary locations just discussed. Applications built using the Windows Runtime (WinRT) for JavaScript can also access folders through the Windows.Storage.KnownFolders class. Table 2-3 lists the KnownFolders properties defined for accessing the underlying folders they represent.

Table 2-3. KnownFolders Properties

Property	Description
documentsLibrary	Gets the Documents Library
homeGroup	Gets the HomeGroup folder
mediaServerDevices	Gets the Media Server Devices (Digital Living Network Alliance [DLNA]) folder
musicLibrary	Gets the Music Library
picturesLibrary	Gets the Pictures Library
removableDevices	Gets the Removable Devices folder
videosLibrary	Gets the Videos Library

In order for an application to access these folders, it needs to ask the user by declaratively indicating that it intends to use a storage location other than the private ones automatically accessible to it. In Windows 8, this is a two-step process. First you enable the target Windows 8 library that you want access to as a *capability* your application is declaring that it uses. You can do this via the Capabilities section of the application manifest. In a standard WinRT for JavaScript Windows 8 app, the app's manifest is located in the project's root folder with the name package.appxmanifest (see Figure 2-1).

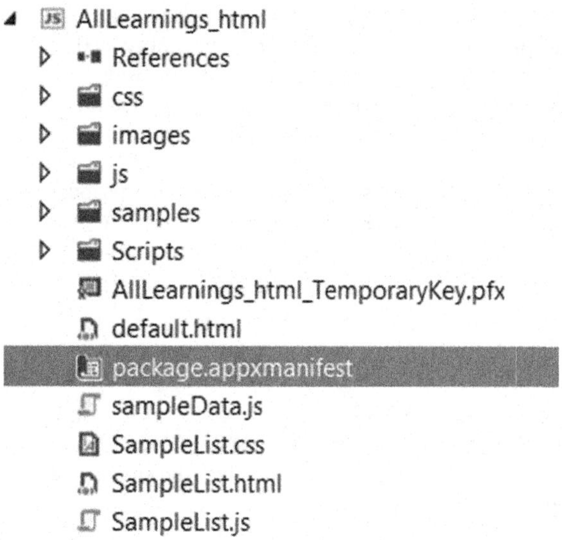

▲ ⬚ AllLearnings_html
   ▷ ▪▪ References
   ▷ 📁 css
   ▷ 📁 images
   ▷ 📁 js
   ▷ 📁 samples
   ▷ 📁 Scripts
      🔲 AllLearnings_html_TemporaryKey.pfx
      🔳 default.html
      📄 package.appxmanifest
      🔲 sampleData.js
      📄 SampleList.css
      🔳 SampleList.html
      🔲 SampleList.js

Figure 2-1. *Application manifest's location in the project structure*

When you open this file, you should see five tabs. Selecting the Capabilities tab opens a screen like the one shown in Figure 2-2.

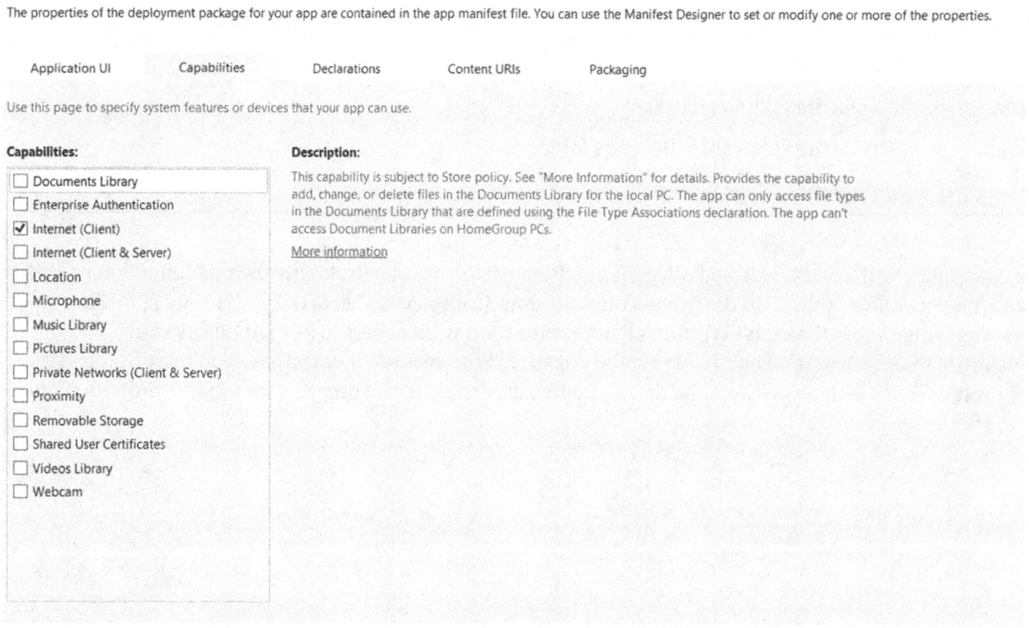

The properties of the deployment package for your app are contained in the app manifest file. You can use the Manifest Designer to set or modify one or more of the properties.

Application UI	Capabilities	Declarations	Content URIs	Packaging

Use this page to specify system features or devices that your app can use.

Capabilities:

  ☐ Documents Library
  ☐ Enterprise Authentication
  ☑ Internet (Client)
  ☐ Internet (Client & Server)
  ☐ Location
  ☐ Microphone
  ☐ Music Library
  ☐ Pictures Library
  ☐ Private Networks (Client & Server)
  ☐ Proximity
  ☐ Removable Storage
  ☐ Shared User Certificates
  ☐ Videos Library
  ☐ Webcam

Description:

This capability is subject to Store policy. See "More Information" for details. Provides the capability to add, change, or delete files in the Documents Library for the local PC. The app can only access file types in the Documents Library that are defined using the File Type Associations declaration. The app can't access Document Libraries on HomeGroup PCs.

More information

Figure 2-2. *Capabilities tab*

Selecting any one of the library capabilities (Documents Library, Music Library, Pictures Library, or Videos Library) enables access to the associated storage location through the appropriate `ApplicationData` property. The section "External Known Folders" discusses how to enable capabilities for the other three `KnownFolders` properties (`homeGroup`, `mediaServerDevices`, and `removableDevices`).

Next, you must explicitly declare which file types your application reads from and writes to. You do so through the Declarations tab of the app's manifest (see Figure 2-3).

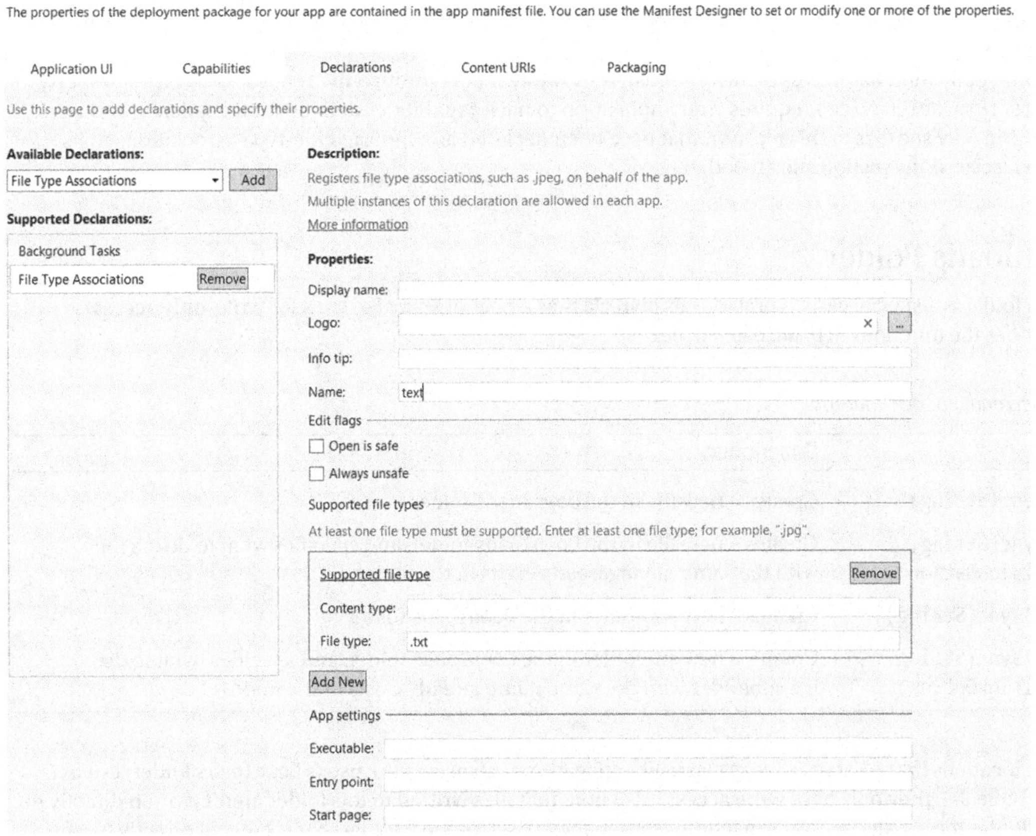

The properties of the deployment package for your app are contained in the app manifest file. You can use the Manifest Designer to set or modify one or more of the properties.

| Application UI | Capabilities | Declarations | Content URIs | Packaging |

Use this page to add declarations and specify their properties.

Available Declarations:

[File Type Associations ▼] [Add]

Supported Declarations:

| Background Tasks | |
| File Type Associations | [Remove] |

Description:

Registers file type associations, such as .jpeg, on behalf of the app.

Multiple instances of this declaration are allowed in each app.

More information

Properties:

Display name:

Logo: [ ] ✕ [...]

Info tip:

Name: text

Edit flags

☐ Open is safe

☐ Always unsafe

Supported file types

At least one file type must be supported. Enter at least one file type; for example, ".jpg".

Supported file type	[Remove]
Content type:	
File type:	.txt

[Add New]

App settings

Executable:

Entry point:

Start page:

Figure 2-3. *Declarations tab*

You need to add a new file-type association to your application. An association must include the file extension (with the extension dot preceding it) and can optionally provide a MIME type. Figure 2-3 shows adding a file association for text files (`.txt`). You can read and write files of any kind that are associated to your application through this interface (as long as your application has access to that folder).

External Known Folders

If you request the Documents Library, Pictures Library, Music Library, or Videos Library, you can also access files on any connected media server as a storage location by using the mediaServerDevices property of KnownFolders. Note that the files you see on the device are scoped based on the capabilities you specify, meaning that if you only declare Music Library capabilities, you see only music files on the media server to which you connect. Also note that, regardless of the capabilities you specify, you don't see documents in the Documents Library of the server you're connected to.

You can also treat your homegroup as a storage location. As with the results of mediaServerDevices, your app can only see the libraries declared in its manifest as capabilities. This also doesn't provide access to the homegroup Documents Library.

Finally, your application has access to files stored in removable media through the removableDevices property of KnownFolders. removableDevices requires your application to have capabilities defined for it explicitly, and the application can only see files in this location that have been declared as supported file-type associations in its manifest in the Declarations section shown earlier.

The Downloads Folder

The Downloads folder is a special case; it provides its own class as a peer of KnownFolders for write-only access. Table 2-4 describes the functions of DownloadsFolder.

Table 2-4. DownloadsFolder Methods

Method	Description
CreateFileAsync(String)	Creates a new file in the Downloads folder
CreateFileAsync(String, CreationCollisionOption)	Creates a new file in the Downloads folder, and specifies what to do if a file with the same name already exists in the folder
CreateFolderAsync(String)	Creates a new subfolder in the Downloads folder
CreateFolderAsync(String, CreationCollisionOption)	Creates a new subfolder in the Downloads folder, and specifies what to do if a subfolder with the same name already exists in the folder

Unlike the locations in the KnownFolders class, all applications can access the user's Downloads folder; but as you can see in Table 2-5, they only have write access. Also note that files written to this folder aren't written directly to the Downloads folder root of an end user's machine. Rather, they're scoped to a folder that is created directly for the application that created the file or folder. As such, the folder name is the name of the application. Take for instance the example application AllLearnings_html. Listing 2-5 shows the event handler for the click event of a UI button called btn_createfile_download. Clicking the button creates a file at the following location on my machine: Edward Moemeka\Downloads\AllLearnings_html\testfile.txt (see Figure 2-4).

Table 2-5. FileIO Methods

Method	Description
`AppendLinesAsync(IStorageFile, IIterable(String))`	Appends lines of text to the specified file
`AppendLinesAsync(IStorageFile, IIterable(String), UnicodeEncoding)`	Appends lines of text to the specified file using the specified character encoding
`AppendTextAsync(IStorageFile, String)`	Appends text to the specified file
`AppendTextAsync(IStorageFile, String, UnicodeEncoding)`	Appends text to the specified file using the specified character encoding
`ReadBufferAsync`	Reads the contents of the specified file and returns a buffer
`ReadLinesAsync(IStorageFile)`	Reads the contents of the specified file and returns lines of text
`ReadLinesAsync(IStorageFile, UnicodeEncoding)`	Reads the contents of the specified file using the specified character encoding and returns lines of text
`ReadTextAsync(IStorageFile)`	Reads the contents of the specified file and returns text
`ReadTextAsync(IStorageFile, UnicodeEncoding)`	Reads the contents of the specified file using the specified character encoding and returns text
`WriteBufferAsync`	Writes data from a buffer to the specified file
`WriteBytesAsync`	Writes an array of bytes of data to the specified file
`WriteLinesAsync(IStorageFile, IIterable(String))`	Writes lines of text to the specified file
`WriteLinesAsync(IStorageFile, IIterable(String), UnicodeEncoding)`	Writes lines of text to the specified file using the specified character encoding
`WriteTextAsync(IStorageFile, String)`	Writes text to the specified file
`WriteTextAsync(IStorageFile, String, UnicodeEncoding)`	Writes text to the specified file using the specified character encoding

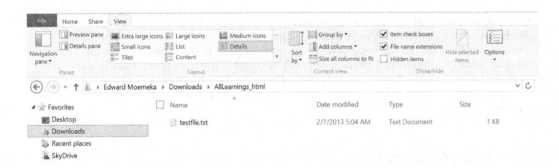

Figure 2-4. Downloads folder root for the AllLearnings_html application

---

■ **Note** The folder location AllLearnings_html is an alias for the actual folder name. If you place mouse or keyboard focus on the navigation bar (the area that shows the current folder location in the figure), the actual path to the file is revealed. On my machine it is C:\Users\Edward\Downloads\8a2843c4-6e36-40f7-8966-85789a855fa8_xctxhvdp4nrje!App.

Listing 2-5. Writing to the *Downloads* Folder

```
btn_createfile_download.onclick = function ()
            {
                Windows.Storage.DownloadsFolder.createFileAsync("testfile.txt")↩
                    .then(function (file)
                {
                    Windows.Storage.FileIO.writeTextAsync(file,↩
                        "this is the content of the file written to the downloads folder");
                });
            };
```

The code in Listing 2-4 creates a text file testfile.txt in the user's Downloads folder using the DownloadsFolder class found in the Windows.Storage namespace.

Final Thoughts on Storage via the ApplicationData Class

Regardless of what store you use for your file I/O functions, the ApplicationData object offers additional services that can help manage it. For instance, ApplicationData.SetVersionAsync allows you to change the application data format used in a future release of your app without causing compatibility problems with previous releases of the app.

You can also use ApplicationData to clear your Windows cache by calling ApplicationData.ClearAsync(). Note that this function clears the data from all storage locations associated with the application. An overloaded method exists for this function that targets a specified location.

Files

File access through the new Windows APIs passes through the StorageFile class. This class provides asynchronous mechanisms for interacting with a given file. As you've seen in the previous section, it works in concert with the StorageFolder class as a tool to create, modify, copy, or delete files. You also saw that in most cases you don't have to use it directly. Instead, WinRT for JavaScript provides a helper class FileIO. FileIO is a static class (meaning you can't create an instance of it) that provides helper methods for reading and writing files represented by objects of the IStorageFile interface. This interface is a generalization of the functions of StorageFile. Table 2-5 provides the full list of what you can do with this class.

The Window 8 Lock Screen

Another developer workflow element that you should familiarize yourself with is lock-screen access. Lock screens can be used to present a user interface with a wait cursor or message to the user while an application with a long-running startup sequence continues to load in the background. It is recommended that you include a lock screen in your app as a way of clearly communicating with your users. Given the lock screen's complexity and potential impact on the visibility of your application and users' ability to interact with the app, we think it's wonderful that the designers of Windows 8 and the Windows 8 Store experience for developers have made it so easy to work with. In fact, we can safely say that this is the least complicated topic discussed in this book.

Before you get started with the code, let's first talk about the functionality exposed to Windows 8 apps seeking to interact with the lock screen. Figure 2-5 shows a Windows 8 lock screen with visual indicators of the areas in which your application information can be surfaced.

Figure 2-5. *Windows 8 lock screen*

As you can see, Windows 8 apps appear in the notification area as tiny icons and associated numbers (ranging from 1 to 99). They may also appear next to the time section with more detailed information. Additionally, as a developer, you can change the lock screen's background image.

■ **Note**   The user can decide which applications are allowed to show detailed status information and which ones show simple notifications. There are eight slots: seven for basic notifications and one for detailed status. If an application isn't selected by the user for lock-screen notification, it doesn't appear on the lock screen.

The Windows 8 lock screen is represented as the static LockScreen class in your application. Lock-screen interaction also uses BackgroundExecutionManager and BadgeUpdateManager. Used in concert with LockScreen, these classes expose mechanisms to change the notification badge (the tiny icon with the number next to it) for your app, ask for access to the lock screen, read and write the lock screen's background image, and post notification updates to it. Table 2-6 shows the members of the LockScreen class.

Table 2-6. *LockScreen Class Members*

Method	Description
getImageStream()	Gets the current lock-screen image as a data stream
getImageFileAsync()	Sets the lock-screen image from a StorageFile object
getImageStreamAsync()	Sets the lock-screen image from a data stream
OriginalImageFile	Gets the current lock-screen image

One thing you have to get used to when working with Windows 8 is the integration of user choice into feature exposure. You saw this earlier in the discussion of how Windows 8 works and in the "The User's Known Folders" section, when it came time to start working with files and folders outside the local data store available to an application. This is no different, although the user workflow is far more explicit. All lock-screen interaction requires user enrollment on one level or another. To access the background image permissions (used to display the image or apply an image of your choosing), you first need to request permissions from the user. You do so by making a call to the static class Windows.ApplicationModel.Background.BackgroundExecutionManager.

Using the requestAccessAsync function, you can prompt the user to enroll your application in lock-screen access scenarios focused on its background image. However, in order for your app to appear on the lock screen for notification purposes, the end user must do more. There is nothing you can do to enable this—the user needs to change a system setting and choose your application specifically (as one of seven) to receive notifications from it. Figure 2-6 shows the PC Settings screen where the user makes this choice.

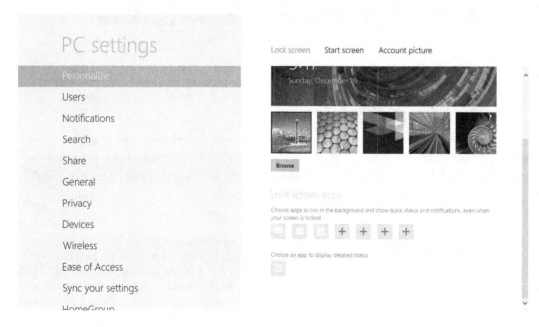

Figure 2-6. *Lock screen personalization by an end user*

Listing 2-6 illustrates how an application might request access to the lock screen.

Listing 2-6. Requesting Access to the Lock Screen and Reading the Result of the Request

```
Windows.ApplicationModel.Background.BackgroundExecutionManager.requestAccessAsync()↩
    .then(function (status)
                {
                    switch (status)
                    {
                        case Windows.ApplicationModel.Background.↩
                            BackgroundAccessStatus.allowedWithAlwaysOnRealTimeConnectivity:
                        txt_display.innerText = "This app is on the lock screen and has↩
                            access to Real Time Connectivity (always on).";
                            break;
                        case Windows.ApplicationModel.Background.BackgroundAccessStatus.↩
                            allowedMayUseActiveRealTimeConnectivity:
                        txt_display.innerText = "This app is on the lock screen,↩
                            and may have access to Real Time Connectivity.";
                            break;
                        case Windows.ApplicationModel.Background.BackgroundAccessStatus.↩
                            denied:
                        txt_display.innerText = "This app is not on the lock screen.";
                            break;
                        case Windows.ApplicationModel.Background.BackgroundAccessStatus.↩
                            unspecified:
                        txt_display.innerText = "The user has not yet taken any action.↩
                            This is the default setting and the app is not on the↩
                            lock screen.";
                            break;
                    }
                });
```

Any application that is on the lock screen can have notifications sent to it. *Badge notification* is the technical term for displaying a notification in the start screen. To use the lock-screen notification feature, you need to use the BadgeUpdateManager class. This class can update the content of an application's lock-screen icon and even present text (if the application has been configured to be the primary lock-screen app—by default, the user's calendar). Listing 2-7 shows how to update an application's badge using the notification mechanisms of BadgeUpdateManager. In the example, you update the number displayed next to the application's lock-screen. Chapter 7 goes into more details on this subject.

Listing 2-7. Lock-Screen Badge Notification

```
var count = 0;
btn_updatebadge.onclick = function ()
{
    count++;
    var badge_xml = Windows.UI.Notifications.BadgeUpdateManager.↩
        getTemplateContent(Windows.UI.Notifications.BadgeTemplateType.BadgeNumber);
    badge_xml.documentElement.setAttribute("value", count.toString());
    var badge = new Windows.UI.Notifications.BadgeNotification(badge_xml);
    var badge_updater = Windows.UI.Notifications.BadgeUpdateManager.↩
        createBadgeUpdaterForApplication();
            badge_updater.update(badge);
};
```

App Bars

If you've used Windows applications like Internet Explorer and Microsoft Word in the past, you may notice that something is missing from Windows 8 apps: main menus. Chapter 1 talked about this: main menus have been removed in Windows 8 apps in favor of application bars. As discussed then, app bars are areas at the top and bottom of the screen that can be activated by either right-clicking, if you have a mouse with which to do that, or touch swiping from the top or bottom on the screen. Figure 2-7 provides an example of how app bars look.

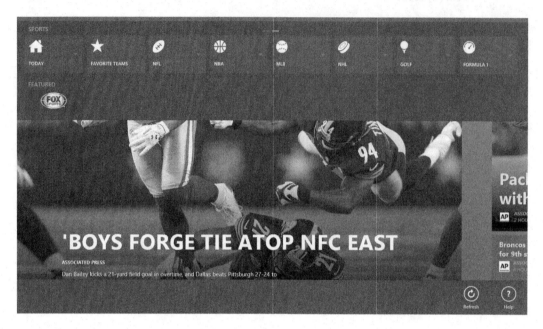

Figure 2-7. *App bar activated in an application*

Menus in the old Windows programming model (native Windows apps like Visual Studio 2012, Microsoft Word, and Internet Explorer) had no constraints on how functionality was exposed. For the most part, the top menus had high-level navigation and application functionality, and context menus focused on context-aware functionality. Microsoft guidance is to maintain this same approach in modern Windows 8 apps. You can see this in the Sports app (which is installed on default Windows 8 installations).

Chapter 1 introduced the concept of author-created attributes, and you created a simple implementation of what is commonly referred to as an *expando* control. This is a JavaScript control that is created on the fly and injected into a placeholder container. In the example in Listings 1-11 and 1-12, you used this technique to create a UI completely generated from JavaScript code. Expando controls are a way to include a combination of UI elements along with behaviors in your application.

The `AppBar` control exposed through the `WinJS.UI` namespace functions like this. It abstracts away the functionality of responding to user swipes and sliding up or down from the top or bottom based on those scenarios. Listing 2-8 illustrates the use of the `data-win-control` attribute to place an app bar on the page.

Listing 2-8. AppBar Control in a Document

```
<!DOCTYPE html>
<html>
<head>
    <meta charset="utf-8" />
    <title>TestAppBars</title>

    <!-- WinJS references -->
    <link href="//Microsoft.WinJS.1.0/css/ui-dark.css" rel="stylesheet" />
    <script src="//Microsoft.WinJS.1.0/js/base.js"></script>
    <script src="//Microsoft.WinJS.1.0/js/ui.js"></script>

    <link href="TestAppBars.css" rel="stylesheet" />
    <script src="TestAppBars.js"></script>
</head>
<body>

        <section aria-label="Main content" role="main" style="margin-left: 100px;">
                <p>This sample tests the app bar functionality</p>
        </section>
    <div data-win-control="WinJS.UI.AppBar" >
        <button id="btn_add" data-win-control="WinJS.UI.AppBarCommand"↵
            data-win-options="{id:'cmdAdd',label:'Add',icon:'add',section:'global',↵
            tooltip:'Add item'}">
        </button>
    </div>
</body>
</html>
```

Notice in the AppBar control that you use a button to which you've added a control decorator. Although you could theoretically place anything in your application's app bar, convention is to use buttons that follow the style guidelines of Windows 8. You can of course build your own UI controls to mimic the look and feel of what users expect, but to simplify things, the Windows Library for JavaScript (WinJS) framework includes an additional control that works with AppBar called the AppBarCommand control. AppBarCommand provides options through its data-win-options properties that allow you to specify the type of command for a given button. Listing 2-8 uses the options attribute to set the label, name, and default icon for the button you add to the app bar. The JavaScript code for this page follows in Listing 2-9

Listing 2-9. Handling AppBarCommand Events

```
(function () {
    "use strict";

    WinJS.UI.Pages.define("/samples/AppBarSample/TestAppBars.html", {

        ready: function (element, options) {
```

```
            btn_add.onclick = function ()
            {
                var v = new Windows.UI.Popups.MessageDialog("this is a test");
                v.showAsync();
            };

        },

        unload: function () {

        },

        updateLayout: function (element, viewState, lastViewState) {

        }
    });
})();
```

Dialogs

Dialogs are a mainstay in the pantheon of Windows applications. They provide a simple, elegant, yet powerful alternative to launching full-blown windows. Dialogs are typically used to prompt the user for some action. But in some special cases (for instance, when you wish to save a file to or load a file from a location chosen by the user) you can use one of several dialog types.

In Windows 8, dialogs used solely for the purpose of notifying the user are vehemently frowned on. This is because dialogs are by nature *modal*, meaning that while they're open, no other interaction with the application is permitted. This is such an intrusive force in the Windows 8 mantra that you run the risk of not passing certification if you overuse modal dialogs such as MessageDialog. (Note that building your own modal dialogs is as bad as using the built-in controls provided by Microsoft. If user interaction is no longer possible because you have a prompt open, it's an easy fail for Microsoft's testers.)

Be that as it may, on some occasions a modal dialog is necessary, such as when there is no further action by the user that can prevent a failure of the application. In such cases, MessageDialog can be a valuable asset. The great thing about this class is that although it presents an interface to the end user, there is no need to lay out anything in your UI in support of it. You saw an example of using the MessageDialog class in Listing 2-9. Listing 2-10 expands on the simple use of MessageDialog, this time showing how it can be customized with a title and selection options.

Listing 2-10. Using MessageDialog

```
(function ()
{
    "use strict";

    WinJS.UI.Pages.define("/samples/DialogSample/TestDialogs.html", {
        // This function is called whenever a user navigates to this page. It
        // populates the page elements with the app's data.
        ready: function (element, options)
        {
            btn_showdialog.onclick = function ()
```

```
        {
            var v = new Windows.UI.Popups.MessageDialog↵
                ("simple dialog with no options");
            v.showAsync();
        };

        btn_showdialog_full.onclick = function ()
        {
            var v = new Windows.UI.Popups.MessageDialog↵
                ("Dialog with options", "Modal dialog");
            var txt_dialogchoice =↵
                document.getElementById("txt_dialogchoice");
            v.commands.append(new Windows.UI.Popups.↵
                UICommand("Yes", function (command)
            {
                txt_dialogchoice.innerText = "User selected yes.";
            }));
            v.commands.append(new Windows.UI.Popups.↵
                UICommand("No", function (command)
            {
                txt_dialogchoice.innerText = "User selected no.";
            }));
            v.commands.append(new Windows.UI.Popups.↵
                UICommand("Maybe", function (command)
            {
                txt_dialogchoice.innerText = "User selected maybe.";
            }));
            v.showAsync();
        };

    },

});
})();
```

Figure 2-8 shows the result of the code when a user clicks the button in the UI associated with btn_showdialog.

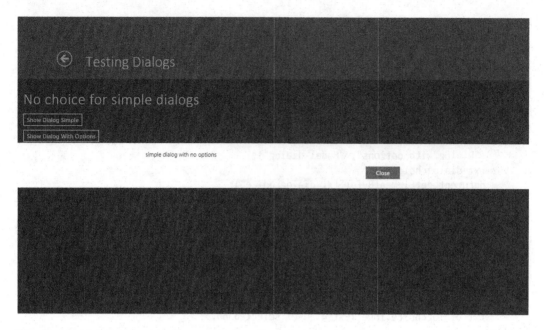

Figure 2-8. *Modal dialog using* `MessageDialog` *through* `AppBar`

When the user clicks `btn_showdialog_full`, the results are slightly different. Figure 2-9 shows that the modal dialog displays three buttons as well as a heading.

Figure 2-9. *Advanced modal dialog using* `MessageDialog`

■ **Note**   The API limits the number of commands you can append the `ModalDialog` commands list to three. Attempting to append more causes an exception. Interestingly, the text isn't limited per se, so it's up to you to ensure that the interface doesn't appear cluttered and confusing when you create dialogs that also serve as prompts to the user for further action.

Consuming Components

At the risk of getting into a heated debate over the prowess of any given language, I'll preface this section with the statement that not all languages are created equal. The popular use of this phrase is usually seen as a hidden slight against one language or another as somehow lesser, but I mean this quite literally. Languages are designed to solve specific problems as understood by their designers. JavaScript is great at what it's great at, .NET languages are great at what they're great at, and of course native languages are excellent when weighed against the design goals that drove their development. Because of this fact, there are gaps that one language or technology covers but that another language doesn't. This is no different with the modern Windows 8 programming interfaces.

Because Windows is primarily native (and all other languages are projections of the native interfaces so developers in a specific language can continue to work in their language and technology of choice), many features in the API landscape remain only in the native world. Audio buffer data, for instance, can at present only be surfaced through native programming. Because the .NET platform offers a mature type-based system, it follows as the second most native layer above C++, sharing many libraries and a common UI paradigm. It doesn't contain all the features available to native applications but has enough to do some major damage. JavaScript-based applications offer the least native programming surface area in the current implementation of WinRT. Although JavaScript provides much of the functionality of WinRT, it lacks the ability to do low-level programming and can't expose functionality as components to other platforms.

Microsoft designed modern Window 8 applications so that apps can share components regardless of the technology with which the components are developed (right now, only .NET and C++/Cx can create shareable components) or the technology with which the consumer is developed. All Windows 8 apps can consume libraries that have been defined as Windows components. Windows components can be consumed in an app by adding a reference to it in the application references area.

Let's see how this works in an example. Listing 2-11 starts by creating a simple .NET web service application that adds two numbers and returns the sum to the caller.

Listing 2-11. Web Service Written in .NET

```
using System;
using System.Web;
using System.Web.Services;

namespace NormalWeb
{

    [WebService(Namespace = "http://tempuri.org/")]
    [WebServiceBinding(ConformsTo = WsiProfiles.BasicProfile1_1)]
    [System.ComponentModel.ToolboxItem(false)]

    public class MathService : System.Web.Services.WebService
    {
        [WebMethod]
        public CalculationResult AddTwoNumbers(int x, int y)
```

```
        {
            var start = DateTime.Now;
            var result = x + y;
            var duration = DateTime.Now.Subtract(start);
            var calc_time_in_seconds = duration.TotalSeconds;

            return new CalculationResult
            {
                CalculationTime = calc_time_in_seconds,
                Result = result,
            };
        }
    }

    public class CalculationResult
    {
        public double CalculationTime { get; set; }
        public int Result { get; set; }
    }
}
```

Unlike normal web services designed specifically for JavaScript—or, at least, designed with web standards in mind—this service returns its result as a complex SOAP type. *SOAP* is a heavy technology used to pass data back and forth between two systems connected via HTTP. For .NET applications, this is a great tool because .NET's communication framework and IDE tooling were designed from the ground up with SOAP in mind back in the early 2000s. Nowadays we use technologies like REST and JSON to communicate with servers. Because SOAP is a heavy protocol that sends relatively large XML documents back, you don't necessarily want to use a JavaScript application to communicate with that service. So, you create a .NET-based WinRT component that connects to it and encapsulates the AddTwoNumbers HTTP-based service call into a function you can easily call; see Listing 2-12.

■ **Note**   If you have Visual Studio, you can easily connect to a web service using C# by using the tool's Add Service Reference feature. In this instance, you must add the connected service to the MathServer namespace.

Listing 2-12. C# Component to Encapsulate a Legacy SOAP Service Call

```
using System;
using System.Runtime.InteropServices.WindowsRuntime;
using System.Threading;
using System.Threading.Tasks;
using Windows.Foundation;

namespace MathComponent
{
    public sealed class MathManager
    {
        public IAsyncOperation<int> AddTwoNumbers(int x, int y)
        {
            MathServer.MathServiceSoapClient client = new MathServer.↵
                MathServiceSoapClient();
```

```
        return AsyncInfo.Run<int>(new Func<CancellationToken,↵
            Task<int>>(async delegate(CancellationToken token)
        {
            var resp = await client.AddTwoNumbersAsync(x, y);
            return resp.Body.AddTwoNumbersResult.Result;
        }));

    }
  }
}
```

Notice that you abstract away more of the complexity of the service call by unwrapping the contents of the response object and returning it as an integer instead of the SOAP-based complex type that returns from AddTwoNumbers.

The final step is to add a reference to the newly created MathComponent WinRT component to your JavaScript application. Once added, the reference is available to all JavaScript in your project. You can call AddTwoNumbers in JavaScript as shown in Listing 2-13. Notice how the function AddTwoNumbers is called in JavaScript as addTwoNumbers; this illustrates that the .NET version of the class is automatically projected into JavaScript in a manner consistent with JavaScript development methodologies. This is the genius of Windows 8 development!

Listing 2-13. Calling a WinRT Component in JavaScript

```
var v = new MathComponent.MathManager();
            v.addTwoNumbers(4, 17).then(function (answer)
            {
                if (answer > 0)
                {
                }
            });
```

Summary

This chapter went through some core workflows that a developer must master when developing Windows 8 apps. You should have gained an understanding of reading from and writing to the file system as well as what storage locations are. Here is an overview of what you covered in Chapter 2:

- The role of storage locations, and that certain locations are available to an application by default and other locations require you to explicitly declare capabilities through the application manifest.

- Application bars and what they're used for. Feel free to go back and review the detailed examples that illustrate creating and using permissions to control a screen.

- Dialogs, how they work in Windows 8, and when to use and not use such devices in your applications.

- A lock screen presents a user interface with a wait cursor or message while an application with a long-running startup sequence loads in the background. The lock screen also prevents that application from shutting down if it takes too long to load.

- Local notifications may be used to notify the user of events happening in your application.

- Windows Runtime components and how they can be used to extend a JavaScript application with functionality that might otherwise be unavailable to it.

CHAPTER 3

■ ■ ■

Incorporating Layout and Controls

Modern Windows user interface programming has always involved some form of controls—reusable user interface elements that encapsulate predictable behavior in the form of user experience. This tenet of Windows development hasn't changed with Windows 8. In this chapter, you learn how controls are exposed to you as a Windows 8 JavaScript developer in the form of interactivity controls such as buttons, list boxes, and so on; and layout controls, which you can use to structure the manner in which your app's user interface is organized.

As stated in Chapter 2, Windows 8 JavaScript development, unlike the other user interface rendering engines available to Windows 8 developers, is based on HTML5. This means layout and controls for your Windows 8 applications start first and foremost with the use of pure HTML +CSS3. In addition, the use of the control integration patterns outlined in the previous chapter allows app developers to extend the HTML5 layout engine with new functionality that closely ties JavaScript apps built using WinJS to the Windows 8 native look and feel. In particular, Chapter 2 discussed the app bar and showed how it can be incorporated into your app user interface.

In this chapter, which covers the incorporation of layout and controls in Windows 8 app development, you start by creating a project. This example project will serve as a template from which you can build basic controls. The chapter discusses and explains these standard controls and then moves into a discussion of data-driven controls and their use of data binding.

Setting Up a Project

Chapter 2 discussed many of the foundational elements of Windows 8 development. You start this chapter with a quick walkthrough of a Windows Runtime (WinRT) for JavaScript project. You create the proverbial "Hello World" application—in this case, "Hello Windows 8 with JavaScript." Although you can do most of your development and user interface layout with any HTML-compatible application (or Notepad, if you desire), you need Visual Studio 2012 in order to compile your application into the app package discussed in Chapter 2. Visual Studio also provides you with some deployment workflow automation tools that can be invaluable to a Windows 8 developer building apps for the Windows Store.

To start, launch Visual Studio 2012. Figure 3-1 shows how the Visual Studio 2012 IDE looks on my machine. If you've changed the color scheme for Visual Studio 2012 or installed add-ins for various other technologies, then it might look different on your computer.

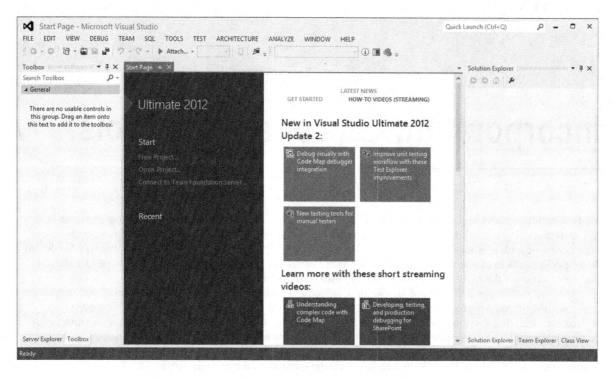

Figure 3-1. *Visual Studio 2012*

This chapter doesn't spend time walking through the various pieces of the IDE. For a detailed discussion, you can reference a book such as *Pro Visual Studio 2012* by Adam Freeman (Apress 2012). For the purpose of this exercise, the important sections to note are the central content area, the Toolbox to the left of that, and the Solution Explorer to the right of it. In a moment, you'll create a new project and see how these areas on the screen "light up" when a project is in scope. This is because they are, like many views in Visual Studio 2010, context aware: based on what is selected (and in some cases what document in the central content area is currently active), the views of other associated Windows may change. Before you move on to the next steps, take a moment to play around with the IDE layout. You can detach and reattach pretty much anything as well as unpin the default pinned side sections (Solution Explorer, Toolbox) to maximize space for the content area. You can even drag the entire content area to another screen and maximize it, effectively dedicating an entire screen to content with no menus, toolbars, or distractions.

You can create a new project by selecting File ➤ New ➤ Project. The resulting dialog looks like Figure 3-2 on my machine.

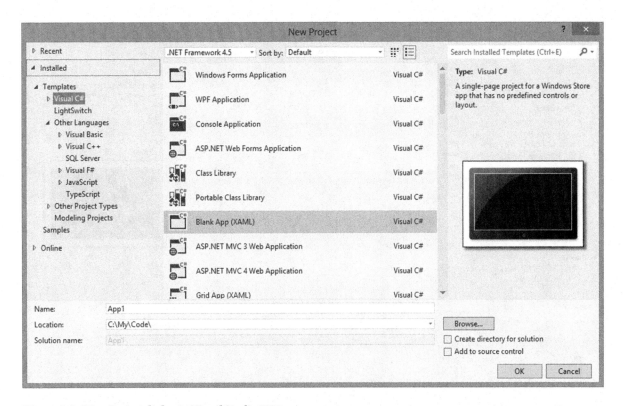

Figure 3-2. *New Project dialog in Visual Studio 2012*

Visual Studio 2012 uses a usage profile mechanism to feature activities a user is interested in over features the user isn't interested in. Depending on how you set up Visual Studio 2012 the first time you ran it, you may be locked in as a C# developer, a Web developer, a database developer, or any number of other profile types. On my machine, C# is the default profile I use; as a result, Visual C# projects are front and center for me to pick from when I launch the new project activity. If I wanted to build Visual Basic, Visual C++, SQL Server, or, of course, JavaScript, I would have to look in the Other Languages section of the New Project dialog box.

The C# profile in Visual Studio 2012 contains many more project types that Visual Studio lets you create. With C#, you can create just about anything from Windows services to Windows Phone 8 applications. These days, companies like Xamarin have taken the C# / Visual Studio 2012 platform to the next level with plug-ins that allow C# developers to even build iOS and Android apps. Figure 3-3 shows the same dialog: this time the JavaScript section is expanded and reveals the Windows Store projects exposed through JavaScript.

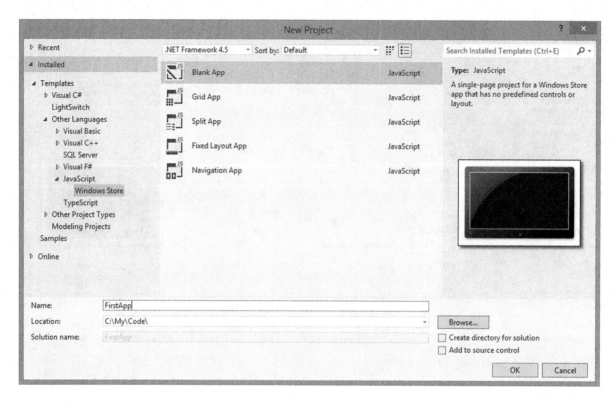

Figure 3-3. New project templates for Windows 8 JavaScript apps

Enter a name in the Name text field that makes sense to you, along with a location where the project files will be stored. Then click the OK button to generate the project. Figure 3-4 shows the Solution Explorer window after the project has been created.

Figure 3-4. Project items of a newly created WinJS project

As is to be expected, the project contains JavaScript, HTML, and CSS files—with default images included solely for the sake of tile icons, not content for the app. Listing 3-1 shows the contents of the default JavaScript file default.js.

Listing 3-1. Default JavaScript File of the New Project

```javascript
// For an introduction to the Blank template, see the following documentation:
// http://go.microsoft.com/fwlink/?LinkId=232509
(function () {
    "use strict";

    WinJS.Binding.optimizeBindingReferences = true;

    var app = WinJS.Application;
    var activation = Windows.ApplicationModel.Activation;

    app.onactivated = function (args) {
        if (args.detail.kind === activation.ActivationKind.launch) {
            if (args.detail.previousExecutionState !== ➥
                activation.ApplicationExecutionState.terminated) {
                // TODO: This application has been newly launched. Initialize
                // your application here.
            } else {
                // TODO: This application has been reactivated from suspension.
                // Restore application state here.
            }
            args.setPromise(WinJS.UI.processAll());
        }
    };

    app.oncheckpoint = function (args) {
        // TODO: This application is about to be suspended. Save any state
        // that needs to persist across suspensions here. You might use the
        // WinJS.Application.sessionState object, which is automatically
        // saved and restored across suspension. If you need to complete an
        // asynchronous operation before your application is suspended, call
        // args.setPromise().
    };

    app.start();
})();
```

The associated HTML content for the app is shown in Listing 3-2.

Listing 3-2. Default HTML File of the New Project

```html
<!DOCTYPE html>
<html>
<head>
    <meta charset="utf-8" />
    <title>FirstApp</title>
```

```
    <!-- WinJS references -->
    <link href="//Microsoft.WinJS.1.0/css/ui-dark.css" rel="stylesheet" />
    <script src="//Microsoft.WinJS.1.0/js/base.js"></script>
    <script src="//Microsoft.WinJS.1.0/js/ui.js"></script>

    <!-- FirstApp references -->
    <link href="/css/default.css" rel="stylesheet" />
    <script src="/js/default.js"></script>
</head>
<body>
    <p>Content goes here</p>
</body>
</html>
```

Now that you've laid out a project example, let's proceed with a discussion of controls. You delve into standard controls before moving on to a discussion of data-driven controls that use data binding.

Incorporating HTML Controls

As mentioned in Chapter 2, a key benefit of using the JavaScript library for Windows is that it's essentially pure HTML. This distinguishing factor from the pure WinRT found in C#- or C++-based Windows 8 apps is no more evident than it is in the case of controls. Because WinJS apps are built using the web standards of HTML, CSS, and JavaScript, they support the use of the HTML control set for application layout, styling, and interactivity programming.

■ **Note** The full list of supported HTML controls supported by Windows Store JavaScript applications can be found on the Microsoft MSDN site at `http://msdn.microsoft.com/library/windows/apps/hh767345.aspx`.

Understanding Controls

In addition to the HTML controls, you also have access to some WinRT controls projected into WinJS as classes. One example of these types of controls is the AppBar control you used in the previous chapter. Note that not all WinRT controls are projected into JavaScript. The Border class, for instance, which is found in the namespace Windows.UI.Xaml.Controls, is available in both C++ and C# through the Toolbox, in XAML, and also in code as a class that can be instantiated and attached to the document tree. As you can see in Figure 3-5, although WinJS is aware of the namespace, it doesn't have a class for Border.

```
        J
        args.setPromise(WinJS.UI.processAll());
    }
};

app.oncheckpoint = function (args) {
    // TODO: This application is about to
    // that needs to persist across suspe
    // WinJS.Application.sessionState obj
    // saved and restored across suspensi
    // asynchronous operation before your
    // args.setPromise().

    var g = new Windows.UI.Xaml.Controls.|
};
```

Autocomplete list:
- constructor — constructor() (+ 1 overload(s))
- hasOwnProperty
- isPrototypeOf — state
- Primitives — se the
- propertyIsEnumerable — lly
- toLocaleString — ete an
- toString — d, call
- valueOf

Figure 3-5. *Lack of XAML controls in WinJS*

Finally, controls can also be in the form of JavaScript classes. These can be classes that you as a developer write in order to reduce the complexity of your user interface construction and increase flexibility in your layout. WinJS comes with a number of controls of this kind, most notably the `ListView` control. Figure 3-6 shows the built-in `ListView` control in action on a default Grid App template. You can create a grid app by selecting Grid App instead of Blank App in the New Project dialog shown in Figure 3-3.

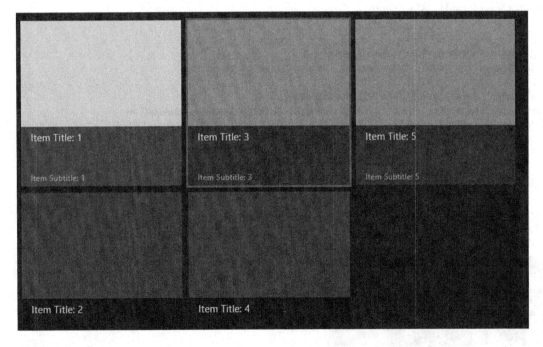

Figure 3-6. *A grid app running*

Applying Controls

As you might imagine, even though these technologies are vastly different from each other, you can use them interchangeably when building Windows 8 apps using JavaScript. In Listing 3-3, you add an app bar and an HTML button to the example project and then use the JavaScript event handler to open a message box that counts how many times the button has been clicked. You start by modifying the user interface. Listing 3-3 shows the new version of default.html with additions in bold.

Listing 3-3. Example App with an App Bar Added

```
<!DOCTYPE html>
<html>
<head>
    <meta charset="utf-8" />
    <title>FirstApp</title>

    <!-- WinJS references -->
    <link href="//Microsoft.WinJS.1.0/css/ui-dark.css" rel="stylesheet" />
    <script src="//Microsoft.WinJS.1.0/js/base.js"></script>
    <script src="//Microsoft.WinJS.1.0/js/ui.js"></script>

    <!-- FirstApp references -->
    <link href="/css/default.css" rel="stylesheet" />
    <script src="/js/default.js"></script>
</head>
<body>
    <p>Using Controls from different paradigms</p>
    <input id="btn_button_count" type="button" value="Click to count" />

    <div id="appbar" data-win-control="WinJS.UI.AppBar">
        <button id="btn_appbar_count" data-win-control="WinJS.UI.AppBarCommand" ↵
            data-win-options="{id:'cmd', label:'Also count', icon:'placeholder'}" ↵
            type="button"></button>
    </div>
</body>
</html>
```

You also change the heading of the form to be more appropriate to your intent. If you run the application now, it should look similar to Figure 3-7.

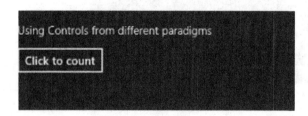

Figure 3-7. *Using a simple HTML button in WinJS*

Right-clicking the screen (or swiping from the button to activate the app bar) reveals the app bar you added to the app's view (see Figure 3-8).

Figure 3-8. *The app bar in the example app*

Now that you've made the layout changes, you can go back to default.js and incorporate the necessary modifications to enable the counting behavior. Listing 3-4 handles the click events for both the pure HTML and WinRT app bar buttons.

Listing 3-4. Event Handling for Both WinJS and Pure HTML Controls

```
// For an introduction to the Blank template, see the following documentation:
// http://go.microsoft.com/fwlink/?LinkId=232509
(function () {
    "use strict";

    WinJS.Binding.optimizeBindingReferences = true;

    var app = WinJS.Application;
    var activation = Windows.ApplicationModel.Activation;
    var _count = 0;

    app.onactivated = function (args) {
        if (args.detail.kind === activation.ActivationKind.launch) {
            if (args.detail.previousExecutionState !== ➥
                activation.ApplicationExecutionState.terminated) {
                // TODO: This application has been newly launched. Initialize
```

```
            // your application here.
        } else {
            // TODO: This application has been reactivated from suspension.
            // Restore application state here.
        }
        args.setPromise(WinJS.UI.processAll());
    }

    _count = 0;
    btn_button_count.onclick = function ()
    {
        _count++;
        var mbox = new Windows.UI.Popups.MessageDialog("Button clicked; you clicked ↵
            something " + _count + " time(s)");
        mbox.showAsync();
    };

    btn_appbar_count.onclick = function () {
        _count++;
        var mbox = new Windows.UI.Popups.MessageDialog("AppBar clicked; you clicked ↵
            something " + _count + " time(s)");
        mbox.showAsync();
    };

};

app.oncheckpoint = function (args) {
    // TODO: This application is about to be suspended. Save any state
    // that needs to persist across suspensions here. You might use the
    // WinJS.Application.sessionState object, which is automatically
    // saved and restored across suspension. If you need to complete an
    // asynchronous operation before your application is suspended, call
    // args.setPromise().

};

app.start();
})();
```

Notice that the third control, MessageDialog, is also used in the example. When the user clicks either the HTML button or the app bar button, the _count variable is incremented by one. Any marshalling that might be necessary to allow this type of transparency between the two technologies is hidden from you. As far as the developer is concerned, the app bar button can be treated like an HTML button when it's clicked by a user, using a standard onclick event handler to process the effects of the click. You see later how powerful and seamless this integration is when you look at some other events the app bar button has—events that aren't available to a standard HTML button. Figure 3-9 shows the user interface for the application when the app bar button is clicked.

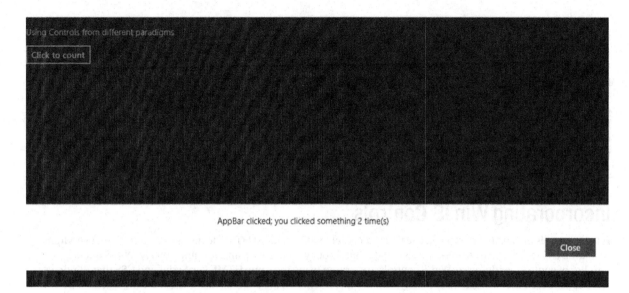

Figure 3-9. *Message dialog when the app bar button is clicked*

When the HTML button is clicked, the _count variable is incremented and rendered as usual, but the message box indicates its originator (see Figure 3-10). The message box text has changed from "AppBar clicked, you clicked ..." to "Button clicked, you clicked...."

Figure 3-10. *Message dialog when the HTML button is clicked*

As you saw from the example, incorporating the standard HTML controls is relatively straightforward—it works in the same manner as web development, so if you're already familiar with HTML you'll have no problem getting accustomed to this or even porting your web-based applications to Windows 8. This is particularly true of single-page applications (SPAs). SPAs are HTML pages hosted on the web that basically incorporate all functionality on a single page. The page calls any back end services it needs, pulls down any additional required HTML or JavaScript, and stores content locally where needed. Gmail is a good example, as is the mail client of Outlook.com. If you've used either of these web-based applications, you may have noticed that they never "go blank"—a typical indicator of the browser clearing the screen because a server request has been made. Sites such as these use HTML and JavaScript extensively and are key examples of the type of applications that can be ported to Windows 8 easily (and also of the power of Windows 8 JavaScript development, because a developer of such an application needs only one version of the application code.)

Incorporating WinJS Controls

HTML controls are great, and you can use them in tandem with standard HTML features to do just about everything that, from a UI perspective, WinJS controls can do. But if you want to get up and running quickly, WinJS offers a number of controls for doing so. WinJS controls are written using the same HTML JavaScript and CSS that Windows store apps use, so they integrate seamlessly with other elements on the page. You saw this in Listing 3-3. Let's add more controls to the page: in Listing 3-5, you add a DatePicker.

Listing 3-5. Using a DatePicker Control in HTML

```
<!DOCTYPE html>
<html>
<head>
    <meta charset="utf-8" />
    <title>FirstApp</title>

    <!-- WinJS references -->
    <link href="//Microsoft.WinJS.1.0/css/ui-dark.css" rel="stylesheet" />
    <script src="//Microsoft.WinJS.1.0/js/base.js"></script>
    <script src="//Microsoft.WinJS.1.0/js/ui.js"></script>

    <!-- FirstApp references -->
    <link href="/css/default.css" rel="stylesheet" />
    <script src="/js/default.js"></script>
</head>
<body>
    <p>Using Controls from different paradigms</p>
    <input id="btn_button_count" type="button" value="Click to count" />
    <div id="control_datepicker" data-win-control="WinJS.UI.DatePicker"></div>
    <div id="appbar" data-win-control="WinJS.UI.AppBar">
        <button id="btn_appbar_count" data-win-control="WinJS.UI.AppBarCommand" ↵
            data-win-options="{id:'cmd', label:'Also count', icon:'placeholder'}" ↵
            type="button"></button>
    </div>
</body>
</html>
```

The new control is highlighted in bold. Figure 3-11 shows the app with the DatePicker control added.

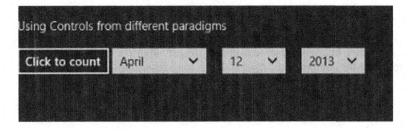

Figure 3-11. *DatePicker control in use*

You should notice two things from looking at this example. First, the control name, found in the data-win-control attribute (custom attributes were discussed in Chapter 2) shares the same namespace as the AppBar control. This WinJS.UI namespace is where you can find all the WinJS controls. Second, controls require a root element to attach themselves to. In this case you use a div, but any element can be used. Try changing the div used in Listing 3-4 to a button, and run the example again: you should notice a white bar around the entire control that functions like a button (meaning it's clickable). Figure 3-12 shows this bizarre UI.

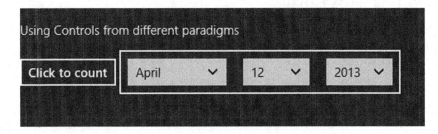

Figure 3-12. *DatePicker applied to a HTML button control*

If you switch the host control to the input element, you get an even more bizarre result: an input text box is displayed! The moral of the story is, be careful what element you apply the control attributes to, because they will still attempt to render themselves. Using a div or span is ideal because they seem to forego their standard behavior when controls are applied to them. For example, based on the HTML layout rules, a div should be on its own line; but as you can see in Figure 3-11, it behaves like an inline element.

This brings up a good point about the "seamless integration" discussed with regard to Listing 3-4. If you look at the UI for the page, the host of btn_appbar_count is not a div but an HTML button. Because of this, you can use the same onclick event for both buttons; they're both simple HTML buttons. This begs the question of how you might access the control-specific features associated with the element, given that the intent is to present a control and not the underlying element. For instance, it's correct to presume that events and properties may be associated with the DatePicker control, which tell you what date is presently selected in the picker and when the selection changed. Controls can also have methods that can be called to automate them in some way programmatically. The AppBar control, for instance, may have methods you can call to show and hide it. All WinJS control-decorated HTML elements have a winControl property attached to them at runtime for this purpose. The winControl property provides the connection from the HTML element hosting the control to the actual WinJS control and can be used to access any events, properties, or methods associated with the control.

Incorporating winControl

Let's modify the ongoing example with some code to show how `winControl` is used. You use this property to handle events that fire when the app bar is shown or hidden, but first you need to update the user interface of the page. In Listing 3-6 you add some basic styling to center the content of the page and also add a new control to display the app bar's current state.

Listing 3-6. Handling App Bar States

```html
<!DOCTYPE html>
<html>
<head>
    <meta charset="utf-8" />
    <title>FirstApp</title>

    <!-- WinJS references -->
    <link href="//Microsoft.WinJS.1.0/css/ui-dark.css" rel="stylesheet" />
    <script src="//Microsoft.WinJS.1.0/js/base.js"></script>
    <script src="//Microsoft.WinJS.1.0/js/ui.js"></script>

    <!-- FirstApp references -->
    <link href="/css/default.css" rel="stylesheet" />
    <script src="/js/default.js"></script>
    <style>
        div {
            padding: 5px;
        }

        .centered {
            margin-top: 50px;
            margin-left: auto;
            margin-right: auto;
            width: 900px;
            box-shadow: 3px 3px 3px #000;
        }
    </style>
</head>
<body>
    <div class="centered">
        <p>Using Controls from different paradigms</p>
        <input id="btn_button_count" type="button" value="Click to count" />
        <div>
            AppBar State: <span id="txt_appbarstate" >AppBar Hidden</span>
        </div>
        <div>
            <div id="control_datepicker" data-win-control="WinJS.UI.DatePicker"></div>
        </div>
    </div>
    <div id="appbar" data-win-control="WinJS.UI.AppBar">
```

```
      <button id="btn_appbar_count" data-win-control="WinJS.UI.AppBarCommand" ↵
          data-win-options="{id:'cmd', label:'Also count', icon:'placeholder'}" ↵
          type="button"></button>
   </div>
</body>
</html>
```

Nothing special here: you've added a new div with a span in it that displays the current state of the application's app bar. You've also added some basic styles that center the content of the page and apply a drop shadow. Figure 3-13 shows how the UI is laid out now.

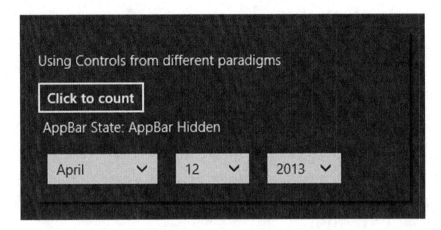

Figure 3-13. *New layout of the page with styling*

The fun stuff happens in the back end, as Listing 3-7 shows.

Listing 3-7. Referencing a WinJS Control from an HTML Element

```
// For an introduction to the Blank template, see the following documentation:
// http://go.microsoft.com/fwlink/?LinkId=232509
(function ()
{
    "use strict";

    WinJS.Binding.optimizeBindingReferences = true;

    var app = WinJS.Application;
    var activation = Windows.ApplicationModel.Activation;
    var _count = 0;

    app.onactivated = function (args)
    {
        if (args.detail.kind === activation.ActivationKind.launch)
        {
            if (args.detail.previousExecutionState !== ↵
                activation.ApplicationExecutionState.terminated)
```

```
            {
                // TODO: This application has been newly launched. Initialize
                // your application here.
            } else
            {
                // TODO: This application has been reactivated from suspension.
                // Restore application state here.
            }
            args.setPromise(WinJS.UI.processAll());

        }

        _count = 0;

        btn_button_count.onclick = function ()
        {
            _count++;
            var mbox = new Windows.UI.Popups.MessageDialog("Button clicked; you clicked ➥
                something " + _count + " time(s)");
            mbox.showAsync();
        };

        btn_appbar_count.onclick = function ()
        {
            _count++;
            var mbox = new Windows.UI.Popups.MessageDialog("AppBar clicked; you clicked ➥
                something " + _count + " time(s)");
            mbox.showAsync();
        };

        appbar.winControl.addEventListener("aftershow", function ()
        {
            txt_appbarstate.innerText = "AppBar Showing";

        });

        appbar.winControl.addEventListener("afterhide", function ()
        {
            txt_appbarstate.innerText = "AppBar Hidden";
        });
    };

    app.oncheckpoint = function (args)
    {

    };
    app.start();
})();
```

Notice that you use the addEventListener convention here when connecting your event handlers. This isn't mandatory; but if you choose to use it, note that the on part of the event name is always excluded. Listing 3-8 shows how the two event handlers would look if you used the other approach. As you can see from the examples, the event names for when the app bar is shown or hidden are onaftershow and onafterhide, even though when using addEventListener you add aftershow and afterhide. This is the convention, so be sure to either remember it or stick to one approach. You use the approach in Listing 3-8 for every other example.

Listing 3-8. Using the Event Handler Convention for Handling WinJS Control Events

```
appbar.winControl.onaftershow = function ()
{
    txt_appbarstate.innerText = "AppBar Showing";
};

appbar.winControl.onafterhide = function ()
{
    txt_appbarstate.innerText = "AppBar Hidden";
};
```

Figure 3-14 shows the user interface for FirstApp when the app bar is opened.

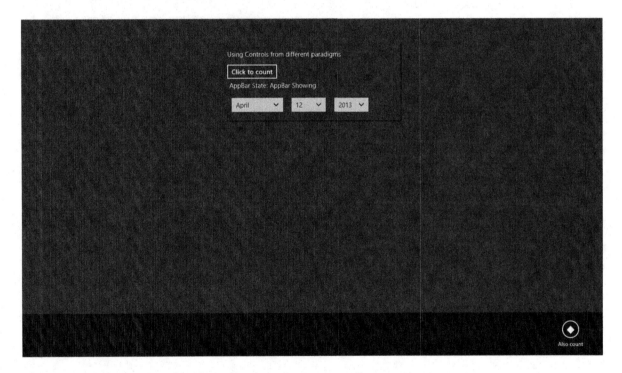

Figure 3-14. *UI for FirstApp when the app bar is open*

The winControl runtime property is a necessary evil for WinJS controls because of the manner in which the controls you've created to date are instantiated. So far you've been adding controls to the page by decorating target HTML elements with the win-data-control attribute (and optionally adding the win-data-options attribute when needed). But the great thing about WinJS controls is that they're first and foremost classes and as such can be instantiated in code. Creating WinJS controls in this manner ensures that you have a handle to the actual control instance. To see this in action, you can make some minor code changes. First, in default.html, change the app bar HTML to match Listing 3-9. Note that that the div has been renamed appbar_host.

Listing 3-9. Changes to the App Bar Layout

```
<div id="appbar_host" >
    <button id="btn_appbar_count" data-win-control="WinJS.UI.AppBarCommand" data-win- ⮯
        options="{id:'cmd', label:'Also count', icon:'placeholder'}" type="button"></button>
</div>
```

Because you've removed the data-win-control declaration from the appbar_host div, all you have now is a simple HTML div with no "special powers," as it were. This is a great time to test the fact that winControl is a runtime property associated with the underlying control that was attached to the host HTML element. If you run the code through the Visual Studio interface (with debugging enabled), you should get an error like that shown in Figure 3-15.

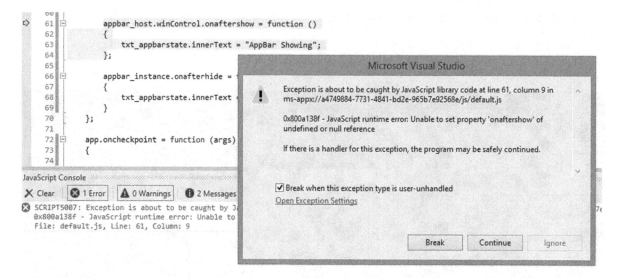

Figure 3-15. *Error using winControl on standard HTML elements*

If you encounter this dialog, click Break and place your mouse over the winControl property. As is to be expected, winControl is undefined—meaning it doesn't exist as a property of the appbar_host object.

Now let's change the code behind by instantiating a new instance of the AppBar class. Replace your current onactivated event handler with the code in Listing 3-10.

Listing 3-10. Instantiating an AppBar Control in JavaScript

```
app.onactivated = function (args)
    {
        if (args.detail.kind === activation.ActivationKind.launch)
        {
            if (args.detail.previousExecutionState !== ⮯
                activation.ApplicationExecutionState.terminated)
            {
                // TODO: This application has been newly launched. Initialize
                // your application here.
            } else
```

```
                {
                    // TODO: This application has been reactivated from suspension.
                    // Restore application state here.
                }
            var appbar_instance = new WinJS.UI.AppBar(appbar_host);
            appbar_instance.onafterhide = function ()
            {
                    txt_appbarstate.innerText = "AppBar Hidden";
            }

            args.setPromise(WinJS.UI.processAll());

        }

    _count = 0;

    btn_button_count.onclick = function ()
    {
        _count++;
        var mbox = new Windows.UI.Popups.MessageDialog("Button clicked; you clicked ↪
            something " + _count + " time(s)");
        mbox.showAsync();
    };

    btn_appbar_count.onclick = function ()
    {
        _count++;
        var mbox = new Windows.UI.Popups.MessageDialog("AppBar clicked; you clicked ↪
            something " + _count + " time(s)");
        mbox.showAsync();
    };

    appbar_host.winControl.onaftershow = function ()
    {
        txt_appbarstate.innerText = "AppBar Showing";
    };

};
```

Instead of declaratively adding the AppBar control, you instantiate it, passing in the target element that will host it. All WinJS controls require the HTML element that will host them as the first parameter of their contructor. This equates to adding the data-win-control attribute to the target element (in this case, appbar_host). If the control has options that you choose to define, you can use the second parameter of the constructor (an optional parameter). If you do so, the options are expressed as a JSON object. For instance, if you were to construct an AppBarCommand class, the second parameter of the contructor would look like Listing 3-11.

Listing 3-11. Example of Configuring Options from JavaScript

```
var appbarbutton_instance = new WinJS.UI.AppBarCommand(btn_appbar_count, { id: 'cmd', label: ↪
    'Also count', icon: 'placeholder' });
```

■ **Note**   The key to WinJS controls, whether defined declaratively through HTML or instantiated in the JavaScript, is the `process` function—specifically, `WinJS.UI.process`. When you're using the declarative approach to instantiate WinJS controls, it doesn't matter much; but it's important to understand that `process` must be called on a control for it to be rendered, and the control renders at the point when `process` is called on it. It's the `process` function that adds the `winControl` runtime property. In Listing 3-10, the JavaScript makes the call `args.setPromise(WinJS.UI.processAll())`, which effectively loops through the DOM, calling process on any elements that have associated controls. As you can imagine, in the case of JavaScript-instantiated controls, the call to create and associate them must happen before `processAll` is called; so be sure to make it a habit of doing so.

Diving In to the WinJS controls

WinJS provides several controls you can use to enhance your Windows 8 JavaScript app. This section goes through several of them in detail, with examples that illustrate how to use them in a general sense. I recommend checking out the `WinJS.UI` topic in MSDN for more details on specific controls. Before you get started with the controls, though, let's take a moment to revisit the pages and navigation topic started in Chapter 1. You do this for two reasons: first, pages are controls, even though they aren't instantiated or used in the same manner as other controls (they're also accessed through the `WinJS.UI` namespace); and second, pages are a great way to organize the examples you're creating for each control.

Pages

The WinJS navigation framework involves both the creation of pages and some application startup calisthenics to get you up and running. Before you begin, let's create a new folder called Demo and another folder in it called AppBarDemo.

To create a folder, right-click the project from the Solution Explorer and select Add and then New Folder from the context menu (see Figure 3-16).

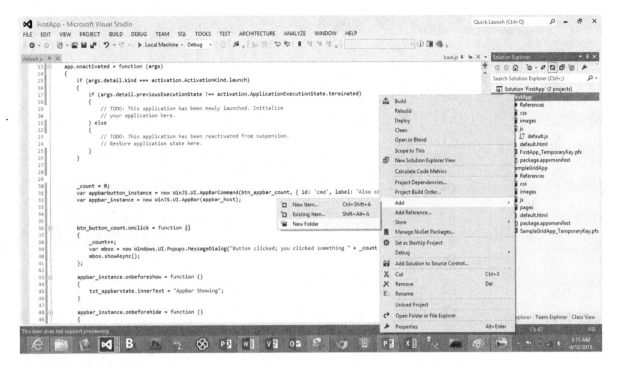

Figure 3-16. *Adding a new folder in Visual Studio 2012*

Adding a Page Control to the Project

In the newly created AppBarDemo folder, right-click and select Add, this time selecting New Item from the context menu. Select Page Control from the resulting Add New Item dialog, as shown in Figure 3-17, give it the name AppBarDemo, and click Add.

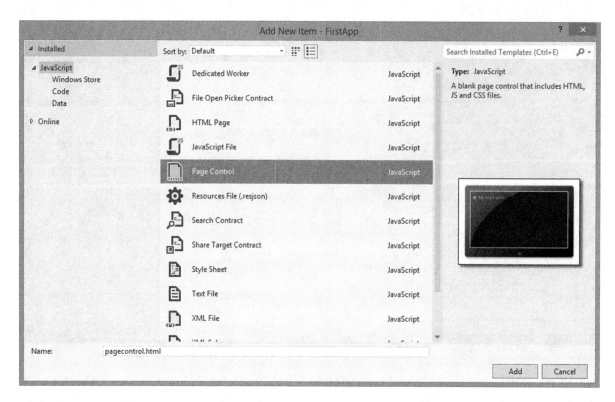

Figure 3-17. *Selecting the Page Control template*

The resulting Solution Explorer view should look like Figure 3-18.

Figure 3-18. *FirstApp project structure*

The thing to note here is that using the Page Control template to create a page adds not only the HTML for the page, but also the JavaScript and CSS. The default HTML added, found in AppBarDemo.html, is shown in Listing 3-12.

Listing 3-12. AppBarDemo UI

```
<!DOCTYPE html>
<html>
<head>
    <meta charset="utf-8" />
    <title>AppBarDemo</title>

    <!-- WinJS references -->
    <link href="//Microsoft.WinJS.1.0/css/ui-dark.css" rel="stylesheet" />
    <script src="//Microsoft.WinJS.1.0/js/base.js"></script>
    <script src="//Microsoft.WinJS.1.0/js/ui.js"></script>

    <link href="AppBarDemo.css" rel="stylesheet" />
    <script src="AppBarDemo.js"></script>
</head>
<body>
    <div class="AppBarDemo fragment">
        <header aria-label="Header content" role="banner">
            <button class="win-backbutton" aria-label="Back" disabled type="button"></button>
            <h1 class="titlearea win-type-ellipsis">
                <span class="pagetitle">Welcome to AppBarDemo</span>
            </h1>
        </header>
        <section aria-label="Main content" role="main">
            <p>Content goes here.</p>
        </section>
    </div>
</body>
</html>
```

The associated default JavaScript is shown in Listing 3-13.

Listing 3-13. AppBarDemo JavaScript

```
// For an introduction to the Page Control template, see the following documentation:
// http://go.microsoft.com/fwlink/?LinkId=232511
(function () {
    "use strict";

    WinJS.UI.Pages.define("/Demos/AppBarDemo/AppBarDemo.html", {
        // This function is called whenever a user navigates to this page. It
        // populates the page elements with the app's data.
        ready: function (element, options) {
            // TODO: Initialize the page here.
        },
```

```
        unload: function () {
            // TODO: Respond to navigations away from this page.
        },

        updateLayout: function (element, viewState, lastViewState) {
            /// <param name="element" domElement="true" />

            // TODO: Respond to changes in viewState.
        }
    });
})();
```

You can see that pages are defined by making a call to WinJS.UI.Pages.define (highlighted in bold) and passing in the path to the page's user interface (in the form /Demos/AppBarDemo/AppBarDemo.html) and a class that represents the page (in this example, you use an anonymous object containing the ready, unload, and updateLayout functions). This class should at a minimum include the ready method, because this is called when the page is fully initialized.

Modifying the Demo to Account for Pages

You need to restructure the original default.html to use the approach highlighted. The default.html file should now look like Listing 3-14.

Listing 3-14. Restructured default.html Page

```html
<!DOCTYPE html>
<html>
<head>
    <meta charset="utf-8" />
    <title>FirstApp</title>

    <!-- WinJS references -->
    <link href="//Microsoft.WinJS.1.0/css/ui-dark.css" rel="stylesheet" />
    <script src="//Microsoft.WinJS.1.0/js/base.js"></script>
    <script src="//Microsoft.WinJS.1.0/js/ui.js"></script>

    <!-- FirstApp references -->
    <link href="/css/default.css" rel="stylesheet" />
    <script src="/js/default.js"></script>

</head>
<body>

    <div id="control_pagehost" style="height:80%"></div>
    <div>
        <button id="btn_appbardemo">AppBar demo</button>
    </div>
</body>
</html>
```

The default.js file looks like Listing 3-15.

Listing 3-15. Restructured default.js

```javascript
// For an introduction to the Blank template, see the following documentation:
// http://go.microsoft.com/fwlink/?LinkId=232509
(function ()
{
    "use strict";

    WinJS.Binding.optimizeBindingReferences = true;

    var app = WinJS.Application;
    var activation = Windows.ApplicationModel.Activation;

    app.onactivated = function (args)
    {
        if (args.detail.kind === activation.ActivationKind.launch)
        {
            if (args.detail.previousExecutionState !== ↪
                activation.ApplicationExecutionState.terminated)
            {
                // TODO: This application has been newly launched. Initialize
                // your application here.
            } else
            {
                // TODO: This application has been reactivated from suspension.
                // Restore application state here.
            }
        }
        args.setPromise(WinJS.UI.processAll());

    };

    app.oncheckpoint = function (args)
    {

    };

    app.start();
})();
```

You now modify the AppBarDemo page that you just created with a new layout and JavaScript code to support it. The original HTML and JavaScript were boilerplate code placed there to enable basic functionality. The new code adds interactivity and a unique user interface layout. AppBarDemo.html is shown in Listing 3-16.

Listing 3-16. Restructured AppBarDemo.html

```html
<!DOCTYPE html>
<html>
<head>
    <meta charset="utf-8" />
    <title>AppBarDemo</title>
```

```html
<!-- WinJS references -->
<link href="//Microsoft.WinJS.1.0/css/ui-dark.css" rel="stylesheet" />
<script src="//Microsoft.WinJS.1.0/js/base.js"></script>
<script src="//Microsoft.WinJS.1.0/js/ui.js"></script>

<link href="AppBarDemo.css" rel="stylesheet" />
<script src="AppBarDemo.js"></script>
<style>
    div {
        padding: 5px;
    }

    .centered {
        margin-top: 50px;
        margin-left: auto;
        margin-right: auto;
        width: 400px;
        box-shadow: 3px 3px 3px #000;
    }
</style>
</head>
<body>
    <div class="centered">
        <p>Using Controls from different paradigms</p>
        <input id="btn_button_count" type="button" value="Click to count" />
        <div>
            AppBar State: <span id="txt_appbarstate">AppBar Hidden</span>
        </div>
        <div>
            <div id="control_datepicker" data-win-control="WinJS.UI.DatePicker"></div>
        </div>
    </div>
    <div id="appbar_host">
        <button id="btn_appbar_count" type="button"></button>
    </div>
</body>
</html>
```

And finally, AppBarDemo.js looks like Listing 3-17.

Listing 3-17. *Restructured* AppBarDemo.js

```javascript
// For an introduction to the Page Control template, see the following documentation:
// http://go.microsoft.com/fwlink/?LinkId=232511
(function () {
    "use strict";
    var _count = 0;
    WinJS.UI.Pages.define("/Demos/AppBarDemo/AppBarDemo.html", {
        // This function is called whenever a user navigates to this page. It
        // populates the page elements with the app's data.
```

```
    ready: function (element, options) {

        _count = 0;
        var appbarbutton_instance = new WinJS.UI.AppBarCommand(btn_appbar_count, ⮡
            { id: 'cmd', label: 'Also count', icon: 'placeholder', });
        var appbar_instance = new WinJS.UI.AppBar(appbar_host);

        btn_button_count.onclick = function ()
        {
            _count++;
            var mbox = new Windows.UI.Popups.MessageDialog("Button clicked; you clicked ⮡
                something " + _count + " time(s)");
            mbox.showAsync();
        };

        appbar_instance.onbeforeshow = function ()
        {
            txt_appbarstate.innerText = "AppBar Showing";
        }

        appbar_instance.onbeforehide = function ()
        {
            txt_appbarstate.innerText = "AppBar Hidden";
        }

        appbarbutton_instance.onclick = function ()
        {
            _count++;
            var mbox = new Windows.UI.Popups.MessageDialog("AppBar clicked; you clicked ⮡
                something " + _count + " time(s)");
            mbox.showAsync();
        }
    },
    });
})();
```

Connecting AppBarDemo to default.html

It should come as no surprise at this point that if you were to run this example, you would see a blank screen. This is because the page hasn't been added to default.html. Unlike typical controls, PageControls don't have to follow the instantiation pattern you saw earlier in the chapter with AppBar. There are a number of ways you can view the page you just created. Regardless of which approach you use, however, you always need a standard HTML control to host it. This is why, in Listing 3-14, you add a new div, control_pagehost.

The easiest way to show the page on your home screen is to call

```
WinJS.UI.Pages.render("/demos/appbardemo/appbardemo.html",control_pagehost);
```

You want to do this only when the `btn_appbardemo` button is clicked and to show a default intro page otherwise. Let's modify the UI to account for this. Listing 3-18 shows the new user interface for the application. You add some content to the `content_pagehost` div that is shown when the application first launches and centers the content that is displayed.

Listing 3-18. Modified User Interface Layout for the FirstApp Example

```
<!DOCTYPE html>
<html>
<head>
    <meta charset="utf-8" />
    <title>FirstApp</title>

    <!-- WinJS references -->
    <link href="//Microsoft.WinJS.1.0/css/ui-dark.css" rel="stylesheet" />
    <script src="//Microsoft.WinJS.1.0/js/base.js"></script>
    <script src="//Microsoft.WinJS.1.0/js/ui.js"></script>

    <!-- FirstApp references -->
    <link href="/css/default.css" rel="stylesheet" />
    <script src="/js/default.js"></script>

</head>
<body>

    <div id="control_pagehost" style="height:80%; width:500px; margin-left:auto; ⤷
        margin-right:auto">
        Welcome to the WinJS controls demo, click a button to open a page that runs the demo
    </div>
    <div>
        <button id="btn_introduction">Introduction</button>
        <button id="btn_appbardemo">AppBar demo</button>
    </div>
</body>
</html>
```

You also add a new button to the page that always takes you back to the default state of the application. Listing 3-19 shows the JavaScript for this page. I've also taken the liberty of cleaning up all the extraneous content auto-generated by Visual Studio.

Listing 3-19. Modified JavaScript for FirstApp

```
(function ()
{
    "use strict";

    WinJS.Binding.optimizeBindingReferences = true;

    var app = WinJS.Application;
    var activation = Windows.ApplicationModel.Activation;
```

```
    app.onactivated = function (args)
    {
        btn_appbardemo.onclick = function ()
        {
            WinJS.UI.Pages.render("/demos/appbardemo/appbardemo.html", control_pagehost);
        }

        btn_introduction.onclick = function ()
        {
            control_pagehost.innerText = "Welcome to the WinJS controls demo, click a ➥
                button to open a page that runs the demo";
        }
    };
    app.start();
})();
```

When you run this application, the default state should resemble Figure 3-19. The image has been cropped to reduce page real estate.

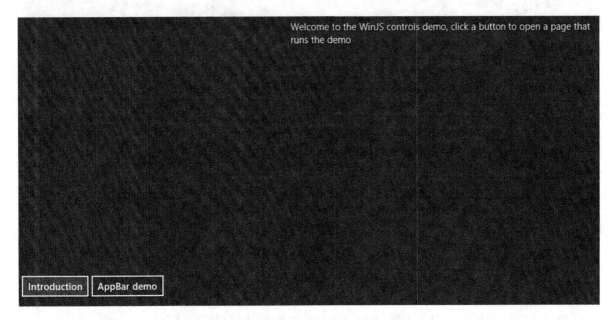

Figure 3-19. *Changing the host for the* DatePicker *control from a* div *to a* button

Using the Empty Function

There is a slight bug in the implementation you've used, tied to the placing of content in HTML elements that are earmarked as hosts for WinJS controls. If you remember, a warning earlier told you to stay away from HTML elements that render their own user interface, because the WinJS rendering process doesn't interfere with the normal rendering of such elements. You saw an example of this when you changed the host for the DatePicker control from a div to a button. When you ran the application, the button user interface surrounded the DatePicker, and the user could still interact with the element as a button! The bug in the example is revealed when you click the AppBar Demo button (see Figure 3-20 illustrates).

Figure 3-20. *Bug revealed*

You should immediately see the problem. The page renders as expected but without tampering with the content that was already in the div! To resolve this issue, WinJS provides a utility function WinJS.Utilities.empty that you can use to clear the contents of an element. (Yes, this can also be done using standard JavaScript/DOM tactics. In fact, you're already using one such tactic. Setting control_pagehost.innerText clears all the content from the div and replaces it with the text you specify).

The empty function takes as an argument the target element you wish to clear of child contents. Listing 3-20 shows the modified code for the event handler.

Listing 3-20. Modified Code for Event Handler

```
btn_appbardemo.onclick = function ()
        {
            WinJS.Utilities.empty(control_pagehost);
            WinJS.UI.Pages.render("/demos/appbardemo/appbardemo.html", control_pagehost);
        }
```

Now, when you click the AppBar Demo button, your screen should look like Figure 3-21.

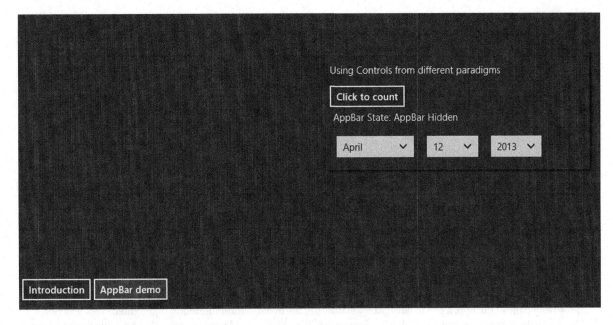

Figure 3-21. *Demo after clicking the AppBar Demo button*

Navigating from Within a Page

Using this approach is fantastic in scenarios where you design a navigation menu into the root user interface. Because you have buttons directly in default.html that invoke event handlers when clicked, which use render to render the PageControl onto your target div, you don't have much to worry about as far as navigation. But what if there was no root navigation menu? It isn't always ideal to define menus at such a high level, and there are plenty of scenarios in which one page may want to navigate directly to another page.

It's for scenarios like this that the WinJS.Navigation APIs were created. Put simply, the WinJS navigation framework provides a global function and event handler that allow your root page (the page that hosts your control host—in this case, default.html) to listen for when navigation is requested within the PageControl JavaScript it hosts. You can then make a call to render, passing in the page requested. To use the example code, instead of calling empty and render every time you add a new button, you can create one function that calls empty and then generically calls render (see Listing 3-21).

Listing 3-21. Global Navigation Handling

```
(function ()
{
    "use strict";

    WinJS.Binding.optimizeBindingReferences = true;

    var app = WinJS.Application;
    var activation = Windows.ApplicationModel.Activation;

    app.onactivated = function (args)
    {
        btn_appbardemo.onclick = function ()
```

```
    {
        WinJS.Navigation.navigate("/demos/appbardemo/appbardemo.html");
    }

    btn_introduction.onclick = function ()
    {
        control_pagehost.innerText = "Welcome to the WinJS controls demo, click a ↪
            button to open a page that runs the demo";
    }
};

WinJS.Navigation.addEventListener("navigated", function (args)
{
    WinJS.Utilities.empty(control_pagehost);
    WinJS.UI.Pages.render(args.detail.location, control_pagehost);
});

app.start();
})();
```

From any page in the app, a call to navigate will now fire the event-handler function highlighted. This function simply passes the location property (which is equivalent to the value passed in to the navigate function) into render.

The remainder of the chapter assumes adding the appropriate button to default.html and the appropriate JavaScript event handlers needed to navigate to the demo page associated with the example you create. I don't include listings for changes to default.html or default.js. Also note that there will be no figures tied to default.html.

AppBar

An AppBar control represents an application toolbar that is used for displaying commands. Earlier in the chapter, you saw how you can listen for when the app bar is opened or closed. You can also listen to the event before the app bar is opened or closed. I've found that the *before* versions of the events appear much faster; so from a usability perspective, they might be better to work with if you plan to update the user interface based on changes to the app bar's visibility. If you need to programmatically show or hide the app bar, you can do so with the show() or hide() method, respectively. The app bar also provides the flexibility to show or hide specific commands.

Let's modify the AppBar you've created thus far to highlight some of these features. Listing 3-22 changes the app bar demo into a simple three-question survey in which the app bar commands represent the questions.

Listing 3-22. Code for the App Bar Demo Page

```
<!DOCTYPE html>
<html>
<head>
    <meta charset="utf-8" />
    <title>AppBarDemo</title>

    <!-- WinJS references -->
    <link href="//Microsoft.WinJS.1.0/css/ui-dark.css" rel="stylesheet" />
    <script src="//Microsoft.WinJS.1.0/js/base.js"></script>
    <script src="//Microsoft.WinJS.1.0/js/ui.js"></script>

    <link href="AppBarDemo.css" rel="stylesheet" />
    <script src="AppBarDemo.js"></script>
```

```
    <style>
        div {
            padding: 5px;
        }

        .panel {
            width: 400px;
        }

        .centered {
            margin-top: 50px;
            margin-left: auto;
            margin-right: auto;
        }

        .shadow {
            box-shadow: 3px 3px 3px #000;
        }
    </style>p
</head>
<body>
    <div class="centered panel">
        <p>AppBar Survey</p>

        <div>
            Question: <span id="txt_appbarquestion">AppBar Hidden</span>
        </div>
        <div>
            <button id="btn_startsurvey">Start Survey</button>
        </div>

    </div>
    <div id="div_overlay" style="position:absolute; left:0px; top:0px; width:100%; ↪
        height:100%; opacity:.65; background-color:blue;visibility:collapse">
        <div class="centered shadow panel" style="margin-top:200px; background-color:white; ↪
            width:400px; height:250px; border-radius:5px;" >
            <span class="centered" style="color:black; font-size:xx-large">Pick a question ↪
                </span>
        </div>
    </div>
    <div id="appbar_host">
        <button id="btn_appbar_question1" data-win-control="WinJS.UI.AppBarCommand" ↪
            data-win-options="{ id: 'cmd1', label: 'Question 1', icon: 'placeholder', }"> ↪
            </button>
        <button id="btn_appbar_question2" data-win-control="WinJS.UI.AppBarCommand" ↪
            data-win-options="{ id: 'cmd2', label: 'Question 2', icon: 'placeholder', }"> ↪
            </button>
        <button id="btn_appbar_question3" data-win-control="WinJS.UI.AppBarCommand" ↪
            data-win-options="{ id: 'cmd3', label: 'Question 3', icon: 'placeholder', }"> ↪
            </button>
    </div>
</body>
</html>
```

The JavaScript code for this page is shown in Listing 3-23.

Listing 3-23. An AppBar Example

```
(function ()
{
    "use strict";

    WinJS.UI.Pages.define("/Demos/AppBarDemo/AppBarDemo.html", {

        ready: function (element, options)
        {
            var appbarbutton_question1 = ➥
                document.getElementById("btn_appbar_question1").winControl;
            var appbarbutton_question2 = ➥
                 document.getElementById("btn_appbar_question2").winControl;
            var appbarbutton_question3 = ➥
                 document.getElementById("btn_appbar_question3").winControl;
            var div_overlay = document.getElementById("div_overlay");

            var appbar_instance = new WinJS.UI.AppBar(appbar_host);
            var command_array = new Array(appbarbutton_question1);
            appbar_instance.showOnlyCommands(command_array);

            appbar_instance.onbeforeshow = function ()
            {
                div_overlay.style.visibility = "visible";
            }

            appbar_instance.onbeforehide = function ()
            {
                div_overlay.style.visibility = "collapse";
            }

            appbarbutton_question1.onclick = function ()
            {
                txt_appbarquestion.innerText = "What is your name?";
                appbar_instance.hide();
                command_array = new Array(appbarbutton_question1, appbarbutton_question2);
                appbar_instance.showOnlyCommands(command_array);
            }

            appbarbutton_question2.onclick = function ()
            {
                txt_appbarquestion.innerText = "What is your age?";
                appbar_instance.hide();
                command_array = new Array(appbarbutton_question1, appbarbutton_question2, ➥
                    appbarbutton_question3);
                appbar_instance.showOnlyCommands(command_array);
            }
```

```
            appbarbutton_question3.onclick = function ()
            {
                txt_appbarquestion.innerText = "Do you know what lies beyond the shadow ➥
                    of the statue?";
                appbar_instance.hide();
            }

            btn_startsurvey.onclick = function ()
            {
                btn_startsurvey.style.visibility = "collapse";
                appbar_instance.show();
            }
        },
    });
})();
```

Each question in the example survey is triggered when the user clicks the appropriate AppBarCommand associated with it. When the app's app bar is opened, a transparent div covers the entire surface of the screen with directions for what to do. Selecting a question from the app bar forcibly closes the bar and displays the question that was selected.

DatePicker

The DatePicker control simply allows users to pick a date. It's no different from any other standard date-picker control you might have been previously exposed to. In Listing 3-5, you saw how the DatePicker looks when it's on a page, but you never got around to incorporating some of its features from a programming perspective. Basically, as with most date-picking controls, the WinJS.UI.DatePicker provides a current property for accessing the currently selected date and an onchange event that notifies you when the current property has been changed. Listing 3-24 lays out the user interface for a simple date-picker demo to show off some of the control's features.

Listing 3-24. User Interface for a Simple Date Picker

```
<!DOCTYPE html>
<html>
<head>
    <meta charset="utf-8" />
    <title>DatePickerDemo</title>

    <!-- WinJS references -->
    <link href="//Microsoft.WinJS.1.0/css/ui-dark.css" rel="stylesheet" />
    <script src="//Microsoft.WinJS.1.0/js/base.js"></script>
    <script src="//Microsoft.WinJS.1.0/js/ui.js"></script>

    <link href="DatePickerDemo.css" rel="stylesheet" />
    <script src="DatePickerDemo.js"></script>
    <style>
        div {
            padding: 5px;
        }
```

```css
    .panel {
        width: 400px;
    }

    .centered {
        margin-top: 50px;
        margin-left: auto;
        margin-right: auto;
    }
</style>
</head>
<body>
    <div class="centered panel div">

        <div>
            Select Your Date of Birth:<div id="datepicker_host"></div>
        </div>

        <div>
            You are  <span id="txt_dob">unknown</span> years old
        </div>
    </div>
</body>
</html>
```

Listing 3-25 provides the JavaScript for the demo page.

Listing 3-25. JavaScript for the Date Picker Demo Page

```javascript
(function () {
    "use strict";

    WinJS.UI.Pages.define("/Demos/DatePickerDemo/DatePickerDemo.html", {

        ready: function (element, options)
        {

            var date_picker = new WinJS.UI.DatePicker(datepicker_host);
            date_picker.maxYear = 1995;
            var today = new Date();
            var dob = null;
            var current_date = Date.parse(Date.now().toString());
            var age = 0;

            date_picker.onchange = function ()
            {
                dob = date_picker.current;
                age = today.getFullYear() - dob.getFullYear();
                txt_dob.innerText = " " + age + " ";
            }
        },

    });
})();
```

The layout is relatively simple, as shown in Figure 3-22. Based on the user's selection, you calculate the user's age. Using the maxYear property of DatePicker, you're able to restrict the usage of the app to those age 18 or older.

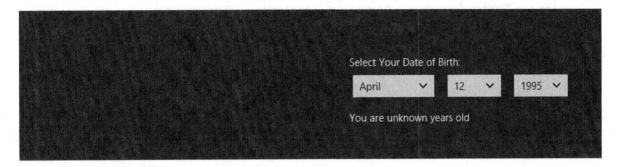

Figure 3-22. *Using the DatePicker control*

Figure 3-23 shows the UI after the user has made a selection.

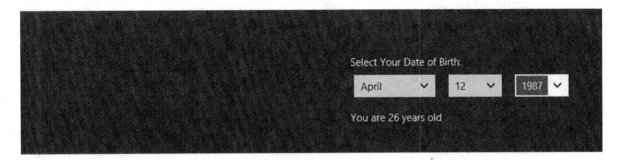

Figure 3-23. *UI following a selection*

Flyout Control

The Flyout control can be used to display a temporary lightweight user interface that disappears when the user clicks a section of the screen that is outside its bounds. It's great for displaying information in a non-interactive way or for consolidating functionality that would otherwise clutter the screen with excess controls. Earlier you created a demo in the form of a questionnaire. Listing 3-26 shows how an individual question (with associated answers) can be implemented using a Flyout control.

Listing 3-26. Implementing an Individual Question Using a Flyout Control

```
<!DOCTYPE html>
<html>
<head>
    <meta charset="utf-8" />
    <title>FlyoutDemo</title>
```

```html
<!-- WinJS references -->
<link href="//Microsoft.WinJS.1.0/css/ui-dark.css" rel="stylesheet" />
<script src="//Microsoft.WinJS.1.0/js/base.js"></script>
<script src="//Microsoft.WinJS.1.0/js/ui.js"></script>

<link href="FlyoutDemo.css" rel="stylesheet" />
<script src="FlyoutDemo.js"></script>
<style>
    div {
        padding: 5px;
    }

    .panel {
        width: 400px;
    }

    .centered {
        margin-top: 50px;
        margin-left: auto;
        margin-right: auto;
    }
</style>
</head>
<body>
    <div class="centered panel div">
        <div>
            How often do you perform a strenuous activity?<button id="btn_answer"> ↪
                Select an answer...</button>
        </div>
        <div id="control_flyouthost" style="width:150px;">
            <div>
                <input type="radio" value="Once a day" name="answer" >Once a day
            </div>
            <div>
                <input type="radio" value="Once a week" name="answer"/>Once a week
            </div>
            <div>
                <input type="radio" value="Once a month" name="answer"/>Once a month
            </div>
            <div>
                <input type="radio" value="Once a year" name="answer"/>Once a year
            </div>
        </div>
    </div>
</body>
</html>
```

The JavaScript for the HTML is provided in Listing 3-27. The application code is as simple and straightforward as the Flyout control itself. When the button is clicked, you call show on the Flyout instance, passing in the HTML element to use as an anchor for it and the position relative to the anchor where it should be shown. The Flyout is nothing more than a container for HTML (like a div that is being shown and hidden with JavaScript).

Listing 3-27. Code Behind for the Flyout Demo Page

```
(function () {
    "use strict";

    WinJS.UI.Pages.define("/Demos/FlyoutDemo/FlyoutDemo.html", {

        ready: function (element, options) {

            var flyout = new WinJS.UI.Flyout(control_flyouthost);
            btn_answer.onclick = function ()
            {
                flyout.show(btn_answer, "bottom");
            }
        },
    });
})();
```

Figure 3-24 shows what this view looks like when it's run.

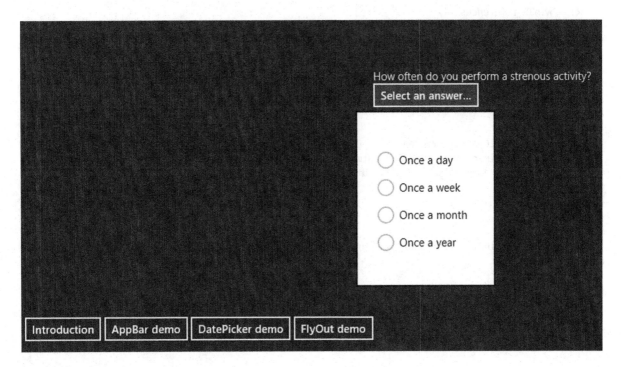

Figure 3-24. *Example of a Flyout control*

HtmlControl

Remember back 20 or so pages ago when I discussed pages and how the PageControl worked? When you created your first page, I explained that there are several ways to display a page on screen. One way, which was showcased in that section, is to use the render function. It takes the HTML, CSS, and JavaScript from the page you specify and intelligently injects it into the host page within the bounds of the host control. It's fascinating how this works, but in most cases it requires a little extra legwork to handle the empty function and all that WinJs.Navigation hullabaloo.

HtmlControl is a pretty nifty shorthand for this. With it you can easily create a navigation app without needing to do much of anything else as far as JavaScript—something the render approach obviously requires. Listing 3-28 creates a simple demo of HtmlControl by loading the Flyout demo from Listing 3-26 into its view.

Listing 3-28. Example of HtmlControl

```
<!DOCTYPE html>
<html>
<head>
    <meta charset="utf-8" />
    <title>HtmlControlDemp</title>

    <!-- WinJS references -->
    <link href="//Microsoft.WinJS.1.0/css/ui-dark.css" rel="stylesheet" />
    <script src="//Microsoft.WinJS.1.0/js/base.js"></script>
    <script src="//Microsoft.WinJS.1.0/js/ui.js"></script>

    <link href="HtmlControlDemo.css" rel="stylesheet" />
    <script src="HtmlControlDemo.js"></script>
</head>
<body>
    <div class="HtmlControl fragment">
        <div data-win-control="WinJS.UI.HtmlControl" data-win-options= ➥
            "{uri:'/demos/flyoutdemo/flyoutdemo.html'}"></div>
    </div>
</body>
</html>
```

The result should be exactly the same as Figure 3-24, with the exception of an extra button for navigating to the demo (see Figure 3-25).

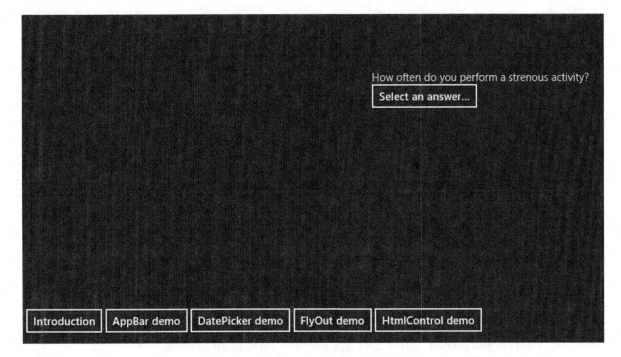

Figure 3-25. Adding an extra navigation button

Menu

The Menu control is relatively similar to Flyout—so much so that the example application you build for it will be essentially the same survey you created earlier, but with a Menu control take on it. You might wonder why two separate controls are needed if they're so similar. The answer is that there is a major difference between them: whereas the Flyout control supports any valid elements being added to it, the Menu control only allows MenuCommand controls to be added. In this way, the Menu control is somewhat like the AppBar control you saw earlier in the chapter.

Both controls add commands through a command property that accepts only a specific type of control (and also only a specific type of HTML element—both controls require that their command objects be hosted in button elements). Listing 3-29 shows the UI for the menu demo.

Listing 3-29. UI for the Menu Demo

```
<!DOCTYPE html>
<html>
<head>
    <meta charset="utf-8" />
    <title>MenuDemo</title>

    <!-- WinJS references -->
    <link href="//Microsoft.WinJS.1.0/css/ui-dark.css" rel="stylesheet" />
    <script src="//Microsoft.WinJS.1.0/js/base.js"></script>
    <script src="//Microsoft.WinJS.1.0/js/ui.js"></script>

    <link href="MenuDemo.css" rel="stylesheet" />
    <script src="MenuDemo.js"></script>
```

```
    <style>
        div {
            padding: 5px;
        }

        .panel {
            width: 400px;
        }

        .centered {
            margin-top: 50px;
            margin-left: auto;
            margin-right: auto;
        }
    </style>
</head>
<body>
    <div class="centered panel div">
        <div>
            How often do you perform a strenuous activity?<button id="btn_answer"> ↪
                Select an answer...</button>
        </div>
        <div id="control_flyouthost" style="width:150px;">
            <button id="control_daily" data-win-control="WinJS.UI.MenuCommand" ↪
                data-win-options="{label:'daily'}"></button>
            <button id="control_weekly" data-win-control="WinJS.UI.MenuCommand" ↪
                data-win-options="{label:'weekly'}"></button>
            <button id="control_monthly" data-win-control="WinJS.UI.MenuCommand" ↪
                data-win-options="{label:'monthly'}"></button>
            <button id="control_yearly" data-win-control="WinJS.UI.MenuCommand" ↪
                data-win-options="{label:'yearly'}"></button>
        </div>
    </div>
</body>
</html>
```

Listing 3-30 shows the JavaScript for this HTML.

Listing 3-30. JavaScript for the HTML Example

```
(function () {
    "use strict";

    WinJS.UI.Pages.define("/Demos/MenuDemo/MenuDemo.html", {

        ready: function (element, options) {
            var menu = new WinJS.UI.Menu(control_flyouthost);
            btn_answer.onclick = function ()
            {
                menu.show(btn_answer, "bottom");
            }
        },
    });
})();
```

Figure 3-26 shows how the page looks when the application is run.

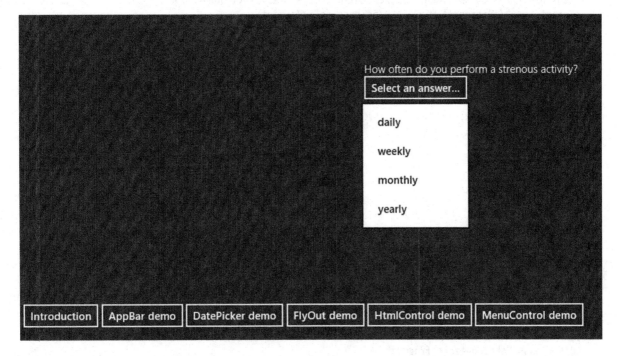

Figure 3-26. *The running application*

Beyond the fact that you're using different controls (the flyout demo used radio buttons, whereas this demo uses mandatory button elements decorated as `WinJS.UI.MenuCommand` objects), this example functions essentially the same way. The choice to use one versus the other ultimately falls to the developer and the style they want projected. Obviously the flyout gives you more flexibility and power, but for small cases (and to align the user with a common motif) the standard `Menu` control might not be so bad. Because you're using commands and not free-form HTML, and because you aren't manipulating the commands in any way, in this case you declaratively add the controls.

RatingsControl, SettingsFlyout, TimePicker, and ToggleSwitch

WinJS contains a number of other fairly simple controls that aren't covered in fine detail in this section. The function of most of them should be self explanatory, so rather than doing a deep dive into each and every control, let's create a single example that illustrates these controls. First you need to build yet another page to host the remainder of the controls. In this case, you create a page that utilizes the settings fly-out the moment it's launched. Listing 3-31 defines the user interface.

Listing 3-31. UI for a Page Utilizing a Settings Flyout

```
<!DOCTYPE html>
<html>
<head>
    <meta charset="utf-8" />
    <title>OtherControls</title>
```

```html
<!-- WinJS references -->
<link href="//Microsoft.WinJS.1.0/css/ui-dark.css" rel="stylesheet" />
<script src="//Microsoft.WinJS.1.0/js/base.js"></script>
<script src="//Microsoft.WinJS.1.0/js/ui.js"></script>

<link href="OtherControls.css" rel="stylesheet" />
<script src="OtherControls.js"></script>
<style>
    div {
        padding: 5px;
        color:black;
    }

    .panel {
        width: 400px;
    }

    .centered {
        margin-top: 50px;
        margin-left: auto;
        margin-right: auto;
    }
</style>
</head>
<body>
    <div class="OtherControls fragment">
        <div id="control_settingsflyouthost" style="background-color:gray">
            <div>Thanks for checking out our demos</div>
            <div>
                Rate this application: <div id="control_ratehost"></div>
            </div>
            <div>
                Enter your date of birth: <div id="control_timepickerhost"></div>
            </div>
            <div>
                Contact me in the future: <div id="control_toggleswitchhost"></div>
            </div>
            <button id="btn_save" >Save</button>
        </div>
    </div>
</body>
</html>
```

Listing 3-32 shows the JavaScript code for this HTML.

Listing 3-32. JavaScript Code for the Example HTML

```javascript
(function ()
{
    "use strict";

    WinJS.UI.Pages.define("/Demos/OtherControls/OtherControls.html", {
```

```
    ready: function (element, options)
    {
        var settings_flyout = new WinJS.UI.SettingsFlyout(control_settingsflyouthost);
        settings_flyout.show();

        var ratings = new WinJS.UI.Rating(control_ratehost);
        var timepicker = new WinJS.UI.TimePicker(control_timepickerhost);
        var toggle_switch = new WinJS.UI.ToggleSwitch(control_toggleswitchhost);

        btn_save.onclick = function ()
        {
            var result = "You rated this app a " + ratings.userRating
                + "\nYou want us to contact you?" + toggle_switch.checked
            + "\nYou rated us on " + timepicker.current.toString();
            var mbox = new Windows.UI.Popups.MessageDialog(result);
            mbox.showAsync();
        }
    },
    });
})();
```

Unlike the other examples in this chapter, Listing 3-32 programmatically creates the controls used for the section. As you can see from the JavaScript, you simply read some common properties from the target controls; when the user clicks the Save button, you present the values of their choices to them in a MessageBox. When this page is selected, the resulting screen should look like Figure 3-27.

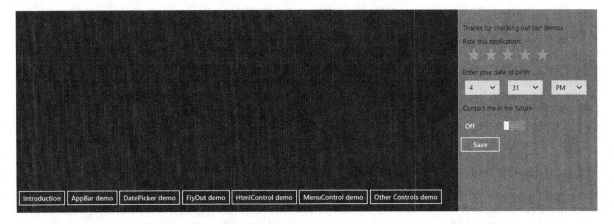

Figure 3-27. *Screen after the user selects the* MessageBox

Finally, Figure 3-28 shows what happens when the Save button is clicked. In this case, the application was rated a 5 by the user ☺.

You rated this app a 5
You want us to contact you?true
You rated us on Fri Jul 15 16:32:00 EDT 2011

Close

Figure 3-28. *Screen after the user clicks the Save button*

Advanced Controls

The previous section looked at a number of the basic controls available to you when working with the WinJS control stack. These controls work in relatively similar ways, requiring only for the control to be declared (or instantiated in code) in order for its user interface to be drawn.

This section introduces the more sophisticated controls offered by the WinJS framework. These controls incorporate data in order to create their user interface. Simply declaring such controls won't "seal the deal," so to speak. You need to also create a data-object list that represents the data the controls present, define a template that represents a view for each item (individual data object) in the list, and bind the two together such that the resulting view displays a list of a given template. Doing this provides a nice introduction to the binding functionality available to Windows 8 apps. The rest of this chapter prepares you to work with common advanced controls, taking you through the Flip View, the List View, and Semantic Zoom.

Working with Advanced Controls

Let's start with a simple explanation of the templating approach to Windows 8 app development. This approach, which did not originate with Windows 8 programming (or Windows programming, for that matter) works in two steps. First the developer defines a template, which is essentially a discrete group of user interface elements laid out in some pattern that is meaningful to the application. If this concept sounds familiar, it's because controls are similar to templates in this respect. Controls are different in that they can be instantiated and can stand alone without data. Templates can't, because they represent data—a template is a user interface view of an element of data. Take for instance the person object defined in Listing 3-33.

Listing 3-33. Code for a person Object

```
var person  = new {
        FirstName: "Azuka",
        LastName: "Moemeka",
        Age: 6.5,
        ImageID: 1234,
    };
```

If you were to represent this visually, it might appear in a list as the first name and last name laid out in a horizontal manner (see Figure 3-29). It might also appear as a details view with an image of the actual person.

Azuka Moemeka

Figure 3-29. *The person object*

Each of these views conceptually represents of the same data. One uses the first name and last name properties of the person object; the other might use the person's last name, their age, and an image that pointed to a picture of that individual. To get these views to work, you have to connect the properties of the object instance with the visual controls that represent them.

Figure 3-29 uses two span elements: one to represent the first name and one to represent the last name. At runtime, you set the innerText property of the appropriate span to the property you want associated with it. Listing 3-34 shows the HTML user interface for Figure 3-29.

Listing 3-34. HTML UI for the person Object Screenshot

```
<span id="span_fname"> </span><span style="margin-left:5px" /><span id="span_lname"> </span>
```

Listing 3-35 shows how to apply the appropriate properties of the object to each span, an activity referred to colloquially as *wiring up*.

Listing 3-35. Binding to Span Elements

```
ready: function (element, options) {
            span_fname.innerText = person.FirstName;
            span_lname.innerText = person.LastName;
        },
```

You can take this one step further. Assume that the specified spans have been designed such that they expect only names (perhaps a style has been applied to them that renders any content they present in a "name" way). You can build a more generalized version of the application using the author-defined attribute functionality discussed in chapter 2. Instead of programmatically setting the values as in Listing 3-5, you can create a generic function that finds the appropriate property and automatically sets the value for you. Listing 3-36 shows the full JavaScript for this new implementation.

Listing 3-36. Homegrown Data Binding

```
(function () {
    "use strict";

    var person = {
        FirstName: "Azuka",
        LastName: "Moemeka",
```

```
        Age: 6.5,
        ImageID: 1234,
    };

    WinJS.UI.Pages.define("/Demos/FlipViewDemo/FlipViewDemo.html", {

        ready: function (element, options) {
            ProcessBindings(person);
        },

    });

    function ProcessBindings(data_source)
    {
        var list = document.getElementsByTagName("span");
        for (var i = 0; i < list.length; i++)
        {
            var node = list.item(i);
            if (node != null)
            {
                if (node.attributes != null)
                {
                    var isboundcontrol = node.hasAttribute("data-binding");
                    if (isboundcontrol)
                    {
                        var property_to_bind = node.getAttribute("data-binding");
                        node.innerText = data_source[property_to_bind];
                    }
                }
            }
        }

    }
})();
```

Listing 3-36 starts by calling a function ProcessBindings, passing in a parameter that serves as the data source object (more on data sources in a moment). Within ProcessBindings, you get all span elements in the document and loop through the list searching for spans that have the author-defined data-binding attribute specified. When you encounter a control like this, you use the value of the data-binding attribute as an index to retrieve the property value of a property of data_source that shares the same name. Listing 3-37 shows how the user interface for this page now looks.

Listing 3-37. Homegrown Data Binding User Interface

```
<!DOCTYPE html>
<html>
<head>
    <meta charset="utf-8" />
    <title>FlipViewDemo</title>
```

```
    <!-- WinJS references -->
    <link href="//Microsoft.WinJS.1.0/css/ui-dark.css" rel="stylesheet" />
    <script src="//Microsoft.WinJS.1.0/js/base.js"></script>
    <script src="//Microsoft.WinJS.1.0/js/ui.js"></script>

    <link href="FlipViewDemo.css" rel="stylesheet" />
    <script src="FlipViewDemo.js"></script>
</head>
<body>
    <div class="FlipViewDemo fragment">
        <div>
            Beautiful children!
        </div>
        <div>
            <span data-binding="FirstName"></span><span style="margin-left:5px" /> ↪
                <span data-binding="LastName"></span>
        </div>
    </div>
</body>
</html>
```

Running this example produces the same result shown in Figure 3-29. The example illustrates some of the major concepts of the binding infrastructure, a principal component of data controls and their use. Templates essentially function like the user interface highlighted in Listing 3-37: they present a UI surface into which data is injected. Data sources represent the source of the data to be injected into the template.

Binding is the activity of associating given properties of the data with elements in the user interface. It encompasses both the binding definition portion (in the example, specifying the data-binding attribute containing the FirstName value—something indicating that FirstName will be placed in that span) and the actual bind action (placing the value in the span).

The example shows the basic mechanics of binding, but it should be easy for you to see how limited it is. First, it only works with spans; a robust data-binding solution would allow for many types of controls to be used. Second, it's limited in binding targets. In the example, you're always binding to innerText on the span element; but what if it was an image? In such a scenario, you would need to use the src attribute.

Given this basic description of data binding and how it applies to data controls, let's now look at some of these controls that WinJS offers. You start with the simplest of these data controls: FlipView. The great thing about using this as the first example is that, because of FlipView's relatively straightforward implementation and programming approach, it's fairly easy to pick up and understand the core concepts behind programming data-driven WinJS controls for Windows 8.

FlipView

The FlipView control can be used to display a list of objects one at a time. An example appears on the app details page of the Windows Marketplace app. This control is great in scenarios in which you need to display detailed views of list items while still providing the end user with the ability to move backward and forward through the list.

Let's expand on the example from Listing 3-27 by switching it to use a FlipView control. First you need to change the person object into a people list, then you create a template to represent each person in this list, and finally you declare the FlipView control and wire it up such that it presents the list.

Listing 3-38 shows the new data source you use. Notice that you add two extra activities to the design. After creating the array of people, you must add them to the WinJS.Binding.List object. The important thing to know about this list, as it relates to data controls of all kinds, is that it's necessary for binding.

Listing 3-38. Setting Up a List for the `FlipView`

```
var people = [
        {
                FirstName: "Alex",
                LastName: "Moemeka",
                Age: 9,
                ImageID: 5678,
        },
        {
        FirstName: "Azuka",
        LastName: "Moemeka",
        Age: 6.5,
        ImageID: 1234,
        }
    ];
    var item_source = new WinJS.Binding.List(people);
```

■ **Note** `FlipView` and `ListView` can't work with anything other that an object that provides the methods and properties exposed by `WinJS.UI.IListDataSource`. While attempting to bind, both controls make calls to methods that are expected to be in the binding type. The good thing about working with this object is that it exposes the same methods and properties as a standard JavaScript array, so it shouldn't be too difficult to pick up how to use it. I recommend using it all the time; but one of the value propositions of WinJS is that it can be easily transformed into standard JS and used in a web-based version of your app. Using any WinJS types that don't translate to standard JavaScript negates this.

You need to do something else with this list in order to get it ready for binding. This is something I haven't talked about to this point, but you need to make the list addressable in the markup. Objects you create in your JavaScript files are by default not accessible to controls that are defined declaratively. To make them visible to the UI layer, you need to declare them as namespaces using the `WinJS.Namespace.define` function. Add the declaration in Listing 3-39.

Listing 3-39. Defining the people List

```
WinJS.Namespace.define("people_list", {
        bindingList: item_source,
        array: people,
    });
```

As with the use of `WinJS.Binding.List`, this notation is something you just have to get used to. In order for binding to work, the object you expose publicly must have a property that represents the list being bound to (in this case, `bindingList`) and an array property defined on it. The `bindingList` property should be set to an instance of your binding list. The `array` property should reference your array.

Now that you have your data source ready to go, you flip over to the user interface and define the template you use to store the data. The template uses the same user interface layout from the homegrown data-binding example, modified to support the official Windows 8 data binding format (see Listing 3-40).

Listing 3-40. Creating a Template

```
<div id="basic_template" data-win-control="WinJS.Binding.Template">
    <span data-win-bind="innerText:FirstName"></span><span style="margin-left: 5px" /><span ↪
        data-win-bind="innerText:LastName"></span>
</div>
```

Based on your understanding of both controls and homegrown binding, Listing 3-40 should be self explanatory. You've created a template control that represents a data template for a person object. In the template control, you define the actual bindings that, as discussed earlier, are the user interface representations of the objects you're trying to display. As with the homegrown example, each person is represented by two spans: one for their first name and one for their last name (with a span that creates a 5-pixel space between them). Notice that in the official WinJS binding approach, the binding string accounts for the type of control being bound to. data-win-bind, equivalent in functionality to data-binding in the homegrown example, takes both the property name to bind to the given control and the attribute name to which the value should be bound. In this case, because both are spans, the value of data-win-bind is innerText:<data source property name>. In general, the pattern is <element's attribute name>:<data source property name>; so if one of the template elements was an image, the data-win-bind attribute would be src:<data source property name>.

Finally you define the control. Note that because the template is referenced and used by the control, it must be defined before any control that uses. Listing 3-41 shows the full user interface HTML with both the template and control.

Listing 3-41. Full UI Code

```
<!DOCTYPE html>
<html>
<head>
    <meta charset="utf-8" />
    <title>FlipViewDemo</title>

    <!-- WinJS references -->
    <link href="//Microsoft.WinJS.1.0/css/ui-dark.css" rel="stylesheet" />
    <script src="//Microsoft.WinJS.1.0/js/base.js"></script>
    <script src="//Microsoft.WinJS.1.0/js/ui.js"></script>

    <link href="FlipViewDemo.css" rel="stylesheet" />
    <script src="FlipViewDemo.js"></script>
</head>
<body>
    <div class="FlipViewDemo fragment">
        <div>
            FlipView Demo
        </div>

        <div aria-label="Main content" role="main">
            <div id="basic_template" data-win-control="WinJS.Binding.Template">
                <span data-win-bind="innerText:FirstName"></span><span style="margin-left: 5px" ↪
                    /><span data-win-bind="innerText:LastName"></span>
            </div>
            <div style="background-color:slategray" data-win-control="WinJS.UI.FlipView" ↪
                data-win-options="{itemTemplate:basic_template, itemDataSource: ↪
                people_list.bindingList.dataSource}">
            </div>
```

```
        </div>
    </div>
</body>
</html>
```

Pay particularly close attention to the `data-win-options` attribute for the `FlipView` control: both this and the `ListView` use this same mechanism. In it you assign the template that the `FlipView` uses to render each item in your data source as well as the data source itself. As the names imply, `itemTemplate` should reference the template for rendering each item (it should be the element ID of the HTML container that will represent each item's user interface), whereas `itemDataSource` should reference the data source—using the publicly scoped name defined in Listing 3-39. If you remember, that object you created contained a property called `bindingList`. In Listing 3-41, you reference a `dataSource` property of this object. This is a property you didn't define but that is attached to the object at runtime; you use it in this context, it's populated with data.

When rendered, this `FlipView` displays the same user interface layout (first name, last name) shown previously, with one exception: on a touch-enabled device, you can swipe right to left on the control to reveal the other list values. (If you don't have a touch-enabled device but have a mouse, the `FlipView` control displays forward and backward arrows you can use to navigate through the elements the control lists.) Figure 3-30 shows the user interface on a machine without touch.

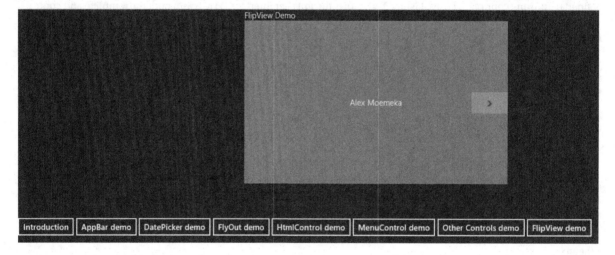

Figure 3-30. *FlipView control example*

ListView

Now that you've seen how to build a `FlipView` control and have a general sense of the primary components of data-driven control development, you should be able to extrapolate how the `ListView` is set up. The `ListView` control is functionally similar from a programming perspective (the only differences are the user interface and interaction pattern for each). This of course is principally due to the usage scenario each control satisfies. Whereas the `FlipView` targets rendering one list item's template at a time, the `ListView` shows them in list form. The simplest way to show this is to change the control type in Listing 3-41 from `WinJS.UI.FlipView` to `WinJS.UI.ListView`. Running the example now shows the same data in list form, as shown in Figure 3-31.

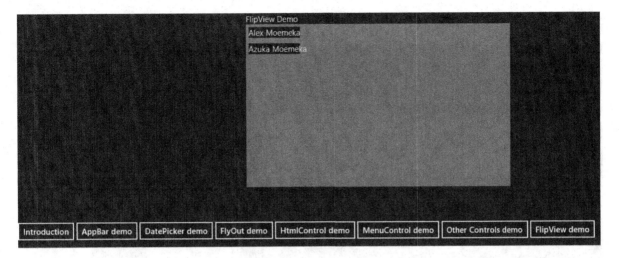

Figure 3-31. *ListView control example*

Visual Studio 2012 includes project templates for creating new projects with all the binding and layout for ListView controls already wired up. Figure 3-32 shows the Add New Project window in which you select the Grid App template. This template provides everything you need to start building a data-driven master-detail application in two formats. In WinJS, the Grid App template creates a grouped view in grid format. The Split App places the master detail all on one page.

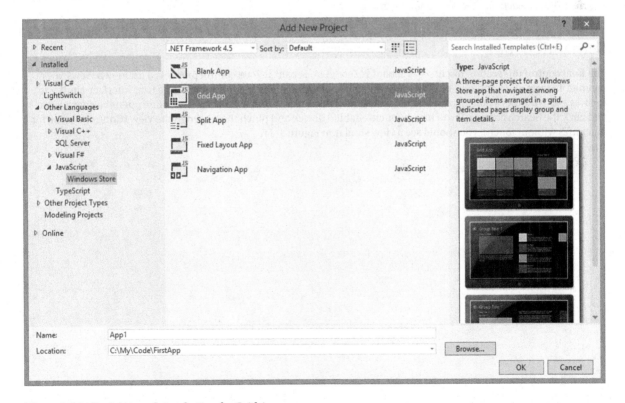

Figure 3-32. *Project template selection for Grid App*

If you create this project and immediately run it, you should have a user interface similar to Figure 3-33.

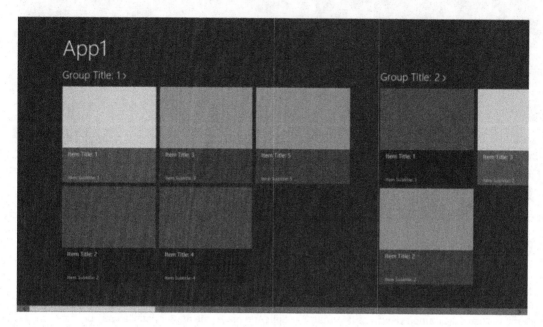

Figure 3-33. *The default Grid App template in action*

SemanticZoom

The final control this section discusses is SemanticZoom. The SemanticZoom control presents a list in two views: a zoomed-in view and a zoomed-out view. You might use this kind of functionality to create a user interface similar to the way the Windows 8 Start screen functions on the All Apps view (from the Start screen, slide open the charms bar, and click the Search charm). If you have a touch-enabled device and pinch the screen in the view (Control + scroll for machines without touch), you should see a view similar to Figure 3-34.

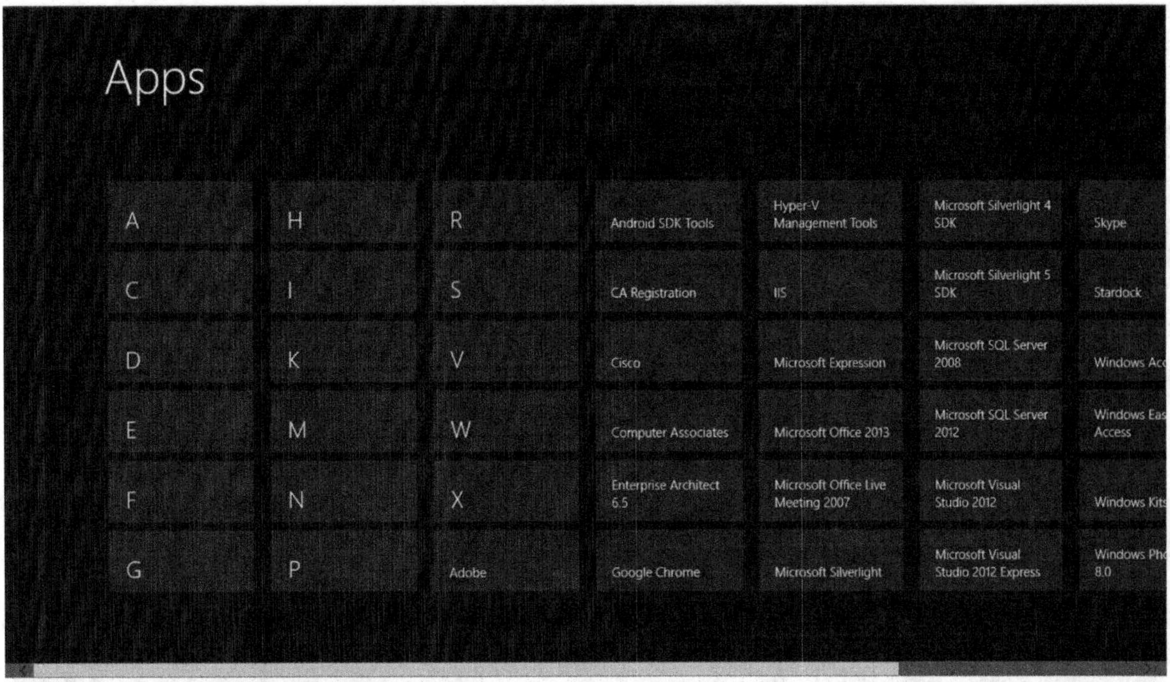

Figure 3-34. *Zoomed-out Start screen*

Being in the zoomed-out state allows the user to navigate quickly to areas of interest to them. In this case, the user can get to apps that start with the letter *X* without having to scroll through every app; but any high-level grouping you felt was relevant to the user would function the same way. Apps in this list could have been zoomed out to show the app publishers' names, date of install, permission set, or any other grouping that makes sense if the Windows 8 developers used one of these sorting mechanisms. As it stands, they chose grouping by the first letter of the app name. Note that desktop applications aren't grouped by application name alone (they don't participate in this first-letter grouping in the same manner as Windows 8 apps). This maps to the root application folder name visible in the Start menu of old. Figure 3-35 shows the zoomed-in view for the All Apps screen.

Figure 3-35. *Zoomed-in view of all apps*

Creating this is relatively straightforward. You simply define a `SemanticZoom` control in HTML and specify two views, using the `ListView` control (or other data controls) to represent the two states it must provide. The first HTML child of the `SemanticZoom` control is the zoomed-in view, and the second HTML child is the zoomed-out view.

The zoomed-out view functions with the use of grouping. Grouping allows you to sort the data you're binding to your control into groups identified via criteria you provide. In Figure 3-34, all the Windows 8 apps are grouped by the first letter of the app name (hence the list of letters). Because you only have two elements in the `people` list, let's modify it such that it you can easily see the grouping function. Listing 3-42 shows a new list (`family_members`) that expands on the `people` list you created earlier.

Listing 3-42. A List of Family Members

```
var family_members = [
        {
            FirstName: "Alex",
            LastName: "Moemeka",
            Age: 9,
            ImageID: 5678,
        },
        {
            FirstName: "Azuka",
            LastName: "Moemeka",
```

```
            Age: 6.5,
            ImageID: 1234,
        },
        {
            FirstName: "Elizabeth",
            LastName: "Moemeka",
            Age: 9,
            ImageID: 910,
        },
        {
            FirstName: "Edward",
            LastName: "Moemeka",
            Age: 9,
            ImageID: 1112,
        },
        {
            FirstName: "Tiki",
            LastName: "The Cat",
            Age: 1,
            ImageID: 1314,
        }
    ];
```

Not much has changed; you've just added more elements to the existing list. You use the first letter of the first name of each family member to group the list (similar to the Start screen approach). If you look at the array elements, you should notice that there are three groupings (A, E, and T) based on the criteria you specified. In previous examples, you created a List object and bound your controls to that object; in this instance, you need to add a few more steps in order to enable grouping of this dataset. The WinJS list object you've been working with fortunately provides everything you need to enable grouping. Using the createGrouped function, you can return a grouped version of the family member list. createGrouped takes three functions as parameters: the first takes an element of the list and identifies a group that it belongs to, the second retrieves the groups to be used for grouping, and the last sorts the elements (both in the list and grouping). See Listing 3-43.

Listing 3-43. Creating a Grouped List that Is Ready for Data Binding

```
var family_members = [
        {
            FirstName: "Alex",
            LastName: "Moemeka",
            Age: 9,
            ImageID: 5678,
        },
        {
            FirstName: "Azuka",
            LastName: "Moemeka",
            Age: 6.5,
            ImageID: 1234,
        },
        {
            FirstName: "Elizabeth",
            LastName: "Moemeka",
```

```
                Age: 9,
                ImageID: 910,
        },
        {

                FirstName: "Edward",
                LastName: "Moemeka",
                Age: 9,
                ImageID: 1112,
        },
        {

                FirstName: "Tiki",
                LastName: "The Cat",
                Age: 1,
                ImageID: 1314,
        },
];
var item_source = new WinJS.Binding.List(family_members);
var grouped_source = item_source.createGrouped(function (item)
{
    // return the string that will be used to evaluate grouping
    return item.FirstName.charAt(0).toString();
}, function (item)
{
    return {
        Title: item.FirstName.charAt(0).toString()
    };
}, function (left, right)
{
    return left.toUpperCase().charAt(0) < right.toUpperCase().charAt(0);
});

WinJS.Namespace.define("familymember_list", {
    bindingList: grouped_source,
    array: family_members,
});
```

In Listing 3-43, two things have changed from the FlipView and ListView examples you saw earlier. First, instead of just creating a list, you now take the additional step of creating a group from the list using the createGrouped function. Second, the grouped item is used to define a public namespace rather than the list itself. The three parameters for createGrouped are relatively simple. The first function returns the first character of every item in the list, so for Edward it would return *E* and for Tiki it would return *T*. This function is called once for each element in the list. The second function, called once per group, returns the group objects with a bindable name associated with them. This is important for binding to templates. In this case, you use the name Title to reference each group name. The final function is used to sort each element in the list and grouped list. It always passes two elements and expects a comparison between the two. You use the Boolean comparison here, but positive and negative numeric values also work. The user interface for the example is provided in Listing 3-44.

Listing 3-44. Semantic Zoom Example

```
<!DOCTYPE html>
<html>
<head>
    <meta charset="utf-8" />
    <title>SZDemo</title>
    <!-- WinJS references -->
    <link href="//Microsoft.WinJS.1.0/css/ui-dark.css" rel="stylesheet" />
    <script src="//Microsoft.WinJS.1.0/js/base.js"></script>
    <script src="//Microsoft.WinJS.1.0/js/ui.js"></script>
    <link href="SZDemo.css" rel="stylesheet" />
    <script src="SZDemo.js"></script>
</head>
<body>
    <div class="SZDemo fragment">
        <div>
            Semantic Zoom
        </div>
        <div id="basic_template" data-win-control="WinJS.Binding.Template">
            <span data-win-bind="innerText:FirstName"></span><span style="margin-left: 5px"
                /><span data-win-bind="innerText:LastName"></span>
        </div>
        <div id="group_header_template" data-win-control="WinJS.Binding.Template">
            <span data-win-bind="innerText:Title"></span>
        </div>
        <div data-win-control="WinJS.UI.SemanticZoom" style="background-color: slategray;
            height: 300px"
            >
            <div id="in" data-win-control="WinJS.UI.ListView" style="background-color:
                slategray; height:300px"
                data-win-options="{itemTemplate:basic_template, itemDataSource:
                    familymember_list.bindingList.dataSource}">
            </div>
            <div id="out" data-win-control="WinJS.UI.ListView" style="background-color:
                slategray; height:300px"
                data-win-options="{itemTemplate:group_header_template, itemDataSource:
                    familymember_list.bindingList.groups.dataSource}">
            </div>
        </div>
    </div>
</body>
</html>
```

Notice a distinct template for the zoomed-out view with bindings to the Title property defined on the group object from Listing 3-43.

As discussed earlier, the SemanticZoom control contains two collection controls: the first represents the zoomed-in view (in this case, a ListView bound to the family_members list), and the second represents the zoomed-out view (you bind to the groups property of the family_members list). This second control you connect to the other template group_header_template because it contains a list of group objects (with the Title property) and not a list of person objects. Figures 3-36 and 3-37 show how the example looks.

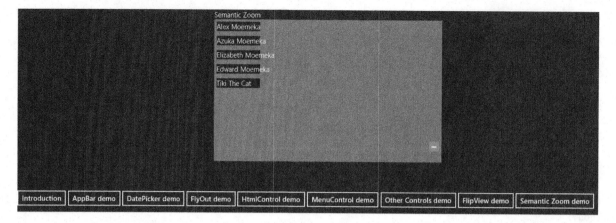

Figure 3-36. *SemanticZoom example in the default zoomed-in view*

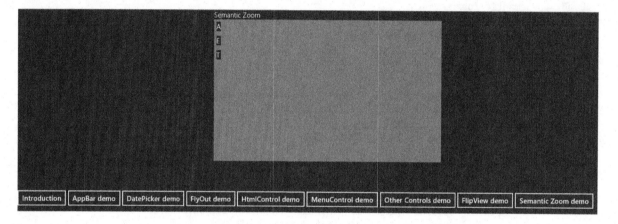

Figure 3-37. *SemanticZoom example in the zoomed-out view*

You can zoom out on the SemanticZoom control using the minus sign at lower-right (for a mouse), using Control + mouse wheel scrolled backward (also for mouse interaction), using Control + minus sign, or, if you have a touch-enabled device, by pinching the SemanticZoom surface.

Creating Your Own Controls

So far you've seen how to incorporate built-in HTML controls like the input, button, image, and span elements. You then examined how to use controls that aren't part of the HTML control set. These controls are great because they encapsulate additional functionality that is relevant to Windows 8 development; they include the AppBar, Flyout, and Ratings controls, among others. You continued by examining templates, binding, and the advanced data-centric controls such as FlipView, ListView, and the exciting new SemanticZoom control.

These controls represent solutions to well-known problems that the developers of the Windows programming APIs saw as important; but what if you have user interface functionality that you want encapsulated for your own libraries? Such controls could be reused across multiple projects to provide a consistent look and feel for the applications you develop. WinJS provides the ability to create your own custom controls if none of the built-in ones meet your demand.

As you saw earlier in this chapter, controls are little more than JavaScript classes that use a pointer in the HTML tree, a host element, to render their content to. You used this mechanism in Chapter 1 to create a homegrown control pattern using the data-win custom attributes. In this section, you create a new control, PersonControl, which essentially functions in a manner similar to the template you created in the previous section for rendering a person object. You need to do two things to do this. First you need to create a class that represents the control—accepting as constructor arguments the host element and the options you're accustomed to. You haven't encountered this before, but creating a class in WinJS is pretty simple. You only need to make a call to WinJS.Class.define, passing in a function that represents the class's constructor. define also takes two other parameters: one that expects an object that represents all the public instance members of the class, and one that expects an object that represents all the public static members of the class. This example doesn't delve into the use of these other two arguments, but you're welcome to explore the use of classes in this manner. You can find out more about them at http://msdn.microsoft.com/en-us/library/windows/apps/br229813.aspx.

You also need to make the class public by defining a namespace for it; you used this same approach in the previous section to make your data lists visible to the HTML markup that declares the controls they bind to. Listing 3-45 shows the JavaScript code for the custom control example. With the class and namespace defined, nothing more needs to be done (if the plan is to declare the control in HTML). As you saw in the "Diving In to the WinJS Controls" section, instantiating the control in JavaScript requires more coding but essentially works in the same manner as the HTML alternative.

Listing 3-45. Creating a Custom Control

```
(function ()
{
    "use strict";

    var person_contructor = WinJS.Class.define(function (element, options)
    {
        element.winControl = this;
        this.element = element;
        var first_name = options.firstname;
        var last_name = options.lastname;

        var firstname_span = document.createElement("span");
        firstname_span.innerText = first_name;
        element.appendChild(firstname_span);

        var space_span = document.createElement("span");
        space_span.innerText = " ";
        element.appendChild(space_span);

        var lastname_span = document.createElement("span");
        lastname_span.innerText = last_name;
        element.appendChild(lastname_span);
    });

    WinJS.Namespace.define("MyControls", {
        PersonControl: person_contructor,
    });

    WinJS.UI.Pages.define("/Demos/CustomDemo/CustomControlDemo.html", {
        // This function is called whenever a user navigates to this page. It
        // populates the page elements with the app's data.
```

```
        ready: function (element, options)
        {
            // TODO: Initialize the page here.
        },
    });
})();
```

The listing is pretty straightforward. You create a class using WinJS.Class.define, passing in the host element and the options specified at declaration time. Within the constructor, you create three <SPAN> elements: one for the first name, one for the space between the first and last names, and one for the last name. You retrieve these values from the options object passed in at declaration time. You set these values to the innerText properties of the appropriate spans and then attach the spans to the host element in the appropriate order.

You next define the namespace for the class so it can be referenced from the HTML markup. In this case, the class is addressable as MyControls.PersonControl. Listing 3-46 shows the HTML markup for this example.

Listing 3-46. Example Custom Control Markup

```
<!DOCTYPE html>
<html>
<head>
    <meta charset="utf-8" />
    <title>CustomControlDemo</title>

    <!-- WinJS references -->
    <link href="//Microsoft.WinJS.1.0/css/ui-dark.css" rel="stylesheet" />
    <script src="//Microsoft.WinJS.1.0/js/base.js"></script>
    <script src="//Microsoft.WinJS.1.0/js/ui.js"></script>

    <link href="CustomControlDemo.css" rel="stylesheet" />
    <script src="CustomControlDemo.js"></script>
</head>
<body>
    <div>
        Semantic Zoom
    </div>
    <div id="control_person" data-win-control="MyControls.PersonControl" data-win-options= ↩
        "{firstname:'chinua',lastname:'achebe'}"></div>
</body>
</html>
```

Just like every other control you worked with in this chapter, you instantiate PersonControl by declaring it through the data-win-control custom attribute attached to a container that represents the host of the control. You then use data-win-options to pass instantiation options in to the control, these options are used to control the ultimate layout of the control when rendered for the first time. Figure 3-38 shows the user interface for this example when the page is navigated to.

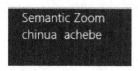

Figure 3-38. *Custom control*

Summary

You just completed a meaty chapter with a comprehensive and in-depth investigation into incorporating layout and controls. Here's a review of the key points:

- The JavaScript library for Windows is essentially pure HTML. This distinguishing factor between the pure Windows Runtime found in C#- or C++-based Windows 8 apps is no more evident than in the case of controls. Because WinJS apps are built using the web standards of HTML, CSS, and JavaScript, they support use of the HTML control set for application layout, styling, and interactivity programming.

- Controls can be in the form of JavaScript classes. These can be classes you write yourself to reduce the complexity of your user interface construction and increase flexibility in your layout.

- WinJS offers a number of controls for getting up and running quickly. WinJS controls are written using the same HTML JavaScript and CSS that Windows store apps use, so they integrate seamlessly with other elements on the page.

- All WinJS control–decorated HTML elements have a property attached to them at runtime for this purpose, called `winControl`. The `winControl` property provides the connection from the HTML element hosting the control to the actual WinJS control and can be used to access any events, properties, or methods associated with the control.

- Using the Page Control template to create a page adds not only the HTML for the page but also the JavaScript and CSS.

- An `AppBar` control represents an application toolbar that (in the case of JavaScript applications) is used to display commands.

- `HtmlControl` can be used to create a page when `PageControl` takes the HTML, CSS, and JavaScript from the specified page and intelligently injects it into the host page within the bounds of the host control.

- Although the `Flyout` and `Menu` controls are similar, the `Flyout` control supports any valid elements being added to it; the `Menu` control allows only for `MenuCommand` controls to be added.

- In addition to HTML controls and functionality provided by controls that aren't part of the HTML control sets, you can use templates, binding, and advanced data-centric controls such as `FlipView`, `ListView`, and `SemanticZoom` for Windows 8 app development.

- Custom controls give you the ability to create reusable user interfaces. This allows you to use controls that have the same layout and behavior in repeated instances.

CHAPTER 4

■ ■ ■

Navigating the Media Maze

Media experiences have long been a weakness in Microsoft platforms, but not because those features aren't inherently available in the system. Windows provides a wide spectrum of built-in playback and management features. The area in which the platform has fallen short is in the exposing of media content-creation and -management facilities to the end user. If you know DirectX or any of the low-level APIs, then you're good to go as far as this. But the reach of such technologies has traditionally not fallen far from organizations with the funding to hire resources with that knowledge.

Microsoft changes this with the release of Windows 8 through Windows Store apps—which have a programming interface that has been designed to ensure the delivery of modern, fast, and fluid applications. As a full-spectrum content-creation and -consumption platform, Windows 8 rises above the rest with its broad range of media support capabilities exposed to developers through the Windows Runtime (Win RT) and Windows Runtime for JavaScript.

Media Playback

If you've ever worked with Windows Forms development, you know how horrible media playback used to be. Before Windows Presentation Foundation / Silverlight, Flash, and HTML 5, media playback on the Windows platform involved embedding the Windows Media Player playback user interface into your playback target using a technology called ActiveX. Whether in a web page or a desktop application, Windows media playback was a totally disconnected experience, even requiring end users to download and install additional components in order to access the media.

In Windows 8 JavaScript applications, Microsoft has chosen to keep the language in total compliance with HTML 5. To that end, media playback follows the pattern of using the familiar video tag. You might have noticed from the previous chapter's discussion of pages and navigation that when you need to reference HTML from within your application, you use relative paths to do so. This is again consistent with standard HTML patterns and practices. Playing back media, as you can imagine, requires specifying at a minimum the location of the media you want to play back. In Windows applications, media for playback can come from one of two places (in general): it can be local to the machine, or it can come from some remote source—a web resource. Local media is placed in the project structure in the same manner as HTML content (and any other kind of content that needs to be referenced in your application). In Figure 4-1, I've placed the video content I plan to play in my project structure. This exercise uses the *Big Buck Bunny* video from www.bigbuckbunny.org. You can directly download a copy of the recording from www.bigbuckbunny.org/index.php/download/.

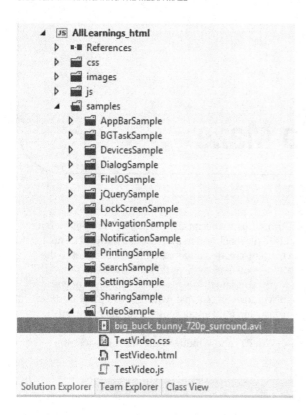

Figure 4-1. *Project structure with video added*

This is of course a far more elaborate project structure than what was used in the previous chapter. Even though it has more folders, the pattern remains the same. You use the application-level navigation to help you move from page to page even when the primary HTML document is no longer the main content area. (Conceptually, of course, it's still the primary document; the other "pages" are merely being injected into it.) This section doesn't go over each example but provides the baseline for the application that will host the rest of the applications. Let's start with the main frame for the application.

Setting Up the Project

In Chapter 3, when you dug deep into navigation mechanisms, you designed the host page `default.html` to display its content in two views. In the top section was the frame that hosted all the pages; below it were buttons that could be used to navigate from example to example. You reuse this formula in this project to create a layout and navigation structure that allow you to build all your examples in a single project. You are of course free to organize your example projects in a manner that makes sense to you. They should run the same regardless of whether they're all in the same projects or separated. (Note that you need to incorporate all appropriate references in scenarios for which you create different projects for different examples.) Listing 4-1 shows the HTML layout for the example browser project.

Listing 4-1. HTML Layout for Example Browser

```html
<!DOCTYPE html>
<html>
<head>
    <meta charset="utf-8" />
    <title>AllLearnings_html</title>

    <!-- WinJS references -->
    <link href="//Microsoft.WinJS.1.0/css/ui-dark.css" rel="stylesheet" />
    <script src="//Microsoft.WinJS.1.0/js/base.js"></script>
    <script src="//Microsoft.WinJS.1.0/js/ui.js"></script>

    <!-- AllLearnings_html references -->
    <link href="/css/default.css" rel="stylesheet" />
    <script src="/js/default.js"></script>
</head>
<body>
    <div style="height: 150px; background-color: #6E1313;">
        <div style="height: 50px;"></div>
        <header aria-label="Header content" role="banner" style="margin-top: 0px;↵
            vertical-align: bottom;">
            <h1 class="titlearea win-type-ellipsis" style="margin-left: 100px;">
                <button id="btn_back" class="win-backbutton" aria-label="Back" type="button"↵
                    style="margin-left: 0px; margin-right: 20px; visibility: collapse;"></button>
                <span id="txt_title" class="pagetitle">Select a sample</span>
            </h1>
        </header>
    </div>
    <div id="frame" style="margin-top: 10px;">
    </div>
</body>
</html>
```

Before you see the user interface for this code, you need to add the code from Listing 4-2 to the application startup section. This ensures that the content host for the example page loads with something when the application starts. In this case, it's loading with a page that lists all your examples as buttons on a page.

Listing 4-2. Application Startup Handler for the Example Browser

```javascript
if (args.detail.kind === activation.ActivationKind.launch)
{
    args.setPromise(WinJS.UI.processAll().then(function ()
    {
        WinJS.Navigation.navigate("/samplelist.html");
    }));
}
```

SampleList.html is basically a list of buttons that represent each example your app can display. As of this chapter, only one of these buttons is applicable, but you add them all here nonetheless. It's up to you to apply the pattern highlighted here each time you start a new chapter with a new example. You know the button to activate based on the subject matter. Listing 4-3 shows the user interface for the example listing page.

Listing 4-3. UI for the Example Listing Page

```html
<!DOCTYPE html>
<html>
<head>
    <meta charset="utf-8" />
    <title>SampleList</title>

    <!-- WinJS references -->
    <link href="//Microsoft.WinJS.1.0/css/ui-dark.css" rel="stylesheet" />
    <script src="//Microsoft.WinJS.1.0/js/base.js"></script>
    <script src="//Microsoft.WinJS.1.0/js/ui.js"></script>

    <link href="SampleList.css" rel="stylesheet" />
    <script src="SampleList.js"></script>
    <script src="sampleData.js" type="text/javascript"></script>
</head>
<body>

    <section aria-label="Main content" role="main" style="margin-top: 5px; margin-left: 100px;">
        <div class="sampleListViewItemTemplate" data-win-control="WinJS.Binding.Template">
            <div>
                <div data-win-bind="textContent:name"></div>
            </div>
        </div>
        <div style="width: auto; height: auto;">
            <div style="height: 0px;"></div>
            <div style="width: auto; height: 39.04px; top: 0px; margin-top: 0px;">
                <input id="btn_navsamples" type="button" value="Navigation Samples" ↵
                    style="width: 353.55px; height: 35.89px;" />
            </div>
            <div style="width: auto; height: 38.32px; ">
                <input id="btn_appbarsamples" type="button" value="AppBar samples">
            </div>
            <div style="width: auto; height: 41.64px;">
                <input id="btn_backgroundtasks" type="button" value="Background Tasks">
            </div>
            <div style="width: auto; height: 41.64px;">
                <input id="btn_jquery" type="button" value="jQuery Samples">
            </div>
            <div style="width: auto; height: 41.64px;">
                <input id="btn_fileio" type="button" value="FileIO Samples">
            </div>
            <div style="width: auto; height: 41.64px;">
                <input id="btn_lockscreen" type="button" value="LockScreen Samples">
            </div>
            <div style="width: auto; height: 41.64px;">
                <input id="btn_video" type="button" value="Video Samples">
            </div>
            <div style="width: auto; height: 41.64px;">
                <input id="btn_search" type="button" value="Search Samples">
            </div>
```

```
        <div style="width: auto; height: 41.64px;">
            <input id="btn_share" type="button" value="Share Samples">
        </div>
        <div style="width: auto; height: 41.64px;">
            <input id="btn_settings" type="button" value="Settings Samples">
        </div>
        <div style="width: auto; height: 41.64px;">
            <input id="btn_printing" type="button" value="Printing Samples">
        </div>
        <div style="width: auto; height: 41.64px;">
            <input id="btn_dialogs" type="button" value="Dialog Samples">
        </div>
        <div style="width: auto; height: 41.64px;">
            <input id="btn_notifications" type="button" value="Notification Samples">
        </div>
        </div>
    </section>
</body>
</html>
```

Figure 4-2 shows how the app looks when it runs.

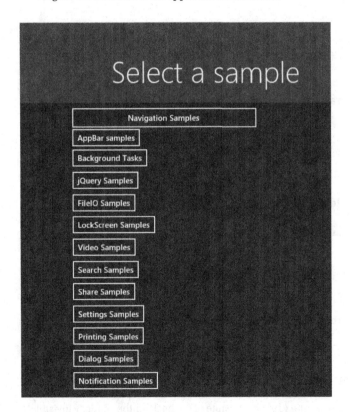

Figure 4-2. *App UI for the example browser*

This page's JavaScript for the button click that launches the video example is shown in Listing 4-4. Event handlers such as this should ideally be placed in the ready function of the page being executed. In this case, that would be samplelist.js.

Listing 4-4. Event Handler Code for When the Video Button Is Clicked

```
btn_video.onclick = function ()
            {
                WinJS.Navigation.navigate("/samples/videosample/testvideo.html",↵
                    "Testing Video Tasks");
            };
```

Notice something interesting about this use of navigate? In Chapter 3, when you used navigate, you passed only one argument: the URL of the HTML file you were navigating to. Now you're passing an extra argument: the string "Testing Video Tasks". This second argument is used to pass state information from the navigating page to the page being navigated to. It's a great way to pass context information between the two pages without having to create global state. Listing 4-5 shows how to use the navigated event of WinJS.Navigation to pass this value to the page-rendering function. If you remember from Chapter 3, global navigation needs to be in the root host page's JavaScript code. This is the JavaScript for the main HTML page hosting all the other pages (similar to how frames work in web-based HTML pages). For this project, this is the default.js file. In the main application function, you can insert this anywhere after the main declarations and before the call to app.start(). Note that in the default project configuration, default.js is located in the project's js folder (see Figure 4-1).

Listing 4-5. JavaScript for the Main HTML Page

```
WinJS.Navigation.addEventListener("navigated", function (args)
        {
            //find the frame
            var frame = document.getElementById("frame");

            //clear the frame
            WinJS.Utilities.empty(frame);


            if (WinJS.Navigation.canGoBack)
                btn_back.style.visibility = "visible";
            else
                btn_back.style.visibility = "collapse";

            if (args.detail.state != null)
                txt_title.textContent = args.detail.state;

            //render the location onto the frame
            args.detail.setPromise(WinJS.UI.Pages.render(args.detail.location, frame,↵
                args.detail.state));

        });
```

You call out two things from this code. First you use the value of state to set a title on the root page—the idea being that a user will always know where they were. Second, you set the visibility state of the back button (initially invisible) based on whether the navigation stack allows for going backward. To enable navigating backward, add the code from Listing 4-6 to the application's activated event handler (the application startup code located in default.js).

Listing 4-6. Code to Handle Backward Navigation

```
var btn_back = document.getElementById("btn_back");
        btn_back.onclick = function ()
        {
            WinJS.Navigation.back();
        };
```

Media Playback

When you click the Video Samples button, you should see the screen shown in Figure 4-3.

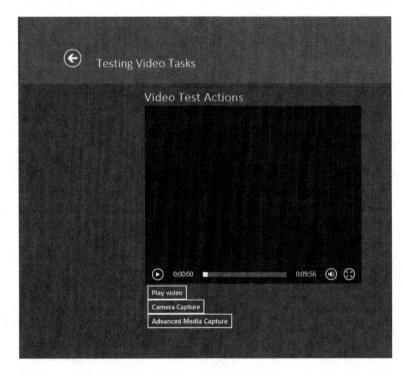

Figure 4-3. *Video sample user interface*

Can you guess what the HTML is to generate this page? Of course, for a seasoned web developer, a page like this is trivial (and made so by design to put the focus primarily on Windows 8 development, not HTML layout practices). Listing 4-7 shows how it's composed. Note that up to this point, no WinJS has been used, so this page could theoretically be ported to the web with no effort.

Listing 4-7. HTML for the Video Sample

```
<!DOCTYPE html>
<html>
<head>
    <meta charset="utf-8" />
    <title>TestVideo</title>
```

```html
    <!-- WinJS references -->
    <link href="//Microsoft.WinJS.1.0/css/ui-dark.css" rel="stylesheet" />
    <script src="//Microsoft.WinJS.1.0/js/base.js"></script>
    <script src="//Microsoft.WinJS.1.0/js/ui.js"></script>

    <link href="TestVideo.css" rel="stylesheet" />
    <script src="TestVideo.js"></script>
    <style>
        div
        {
            margin-left: 5px;
        }

        span
        {
            font-size: 22pt;
            font-family: Calibri;
        }

            span.notification
            {
                background-color: red;
            }

        input[type=file]
        {
            width: 100%;
        }

        .centered
        {
            margin-left: auto;
            margin-right: auto;
            width: 800px;
            box-shadow: 0px 0px 5px #000;
        }
    </style>

    <script type="text/javascript">

    </script>
</head>
<body>
    <div class="TestVideo fragment">
        <div class="centered">
            <div>
                <span class="heading">Video Test Actions</span>
            </div>
            <div>
                <video id="player_video" style="width: 500px; height: 400px"↵
                    src="/samples/videosample/big_buck_bunny_720p_surround.avi" autoplay></video>
            </div>
```

```
        <div>
            <div style="display: table-cell">
                <div>
                    <button id="btn_playvideo">Play video</button>
                </div>
                <div>

                    <button id="btn_capture">Camera Capture</button>
                </div>
                <div>
                    <button id="btn_advancedcapture">Advanced Media Capture</button>
                </div>

            </div>

        </div>
    </div>
</body>
</html>
```

Don't worry about the buttons btn_capture and btn_advancecapture for right now; they're discussed in detail when you get into the mechanisms of media capture in Windows 8 apps. In the example, the end user has no control over when the playback begins. Playback starts immediately here because of the autoplay attribute. You can delegate playback control to the user by making the playback controls visible as shown in Listing 4-8 (and of course removing the autoplay feedback).

Listing 4-8. Video Playback

```
<video id="player_video" style="width:500px; height:400px" ↵
    src="/samples/videosample/big_buck_bunny_720p_surround.avi" controls></video>
```

Of course, you can also control playback through the application using JavaScript. Listing 4-9 uses JavaScript to play video (you can also use JavaScript to stop or pause video using the pause() function).

Listing 4-9. JavaScript Video Playback (Playing Video)

```
btn_playvideo.onclick = function ()
            {
                player_video.play();
            };
```

In addition to autoplay and controls, you can apply various other attributes to the video tag. These include but are of course not limited to the following:

- muted: Tells the video control to mute audio

- poster: Allows you to specify a URL the points to an image that is displayed while the video isn't playing

- loop: Tells the video control to restart the video after it has completed

Listing 4-10 shows the use of the poster property. As you can imagine, it can be quite useful for depicting the contents of the video before the user decides to play it. You might have seen this type of technique used on such popular sites as YouTube, AOL, and MSN, enticing you to play a video.

Listing 4-10. Adding a Poster to the Video Tag

```
<video id="player_video" style="width: 500px; height: 400px"↵
    src="/samples/videosample/big_buck_bunny_720p_surround.avi"↵
    poster="/samples/videosample/Big_buck_bunny_poster_big.jpg" controls></video>
```

In this case, you're using a file in your project folder to serve as the image (this image file can come from any web resource as well). I chose to use the poster for the *Big Buck Bunny* movie, which can be found at the following wiki commons web address: `https://commons.wikimedia.org/wiki/File:Big_buck_bunny_poster_big.jpg`. You are of course welcome to use any image that makes sense to you.

When you run this example, you can see the image displayed directly in the video control. It stays there as long as the video is in a stopped state (media such as this can be playing, paused, or stopped). Figure 4-4 shows how the video control looks before playback begins.

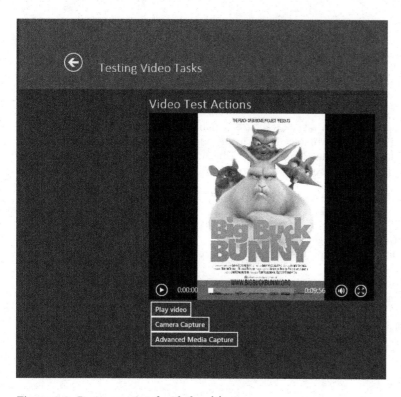

Figure 4-4. Poster associated with the `video` tag

Using the `video` tag, you can also play back media directly from a backend web server. Listing 4-11 shows this at work.

Listing 4-11. Server-side Video Playback

```
<video id="player_video" style="width:500px; height:400px"↵
    src="http://sample.com/samples/videosample/big_buck_bunny_720p_surround.avi"↵
    controls></video>
```

For this example to work, you have to add the *Internet Client* capabilities to your application manifest as described in Chapter 1. Internet Client grants a Windows 8 app permission to access the Internet. Without it, you can't connect to any cloud-based resource through any API.

The video control in Windows 8 is a subclass of HTMLMediaElement. It can be used to play both video and audio. If you're sure there is no need for anything more than audio (perhaps a game intro sequence or a music streaming application), then you can use the audio tag. Like the video tag, the audio tag can be used to play back both video and audio content, with the caveat that the audio tag plays back only audio (no video is rendered). Try replacing the HTML in Listing 4-11 with the code in Listing 4-12.

Listing 4-12. Playing Only Audio

```
<audio id="player_video"  src="/samples/videosample/big_buck_bunny_720p_surround.avi" ↵
    controls></audio>
```

Now, when you click the Play Video button, only the sounds associated with the *Big Buck Bunny* video play. You might also notice that only the bottom portion of the video control (the part with the Play/Pause button) is visible now. When I said the audio tag doesn't play any video, I meant it.

Of course, as Listing 4-13 shows, the audio tag may also be used to stream audio from a remote server in the same manner as the video tag.

Listing 4-13. Streaming Only Audio from a Remote Server

```
<audio id="player_video"  src="http://sample.com/samples/videosample/ ↵
    big_buck_bunny_720p_surround.avi" controls></audio>
```

The examples to this point have used a video, *Big Buck Bunny*, which uses the AVI file format. Windows 8 supports a number of encoding types and file formats for audio and video playback. Table 4-1, pulled from MSDN, shows all the supported media formats.

Table 4-1. *Supported Media Playback Formats*

Media File Container or File Format	File Extension	Media Stream Formats (Codecs)	
		Video	Audio
MPEG-4	.3g2	H.263	AAC (LC, HE)
	.3gp2	H.264 (Baseline, Main, High)	
	.3gp	MPEG-4 Part 2 SP and ASP	
	.3gpp		
	.m4a	n/a	AAC (LC, HE)
	.m4v	H.263	MP3
	.mp4v	H.264 (Baseline, Main, High)	AC3 (DD, DD+)
	.mp4	MPEG-4 Part 2 SP and ASP	
	.mov		
MPEG-2	.m2ts (such as AVCHD)	H.264	MPEG-2 (L1, L2, stereo only)
			MPEG-1 (L1, L2)
			AAC (LC, HE)
			AC3 (DD, DD+)

(continued)

Table 4-1. (*continued*)

Media File Container or File Format	File Extension	Media Stream Formats (Codecs)	
		Video	Audio
ASF	.asf	VC-1	WMA standard
	.wm	WMV9	WMA voice
			WMA lossless
	.wmv		WMA Pro
	.wma	n/a	AC3 (DD, DD+)
ADTS	.aac	n/a	AAC (LC, HE)
	.adt		
	.adts		
MP3	.mp3	n/a	MP3
WAV	.wav	n/a	PCM
			MP3
			MS ADPCM
			IMA ADPCM
			MS CCITT G.711
			MS GSM 6.10
			AC3 (DD, DD+)
AVI	.avi	MPEG-4 Part2 SP and ASP	PCM
		Motion-JPG	MP3
		H.263	MS ADPCM
		Uncompressed	IMA ADPCM
			MS CCITT G.711
			MS GSM 6.10
			AC3 (DD, DD+)
AC-3	.ac3	n/a	AC3 (DD, DD+)
	.ec3		

You can access the table directly at `http://msdn.microsoft.com/en-us/library/windows/apps/hh986969.aspx`.

Video/Audio Effects

You can add effects to videos or audio playing in the Video Player. To add any effect, you use the `msInsertVideoEffect` method of the `video` class. Listing 4-14 adds a new line to the `btn_playvideo` event handler.

Listing 4-14. Adding a Video Stabilization Effect to a Video Being Played Back

```
btn_playvideo.onclick = function ()
        {
            player_video.msInsertVideoEffect ↵
                ("Windows.Media.VideoEffects.videoStabilization", false);
            player_video.play();
        };
```

Listing 4-14 applies the video stabilization effect built into the framework. This effect can be found in the specified namespace. Note that videoStabilization isn't a class but a string that represents a unique identifier (ClassID) that maps to this effect. In an animated video such as this, stabilization is naturally ineffectual. But if you have video taken with a camcorder or camera and that you have access to on your development PC, you're welcome to try this on your PC.

Background Audio

The previous section started delving into the intricacies of the audio element. You saw how the audio tag can be used to play audio data located on the user's machine or from a remote server. When these audio files play, however, they're designed by default to only play in the foreground. In the world of Windows 8, this means once you switch away from your application, the sound stops. You can try this now by adding a new audio control to the example code you've been using. (You previously modified the video tag to an audio tag to see the difference between the two; you don't need to create a separate dedicated tag for audio.) Listing 4-15 shows an excerpt of the modified user interface you have been using so far, now with a dedicated audio control. This control is declaratively configured to autoplay when the page is loaded. The video control's size has also been reduced.

Listing 4-15. UI with a Dedicated Audio Control

```
<div>
    <video id="player_video" style="width: 300px; height: 200px" ↵
        src="/samples/videosample/big_buck_bunny_720p_surround.avi" ↵
        poster="/samples/videosample/Big_buck_bunny_poster_big.jpg" controls></video>
</div>
<div>
    <audio id="player_audio" src="/samples/videosample/big_buck_bunny_720p_surround.avi" ↵
        controls autoplay></audio>
</div>
```

This code should replace the section of the former listing, which contained just the div for the video element. Alternatively, you can add the second audio div and modify the video div to fit the listing. In either case, you should end up with two media controls, one above the other, with all built-in playback controls enabled on both of them. Figure 4-5 shows how this user interface looks. Notice that when you run this, the audio starts playing immediately (based on the autoplay attribute you assigned to it). Also notice that when you switch to another application or to the Windows 8 Start screen, the audio quickly fades out.

Figure 4-5. *Test video UI with both video and audio controls*

Navigate back to the application, and the audio starts again. If you paid close attention to the playback time of the media when you navigated away, notice that it has increased in value from the point at which you navigated away (and also notice that the media is playing from a later position). This is because the audio has been playing while your example app was shifted to the background. However, because audio configured in this manner can't be heard when the app hosting it is no longer visible to the user, you hear nothing when you switch to a different app.

Enabling background playback requires need three steps. First you need to declaratively tell Windows that the audio player is designed for background audio playback. You then need to inform Windows of your intent to have the application running in the background (for the purpose of playing the audio). Finally, you need to hook your application up to the background audio playback infrastructure so that a user can use the Windows media playback controls to control the background audio. Let's get started.

In this audio tag, you set one of a few properties that would be useless if set on the video element: the msAudioCategory property. The system uses this property to help identify and manage the performance and integration of audio. When its value is set to BackgroundCapableMedia, it earmarks audio being played through the audio element as available to the background audio player. Listing 4-16 shows the modified audio tag.

Listing 4-16. audio Tag Configured for Background Audio Playback

```
<audio id="player_audio" src="/samples/videosample/big_buck_bunny_720p_surround.avi"↵
    msAudioCategory="BackgroundCapableMedia" controls autoplay></audio>
```

Now that you've completed the necessary user interface modifications, the next step is to mosey on over to the handy Declarations tab of your project's package.appxmanifest configuration file. You're adding a new Background Task declaration to the app, which supports audio tasks. Be sure to specify the project Start page in the Start Page text box, as shown in Figure 4-6.

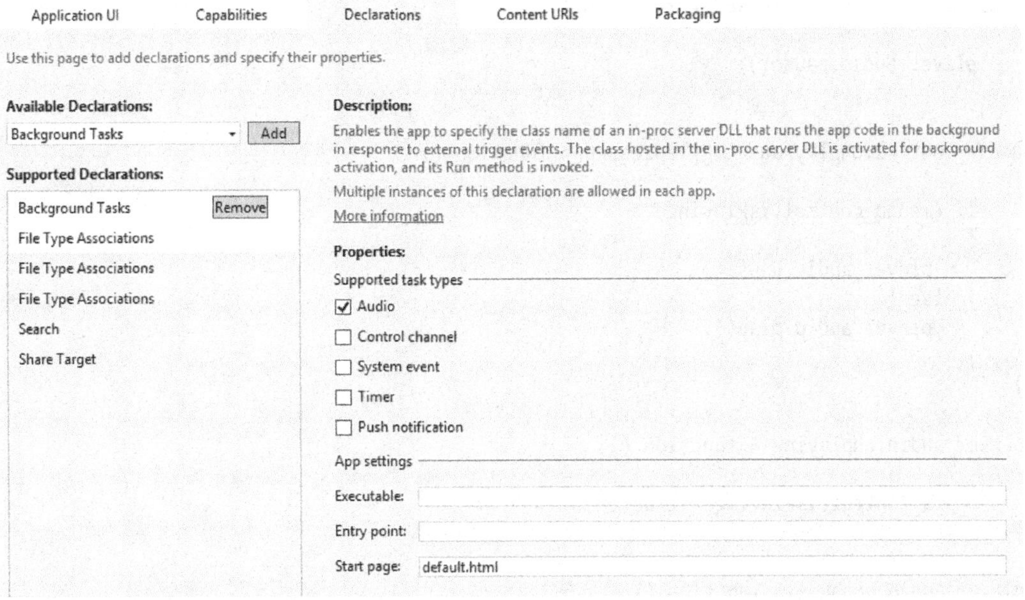

Application UI   Capabilities   Declarations   Content URIs   Packaging

Use this page to add declarations and specify their properties.

Available Declarations:

Background Tasks   ▼ Add

Supported Declarations:

Background Tasks   Remove

File Type Associations

File Type Associations

File Type Associations

Search

Share Target

Description:

Enables the app to specify the class name of an in-proc server DLL that runs the app code in the background in response to external trigger events. The class hosted in the in-proc server DLL is activated for background activation, and its Run method is invoked.

Multiple instances of this declaration are allowed in each app.

More information

Properties:

Supported task types

☑ Audio

☐ Control channel

☐ System event

☐ Timer

☐ Push notification

App settings

Executable:

Entry point:

Start page: default.html

Figure 4-6. *Background audio declaration*

You're almost done. You now must modify the code behind to enable the hooks into the background audio subsystem. This is needed so the user can identify and control the audio while using another application. Listing 4-17 adds the code for managing this. Notice the use of some of the audio element events like onplay and onstop. These are powerful events for figuring out when your video control is playing, paused, errored out, and in many other states, so get to know them if you plan to build rich media applications.

Listing 4-17. Enabling Background Audio

```
(function ()
{
    "use strict";
    var media_control = null;
    WinJS.UI.Pages.define("/samples/VideoSample/TestVideo.html", {


        ready: function (element, options)
        {
            media_control = Windows.Media.MediaControl;
            media_control.onplaypressed = function ()
            {
                player_audio.play();
            }

            media_control.onpausepressed = function ()
            {
                player_audio.pause();
            }
```

```
    media_control.onstoppressed = function ()
    {
        player_audio.pause();
    }

    media_control.onplaypausetogglepressed = function ()
    {
        if (media_control.isPlaying)
        {
            player_audio.pause();
        } else {
            player_audio.play();
        }
    }

    player_audio.onplaying = function ()
    {
        media_control.isPlaying = true;
    }

    player_audio.onpause = function ()
    {
        media_control.isPlaying = false;
    }

    player_audio.onended = function ()
    {
        media_control.isPlaying = false;
    }

    Windows.Media.MediaControl.isPlaying = false;
    Windows.Media.MediaControl.artistName = "The Peach Open Movie Project";
    Windows.Media.MediaControl.trackName = "Big Buck Bunny";

    btn_playvideo.onclick = function ()
    {
        player_audio.play();
    };


    },



    });
})();
```

In order for background playback to work, your code must provide an event handler for onplaypressed, onpausepressed, onstoppressed, and onplaypausetoggle at a minimum. If any one of these events isn't handled, the background playback won't work. Figure 4-7 shows the background audio controller while the *Big Buck Bunny* audio is running in the background.

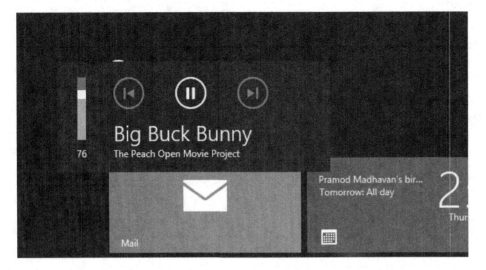

Figure 4-7. Audio being controlled through the background audio controller

Streaming Media to Other Devices

You can connect media you're playing back in your app to any Digital Living Network Alliance (DLNA) compatible device that supports the media type that you intend to stream. DLNA is a non-profit trade organization that defines and manages interoperability standards that enable sharing of digital content among devices. DLNA-enabled televisions can receive input from mobile devices wirelessly over a home network, for instance. Play To is a technology that allows users to stream media content from their devices to a screen of their choosing using these DLNA standards.

When a user selects the Devices charm while in an app that is showing or playing media, a list of potential Play To devices is presented to them. Picking one of the Play To targets sends a request to an app that has been configured to stream content to the Play To infrastructure, signaling the app to present a stream that it intends to stream. The programming interface is complete when the app attaches a stream. Listing 4-18 modifies the previous example's user interface to introduce a dedicated button for playing audio as well as one for video.

Listing 4-18. New UI for the Example App

```
<!DOCTYPE html>
<html>
<head>
    <meta charset="utf-8" />
    <title>TestVideo</title>

    <!-- WinJS references -->
    <link href="//Microsoft.WinJS.1.0/css/ui-dark.css" rel="stylesheet" />
    <script src="//Microsoft.WinJS.1.0/js/base.js"></script>
    <script src="//Microsoft.WinJS.1.0/js/ui.js"></script>

    <link href="TestVideo.css" rel="stylesheet" />
    <script src="TestVideo.js"></script>
```

```html
    <style>
        div {
            margin-left: 5px;
        }

        span {
            font-size: 22pt;
            font-family: Calibri;
        }

        span.notification {
            background-color: red;
        }

        input[type=file] {
            width: 100%;
        }

        .centered {
            margin-left: auto;
            margin-right: auto;
            width: 800px;
            box-shadow: 0px 0px 5px #000;
        }
    </style>

    <script type="text/javascript">

    </script>
</head>
<body>
    <div class="TestVideo fragment">
        <div class="centered">
            <div>
                <span class="heading">Video Test Actions</span>
            </div>
            <div>
                <video id="player_video" style="width: 300px; height: 200px"
                    src="/samples/videosample/big_buck_bunny_720p_surround.avi"
                    poster="/samples/videosample/Big_buck_bunny_poster_big.jpg" controls>
                </video>
            </div>
            <div>
                <audio id="player_audio"
                    src="/samples/videosample/big_buck_bunny_720p_surround.avi"
                    msaudiocategory="BackgroundCapableMedia" controls>
                </audio>
            </div>
            <div>
                <div style="display: table-cell">
                    <div>
                        <button id="btn_playvideo">Play video</button>
```

```
                <span style="width: 10px" />
                <button id="btn_playaudio">Play audio</button>
            </div>
            <div>

                <button id="btn_capture">Camera Capture</button>
            </div>
            <div>
                <button id="btn_advancedcapture">Advanced Media Capture</button>
            </div>

        </div>

    </div>
    </div>
</div>
</body>
</html>
```

Listing 4-19 shows the JavaScript code for this, including the code for incorporating Play To functionality.

Listing 4-19. Implementing Play To in the Example App

```
(function ()
{
    "use strict";
    var media_control = null;
    var manager = null;
    WinJS.UI.Pages.define("/samples/VideoSample/TestVideo.html", {

        ready: function (element, options)
        {
            media_control = Windows.Media.MediaControl;
            media_control.onplaypressed = function ()
            {
                player_audio.play();
            }

            media_control.onpausepressed = function ()
            {
                player_audio.pause();
            }

            media_control.onstoppressed = function ()
            {
                player_audio.pause();
            }

            media_control.onplaypausetogglepressed = function ()
            {
                if (media_control.isPlaying)
```

```
            {
                player_audio.pause();
            } else
            {
                player_audio.play();
            }
        }

        player_audio.onplaying = function ()
        {
            media_control.isPlaying = true;
        }

        player_audio.onpause = function ()
        {
            media_control.isPlaying = false;
        }

        player_audio.onended = function ()
        {
            media_control.isPlaying = false;
        }

        Windows.Media.MediaControl.isPlaying = false;
        Windows.Media.MediaControl.artistName = "The Peach Open Movie Project";
        Windows.Media.MediaControl.trackName = "Big Buck Bunny";

        btn_playvideo.onclick = function ()
        {
            player_video.play();
        };

        btn_playaudio.onclick = function ()
        {
            player_audio.play();
        }

        manager = Windows.Media.PlayTo.PlayToManager.getForCurrentView();
        manager.onsourcerequested = function (e)
        {
            e.sourceRequest.setSource(player_video.msPlayToSource);
        }


    },


    });
})();
```

The critical ingredient in enabling Play To is the PlayToManager class. To talk about this, I have to delve momentarily into the subject of the charms bar and charms bar programming (something covered in greater detail in Chapter 5). In general, when a user selects an action by clicking one of the charms bar buttons while your application is active (there are other advanced scenarios in which your application isn't active, as discussed in Chapter 5), Windows queries your app to see whether it supports the functionality the user is requesting. As you saw in the introductory chapters, this can be searching, sharing, settings, or devices. Play To functionality is requested through the multipurpose Devices charm. When the user clicks the Devices charm while your app is running, a query is made to your app to see if it has a playing video that it's willing to send over the network using Play To. Windows determines that you're at least interested in Play To by your app handling the onsourcerequested event of the aforementioned PlayToManager class. To publish your content, simply call the setSource function as shown in Listing 4-19, passing in a handle to the source media you want streamed via a call to its msPlayToSource property.

Here are some parting guidelines on Play To, should you decide to use (or not use) it in your app. Microsoft expects that if you have playback media as part of your app functionality, you expose a Play To contract (a fancy word for connecting Play To that you hear used in conjunction with other charms). For now this is a request and not a mandate. Additionally, because Play To exists as a Windows feature that can be requested at any point in time by the user through the charms bar, it's recommended that the media player used remain in scope for the lifetime of the application. In the example you created, a user isn't aware of the Play To functionality until they reach the video sample page; when they navigate away from that page, they lose the ability to stream the *Big Buck Bunny* movie because the page is removed from memory. If you had a root video tag available on the default.html page that you used for Play To purposes, however, the user could navigate freely through the example application without issue.

Media Capture

The Windows 8 capture framework provides app developers with the ability to capture media in the form of photos, audio recordings, and video recordings in an app. For any Windows 8 device possessing a camera, you can use the camera capture programming interfaces to record videos or to take pictures. The easiest way to do this is by using the built-in CameraCaptureUI dialog.

Before you get into what this dialog does, I should mention that as with most things with Windows 8, user permission is required for your app to access the onboard camera of the device it's running on. This means you need to add some capabilities to your package.appxmanifest file. For access to the camera, microphone, and video recorder, the Webcam capability must be enabled. I also recommend requesting permissions to store images in the pictures library in tandem with the Webcam capability. This is called the Pictures Library capability. (You need both these capabilities as well as the Music Library capability to run the example in this section, so be sure to enable them.)

CameraCaptureUI opens a full-screen modal dialog that represents the viewfinder for the camera. When this dialog is enabled, the user's screen looks something like Figure 4-8.

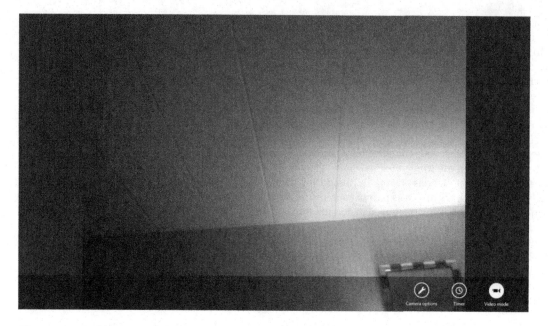

Figure 4-8. *Camera capture dialog*

You can specify what options are available to the user when the camera capture dialog is launched through the function that launches it:

- For pictures only, select `Windows.Media.Capture.CameraCaptureUIMode.photo`.

- For videos, select `Windows.Media.Capture.CameraCaptureUIMode.video`.

- If you want the user to have the choice to use the dialog to capture either pictures or video, there is an option for that as well: `Windows.Media.Capture.CameraCaptureUIMode.photoOrVideo`.

`CameraCaptureUI` also exposes a property called `PhotoSettings` that is of type `CameraCaptureUIVideoCaptureSettings` (same namespace). This property can be used to perform additional configuration on the dialog. For instance, you can use this setting to toggle whether you want the user to have cropping enabled. Let's look at an example of using the `CameraCaptureUI` class to take pictures.

To start out, recall that the previous examples had extra `btn_capture` and `btn_advancecapture` buttons that you disregarded. In Listing 4-20, you finally add an event handler for `btn_capture` to show how easy capturing media can be.

Listing 4-20. Using the Camera Capture Interface to Capture an Image and Place It in the Pictures Library

```
btn_capture.onclick = function ()
        {
            var capture = Windows.Media.Capture.CameraCaptureUI();
            capture.captureFileAsync(Windows.Media.Capture.CameraCaptureUIMode.photoOrVideo)↵
.then(function (file)
            {
                if (file != null)
                    file.copyAsync(Windows.Storage.KnownFolders.picturesLibrary);
            });
        };
```

CameraCaptureUI is great for straightforward scenarios, but it has two drawbacks. First, the full-screen modal dialog covers the entire application user interface, which you may not want based on the type of application you're building. Second, it only allows for video and image capture. If you want deeper control over your app's ability to capture media—for instance, if you need to capture audio—you use the MediaCapture class to do so. You can use the code in Listing 4-21 to create and initialize a MediaCapture object in JavaScript.

Listing 4-21. Capturing Media Using the MediaCapture Object

```
// Create and initialize the MediaCapture object.
function initMediaCapture() {
    var capture = null;
    capture = new Windows.Media.Capture.MediaCapture();
    capture.initializeAsync().then (function (result) {
    }, errorHandler);
}
```

If you need to tweak the media capture mechanism a bit, WinRT provides the mechanisms to do this through the MediaCaptureInitializationSettings object. Configuring this setting lets your app specify details about how you want the captures to occur. You can use it to target audio capture instead of video and to set the format of a capture. Because certain use cases are common when it comes to media capture, the API also provides for encoding profiles that can be used to quickly set up a recording format and structure for you. Listing 4-22 adds an event handler for the btn_advancedcapture button that shows the use of profiles to set up an audio recording.

Listing 4-22. Capturing an Audio Recording

```
btn_advancedcapture.onclick = function ()
        {

            var capture = new Windows.Media.Capture.MediaCapture();
            var profile = Windows.Media.MediaProperties.MediaEncodingProfile.createMp3↵
                (Windows.Media.MediaProperties.AudioEncodingQuality.High);
        Windows.Storage.KnownFolders.musicLibrary.createFileAsync("recordings.mp3",↵
            Windows.Storage.CreationCollisionOption.generateUniqueName).then(function (file)
            {
                capture.initializeAsync().then(function ()
                {
                    capture.startRecordToStorageFileAsync(profile, file);
                });
            });

        };
```

Listing 4-23 uses this same pattern to create a profile for capturing video using the WMV format.

Listing 4-23. Capturing Video

```
btn_advancedcapture.onclick = function ()
        {

            var capture = new Windows.Media.Capture.MediaCapture();
            var profile = Windows.Media.MediaProperties.MediaEncodingProfile.createWmv↵
                (Windows.Media.MediaProperties.VideoEncodingPropertiesHigh);
        Windows.Storage.KnownFolders.musicLibrary.createFileAsync("video.wmv",↵
```

```
        Windows.Storage.CreationCollisionOption.generateUniqueName).then(function (file)
        {
            capture.initializeAsync().then(function ()
            {
                capture.startRecordToStorageFileAsync(profile, file);
            });
        });


    };
```

If you embed the code in Listing 4-23 in an application, you might notice that something is missing. While the application is capturing the video, you have no viewfinder to see what the camera is presently pointing to. When you're working with the MediaCapture class for video capture, there is no built-in user interface for displaying the contents of the viewfinder (in essence, previewing what is being recorded). WinRT for JavaScript applications differ from traditional .NET and native Windows Store applications in this regard because they don't have a built-in control (called CaptureElement) for rendering the media capture preview. Instead, WinJS reuses the video tag to accomplish this. The example in Listing 4-24 shows how you can enable video capture previewing in the application.

Listing 4-24. Enabling Video Preview

```
var capture = new Windows.Media.Capture.MediaCapture();
...
var myVideo = document.getElementById("player_video");
myVideo.src = URL.createObjectURL(capture);
myVideo.play();
```

In the preceding example, once capture is initialized, the source of a video tag on the page is set to the object URL of that MediaCapture object, obtained via a call to URL.createObjectURL. Adding this code to Listing 4-23 results in the captured content being previewed in the frame of the video tags (where *Big Buck Bunny* was previously showing).

Summary

In this chapter, you learned about the many ways media can be used in your application. The findings in this chapter include:

- The integration of media playback into your app from local sources as well as remote websites

- Media capture and the many approaches you can take to facilitate it in your application, and the multitude of things you can do using the CameraCaptureUI

- The more powerful MediaCapture class, which provides functionality to capture audio and create custom viewfinders for capturing video

- Using the MediaCapture API in scenarios where it's important to stay in your application's user interface (and, of course, in advanced scenarios when you need lower-level refinement of the capture pipeline)

■ ■ ■

CHAPTER 5

Making the Most Out of Charms and Contracts

Contracts and charms are two new concepts introduced in Windows 8 that not only revolutionize the activity of app-to-app communication, but also introduce new usage scenarios for developers to work with. Using charms, the user can search across the entire device as well as in applications, send content to other applications or devices, and access settings in a standardized manner. Interoperability between applications can be further enhanced with the use of contracts. The beauty of this approach is that each application installed on a Windows 8 system enhances the system capabilities through well-defined extensions to formal interactions such as opening a file or choosing a contact from the contact store. As a Windows 8 app developer, you use contracts as a mechanism to handle a user's interaction through charms; you also use contracts to facilitate this implicit interaction between applications. This chapter talks more about contracts later. Let's get started.

Charms

Chapter 1 introduced the concept of charms, when you walked through the core activities available to the end user. If you recall, swiping from the right at any time produces the charms menu, which you can use to perform five (on Windows 8, although not on Windows Server 2012 by default) basic activities: Search, Share, Start, Devices, and Settings. Figure 5-1 shows how the charms menu looks when it's visible.

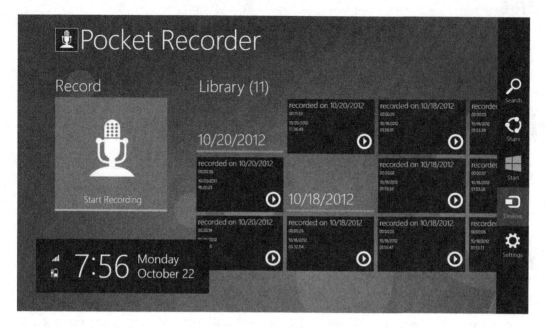

Figure 5-1. *Windows charms*

Search Charm

This section introduces you to the Search charm functionality in Windows 8, going into detail on how you as an app developer can incorporate system-wide searches into your app and even present auto-completion hints. If you've used Windows 7 in the past, then you're familiar with the workings of the Search charm, because it replaces the search box found on the Windows 7 Start menu. With the Search charm, you can find apps, settings, and files on your PC.

Search Charm Usage

The Search charm is used to perform system-wide searches across all applications, files, and settings. In addition, Windows 8 provides an extensibility framework that applications can use to explicitly plug in to the search infrastructure. You can see the Search charm at work anytime you start typing while on the Start screen. By default, Windows 8 searches all applications by name and filters the app list to applications that match the text you type in. You should also notice that the Search charm fly-out appears with the search text box in focus (see Figure 5-2).

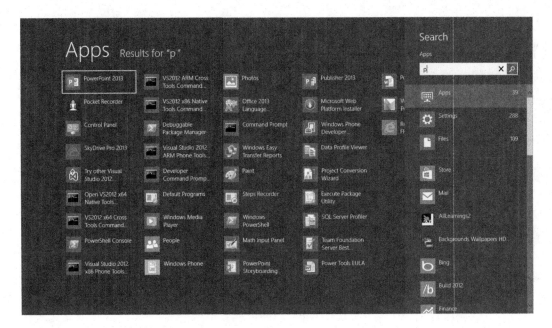

Figure 5-2. *Search charm at work*

The Search Experience

As stated earlier, the search experience provides many extensibility points for an application to hook in to. To start with, let's look at how to launch the search experience directly from an application. The call to do this from JavaScript is as simple as this:

```
Windows.ApplicationModel.Search.SearchPane.getForCurrentView().show();
```

As you've seen many times with the new Windows 8 model, however, making this kind of calls requires user involvement on some level. In the case of search, this involvement is through the application manifest, which is surfaced in the Windows Store as a set of features that a given application requires.

Figure 5-3 shows how an application's permissions look from an end user's point of view. From here the user can decide if they want to download and install the application (considering that in this case, Skype requires the use of the user's webcam).

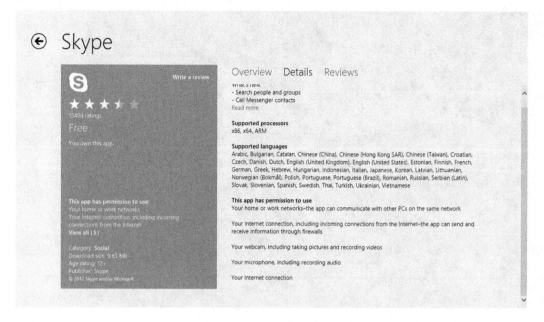

Figure 5-3. *Application permissions listed for the user in the Windows Store*

It's a silly example; of course, given the popularity of Skype and the fact that most users already have a sense of what it does, the typical user will download and install it. In fact, it's currently (at the time of this writing) the top application in the Social category.

Listing 5-1 shows a simple search user interface for an application called TestSearch with a default page called TestSearch.html. We first define a rudimentary user interface with a single button that is used to launch the search pane. Although there are other user interface elements on the page, this discussion is focused on the button (btn_startsearch).

Listing 5-1. Search Example UI (TestSearch.html)

```
<!DOCTYPE html>
<html>
<head>
    <meta charset="utf-8" />
    <title>Test Search</title>

    <!-- WinJS references -->
    <link href="//Microsoft.WinJS.1.0/css/ui-dark.css" rel="stylesheet" />
    <script src="//Microsoft.WinJS.1.0/js/base.js"></script>
    <script src="//Microsoft.WinJS.1.0/js/ui.js"></script>

    <link href="TestSearch.css" rel="stylesheet" />
    <script src="TestSearch.js"></script>
</head>
<body>
    <div class="TestSearch fragment">
        <section aria-label="Main content" role="main">
            <p id="txt_searchtext">Search Text Goes Here</p>
```

```
        </section>
        <section aria-label="Main content" role="main">
            <p>Use the search charm to initiate a search.</p>
        </section>
        <section aria-label="Main content" role="main">
            <p><input type="button" id="btn_startsearch" value="Open Search Pane" /></p>
        </section>
    </div>
</body>
</html>
```

We now add an event handler for the clicked event of btn_search (see Listing 5-2).

Listing 5-2. Search Example JavaScript Code (TestSearch.js)

```
(function () {
    "use strict";

    WinJS.UI.Pages.define("/samples/SearchSample/TestSearch.html", {
        // This function is called whenever a user navigates to this page. It
        // populates the page elements with the app's data.
        ready: function (element, options) {

            btn_startsearch.onclick = function ()
            {
                Windows.ApplicationModel.Search.SearchPane.getForCurrentView().show();
            };
        },
    });
})();
```

If we compile and run this example, everything should work well until we actually click the button. If we run without debugging, the application simply crashes, and we're returned to the Windows 8 Start screen after clicking the button. If we're debugging using Visual Studio 2012, the window switches to the IDE with the following error:

```
Unhandled exception at line 13, column 17 in ms-appx://8a2843c4-6e36-40f7-8966 85789a855fa8
/samples/searchsample/TestSearch.js

0x80070005 - JavaScript runtime error: Access is denied.

WinRT information: The search extension must be specified in the manifest in order to use the Search
Pane APIs.
```

As you can see from the error message, the application can't make calls into the search infrastructure by default. To enable access to be granted, the application must first explicitly declare that it's planning on integrating with search.

Without altering the code in any way, we can get the application running properly by adding the right declarations to the package manifest for the app. To begin, we need to locate the file in the project labeled package.appxmanifest. Figure 5-4 shows the location of a typical application manifest for a Windows 8 app project. (Get used to this file; it's used for many examples in this book.)

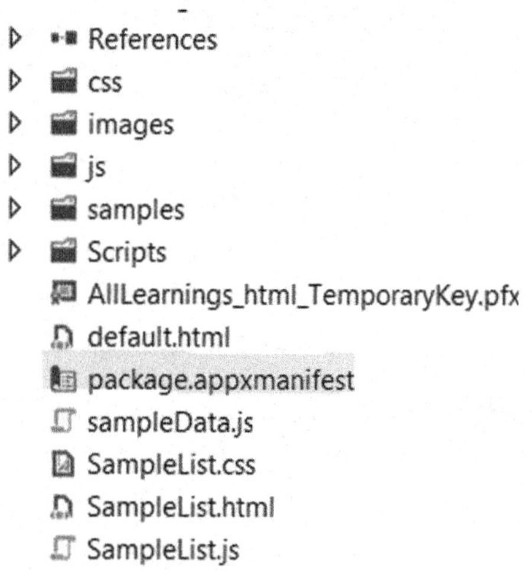

▷ ▪▪ References
▷ 📁 css
▷ 📁 images
▷ 📁 js
▷ 📁 samples
▷ 📁 Scripts
   📄 AllLearnings_html_TemporaryKey.pfx
   📄 default.html
   📄 package.appxmanifest
   📄 sampleData.js
   📄 SampleList.css
   📄 SampleList.html
   📄 SampleList.js

Figure 5-4. *Application manifest in a Visual Studio 2012 project structure*

Search Declarations

If you recall, Chapter 2 discussed some of the package manifest features when it talked about known folders and configuring file-type associations. Figure 5-5 shows the Declarations tab after the Search declaration has been added (to add a declaration, click the drop-down of available declarations, select the one you want, and the click the Add button).

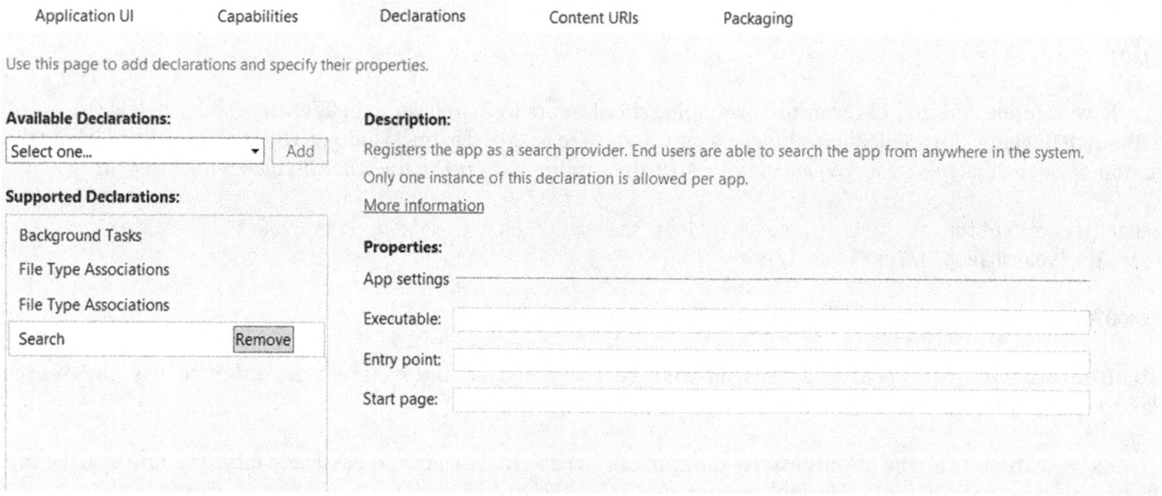

| Application UI | Capabilities | Declarations | Content URIs | Packaging |

Use this page to add declarations and specify their properties.

Available Declarations:

Select one... ▼ [Add]

Description:

Registers the app as a search provider. End users are able to search the app from anywhere in the system. Only one instance of this declaration is allowed per app.

More information

Supported Declarations:

Background Tasks
File Type Associations
File Type Associations
Search [Remove]

Properties:

App settings

Executable:

Entry point:

Start page:

Figure 5-5. *Declarations tab with Search declaration added*

Adding Permissions

Now that you've seen how permissions are consumed by the end user, let's look at how you add the appropriate permissions to an application. With the Executable, Entry Point, and Start Page fields blank, rebuild the application and run it again. Notice that clicking the Search button no longer causes an error; instead, it activates the Windows 8 search experience (see Figure 5-6).

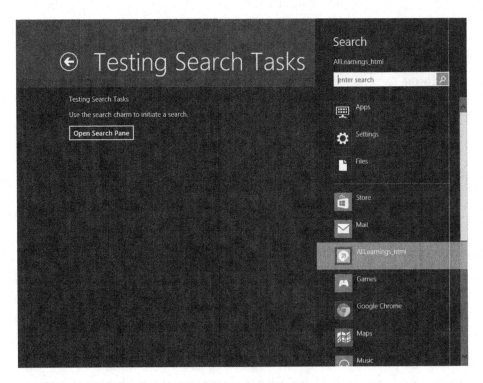

Figure 5-6. *Search experience launched from an application*

The following tables highlight all the members of the SearchPane class: events in Table 5-1, properties in Table 5-2, and methods in Table 5-3.

Table 5-1. *SearchPane Events*

Name	Description
onquerychanged	Fires when the user changes the text in the search box
onquerysubmitted	Fires when the user submits the text in the search box and the app needs to display search results
onresultsuggestionchosen	Fires when the user selects one of the suggested results that is provided by the app and displayed in the search pane
onsuggestionsrequested	Fires when the user's query text changes and the app needs to provide new suggestions to display in the search pane
onvisibilitychanged	Fires when the user opens or closes the search pane

Table 5-2. *SearchPane Properties*

Name	Accessibility	Description
language	Read-only	Identifies the language currently associated with the user's text input device
placeholderText	Read/write	The placeholder text in the search box when the user hasn't entered any characters
queryText	Read-only	The current text in the search box of the search pane
searchHistoryContext	Read/write	A string that identifies the context of the search and is used to store the user's search history with the app
searchHistoryEnabled	Read/write	Indicates whether the user's previous searches with the app are automatically tracked and used to provide suggestions
showOnKeyboardInput	Read/write	Gets or sets whether the user can open the search pane by typing
visible	Read-only	Indicates whether the search pane is open

Table 5-3. *SearchPane Methods*

Name	Description
getForCurrentView	Retrieves an instance of the search pane from which users can search within the app
setLocalContentSuggestionSettings	Specifies whether suggestions based on local files are automatically displayed in the search pane, and defines the criteria that Windows uses to locate and filter these suggestions
show()	Shows the search pane
show(String)	Shows the search pane with the specified initial query string
trySetQueryText	Attempts to set the text in the search box of the search pane

The search application we created before was rudimentary, but it serves as a base from which to incorporate more functionality. Text entered in the example isn't presently pushed back to the application, so let's change that. Listing 5-3 modifies the example to include handling user input from the search pane. Now, when we click the button to open the Search pane, the search text box shows the text "enter search". Also, as we type text into the search text box, the text appears in the application.

Listing 5-3. Search Notification

```
(function () {
    "use strict";

    WinJS.UI.Pages.define("/samples/SearchSample/TestSearch.html", {
        // This function is called whenever a user navigates to this page. It
        // populates the page elements with the app's data.
        ready: function (element, options) {

            btn_startsearch.onclick = function ()
            {
                var search = ↵
                    Windows.ApplicationModel.Search.SearchPane.getForCurrentView();
```

```
            search.placeholderText = "enter search";
            search.onquerychanged = function (e)
            {
                txt_searchtext.innerText = e.queryText;
            };
            search.show();
        };
    },
    });
})();
```

The listing modifies the search example we started with by adding an event listener for the queryChanged event. The results of the event are printed in the Search content region in the HTML interface. Figure 5-7 shows the resulting cloned, meaning replicated, application.

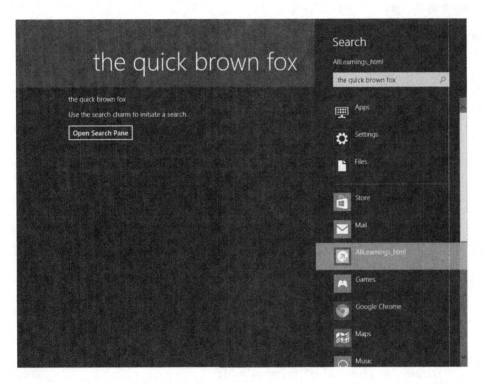

Figure 5-7. *Cloning search input*

The search framework also allows applications to inject auto-suggest values. Listing 5-4 uses this feature to create suggestions based on the first character the user types into the global search box. Note that in real-world scenarios, search suggestions are ideally loaded asynchronously from an external source like a database or web service.

Listing 5-4. Search Auto-Suggestion Example

```
(function () {
    "use strict";

    WinJS.UI.Pages.define("/samples/SearchSample/TestSearch.html", {
        // This function is called whenever a user navigates to this page. It
        // populates the page elements with the app's data.
        ready: function (element, options) {

            btn_startsearch.onclick = function ()
            {
                var search = ↵
                    Windows.ApplicationModel.Search.SearchPane.getForCurrentView();
                search.placeholderText = "enter search";
                search.onquerychanged = function (args)
                {
                    txt_searchtext.innerText = args.queryText;
                };
                search.onsuggestionsrequested = function (args)
                {
                    if (search.queryText.charAt(0) == "a")
                    {
                        args.request.searchSuggestionCollection ↵
                            .appendQuerySuggestion("Avengers");
                        args.request.searchSuggestionCollection ↵
                            .appendQuerySuggestion("Aliens");
                        args.request.searchSuggestionCollection ↵
                            .appendQuerySuggestion("A Man Apart");
                        args.request.searchSuggestionCollection ↵
                            .appendQuerySuggestion("Anaconda");
                    } else if (search.queryText.charAt(0) == "b")
                    {
                        args.request.searchSuggestionCollection ↵
                            .appendQuerySuggestion("Braveheart");
                        args.request.searchSuggestionCollection ↵
                            .appendQuerySuggestion("Birds");
                        args.request.searchSuggestionCollection ↵
                            .appendQuerySuggestion("Baby's Day Out");
                        args.request.searchSuggestionCollection ↵
                            .appendQuerySuggestion("Bridesmaids");
                    } else
                    {
                        args.request.searchSuggestionCollection ↵
                            .appendQuerySuggestion("Catwoman");
                        args.request.searchSuggestionCollection ↵
                            .appendQuerySuggestion("Dances With Wolves");
                        args.request.searchSuggestionCollection ↵
                            .appendQuerySuggestion("Empire Strikes Back");
```

```
                        args.request.searchSuggestionCollection ↵
                            .appendQuerySuggestion("Ferris Bueller's Day Off");
                    }

            };
            search.show();
        };
    },
  });
})();
```

Figure 5-8 shows the resulting user experience. As you can see, a list of possible choices is presented based on what text is entered in the search text box. In the example, the letter *d* is typed in, which results in a list of suggestions that contain *d*. As stated earlier, in the ideal scenario, these suggestions would be retrieved from a source external to the application, such as a database or web service. Bear in mind when using this technique that there may be latency associated with suggestions being presented to the user.

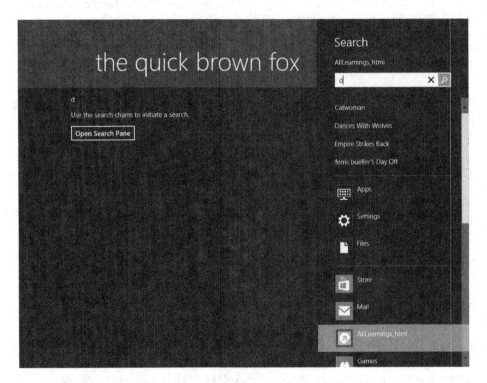

Figure 5-8. *Auto-suggesting search*

So far, all the examples have focused on searching the application while the application is running. If you examine the examples, you see that the application doesn't subscribe to search until the Search button is clicked. Ideally, an application that allows for search subscribes to it at the global level and displays the appropriate interface based on the search criteria. We can easily remedy this by moving the search initialization code out of the btn_startsearch click handler, but what about the other issue?

Search Within Applications

If you examine the Windows 8 search experience, notice that in addition to searching through apps, files, and settings content, a user can also search directly within applications. The examples in Listings 5-3 and 5-4 touched on this briefly; however, the previous examples all start with the application running, and a search is performed while it remains in that state. It's also possible to search within applications that aren't presently running. In these scenarios, you select an application within which to search; the application is launched with the search information already present and, in many cases, the search already performed. Try this with the example application we're developing. It launches but doesn't respond to the search string as you expect it to. This is because the application requires some modifications to its startup code in support of such scenarios.

Ordinarily, a Windows 8 app is launched by the user clicking the tile representing it. In the case of search, however, the application is launched by clicking an icon representing it on the search pane. When this happens, the ideal experience is to launch directly into an application-specific search screen; but as you saw with the example, unless an app knows it's being started as part of a search (as opposed to normal activation), the app continues to show its standard activation user experience. To help remedy this, Windows 8 apps are passed parameters that identify the source of the activation during the launch process. Hence when the app is launched through search, it has a *search* activation kind rather than the standard *launch* activation. By testing for this in the application's onactivated event handler, you can bootstrap the application with all the correct information when it's launched using search. Listing 5-5 illustrates.

Listing 5-5. Handling Search Activation (default.js)

```
"use strict";

    var app = WinJS.Application;
    var activation = Windows.ApplicationModel.Activation;

    app.onactivated = function (args)
    {
        if (args.detail.kind === activation.ActivationKind.launch)
        {
            args.setPromise(WinJS.UI.processAll().then(function ()
            {
                WinJS.Navigation.navigate("samplelist.html");
            }));
        } else if (args.detail.kind === activation.ActivationKind.search)
        {
            WinJS.Navigation.navigate
                ("/samples/searchsample/testsearch.html", args.detail.detail[0].queryText);
        }
    };
```

In the example, we modify the onactivated event handler for our example application to test for search activation. Whereas the application would normally launch the page **samplelist.html**, in scenarios where the activation kind is search, we instead launch **testsearch.html**. If we find that the application has been activated via search, we navigate the user directly to the search example and propagate the queryText value (the text that is presently in the global search box) into that page. Listing 5-6 shows how the search page example is modified to support this change.

Listing 5-6. Handling Search Activation

```
(function () {
    "use strict";

    WinJS.UI.Pages.define("/samples/SearchSample/TestSearch.html", {
        // This function is called whenever a user navigates to this page. It
        // populates the page elements with the app's data.
        ready: function (element, options)
        {

            var state = WinJS.Navigation.state;
            var search = ↵
                Windows.ApplicationModel.Search.SearchPane.getForCurrentView();
            if (state != null)
            {
                txt_searchtext.innerText = state;
            }
            search.onquerychanged = function (args)
            {
                txt_searchtext.innerText = args.queryText;
             //perform search against back end and present the results
            };
            search.onsuggestionsrequested = function (args)
            {
                if (search.queryText.charAt(0) == "a")
                {
                    args.request.searchSuggestionCollection ↵
                        .appendQuerySuggestion("Avengers");
                    args.request.searchSuggestionCollection ↵
                        .appendQuerySuggestion("Aliens");
                    args.request.searchSuggestionCollection ↵
                        .appendQuerySuggestion("A Man Apart");
                    args.request.searchSuggestionCollection ↵
                        .appendQuerySuggestion("Anaconda");
                } else if (search.queryText.charAt(0) == "b")
                {
                    args.request.searchSuggestionCollection ↵
                        .appendQuerySuggestion("Braveheart");
                    args.request.searchSuggestionCollection ↵
                        .appendQuerySuggestion("Birds");
                    args.request.searchSuggestionCollection ↵
                        .appendQuerySuggestion("Baby's Day Out");
                    args.request.searchSuggestionCollection ↵
                        .appendQuerySuggestion("Bridesmaids");
                } else
```

```
            {
                args.request.searchSuggestionCollection ↵
                    .appendQuerySuggestion("Catwoman");
                args.request.searchSuggestionCollection ↵
                    .appendQuerySuggestion("Dances With Wolves");
                args.request.searchSuggestionCollection ↵
                    .appendQuerySuggestion("Empire Strikes Back");
                args.request.searchSuggestionCollection ↵
                    .appendQuerySuggestion("Ferris Bueller's Day Off");
            }

        };

        btn_startsearch.onclick = function ()
        {

            search.placeholderText = "enter search";

            search.show();
        };
    },
    });
})();
```

Share Charm

The Share charm is the most prominent means of sharing between applications. It's specifically designed for such functionality and in that way is the resident first-class inter-app communication mechanism for Windows 8. When an application subscribes to the sharing experience, it can send and receive content in various forms ranging from plain text and HTML content to complex structures.

Sharing follows a pattern similar to searching when it comes to permissions—in this case the Share Target declaration is required. As with search, when a declaration is needed, it's surfaced as a permission that the user can explore when deciding whether to download and install your app. Should they miss this out of sheer excitement, they need only use the Settings menu to access the same list of permissions required for a given app to run. Figure 5-9 shows the very popular ESPN app with the Permissions screen of the settings pane exposed.

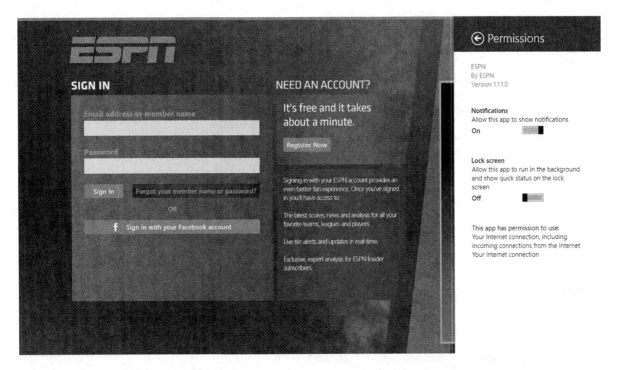

Figure 5-9. *Permissions available through Settings menu*

The Sharing charm supports two types of contracts: essentially, one for giving content and one for receiving content. Because the giving side of the equation can only ever be activated by the end user through the Share charm, there is no requirement to explicitly define anything to get it going.

Sharing as Source

As far as a Windows 8 app is concerned, it can always "share" content that it deems meaningful to share. Let's look at a simple example. We'll share some text from the example application with the Windows Mail application (but really with any application that supports text sharing). The code to initiate this is shown in Listing 5-7.

Listing 5-7. Basic Sharing

```
<!DOCTYPE html>
<html>
<head>
    <meta charset="utf-8" />
    <title>TestSharing</title>

    <!-- WinJS references -->
    <link href="//Microsoft.WinJS.1.0/css/ui-dark.css" rel="stylesheet" />
    <script src="//Microsoft.WinJS.1.0/js/base.js"></script>
    <script src="//Microsoft.WinJS.1.0/js/ui.js"></script>
```

```html
    <link href="TestSharing.css" rel="stylesheet" />
    <script src="TestSharing.js"></script>
</head>
<body>
    <div class="TestSharing fragment">
        <section aria-label="Main content" role="main">
            <p><input type="text" id="txt_content" /></p>
        </section>
        <section aria-label="Main content" role="main">
            <p><input type="button" id="btn_openshare" value="Open Share" /></p>
        </section>

    </div>
</body>
</html>
```

```javascript
(function () {
    "use strict";

    WinJS.UI.Pages.define("/samples/SharingSample/TestSharing.html", {

        ready: function (element, options)
        {
            var transfer = Windows.ApplicationModel. ↵
                DataTransfer.DataTransferManager;
            var share = transfer.getForCurrentView();
            share.ondatarequested = function ( args)
            {
                args.request.data.properties.title = "Sample Sharing Text";
                args.request.data.properties ↵
                    .description = "Description of the text being sent";
                args.request.data.setText(txt_content.value);
            };

            btn_openshare.onclick = function ()
            {
                transfer.showShareUI();
            };
        },
    });
})();
```

When we run this application and click the Open Share button, the code in ondatarequested is called. It populates the sharing context with the text from the txt_content text box. Based on the content specified (in this case, text), a list of applications that can handle receiving this content type appears in the sharing pane (see Figure 5-10).

Figure 5-10. *Sharing pane with compatible applications for the shared content type*

When one of the applications is clicked, the application is launched in a share view, and the user is given the option to make last-minute edits and complete the share procedure. Figure 5-11 shows what happens when the Windows Mail application is clicked.

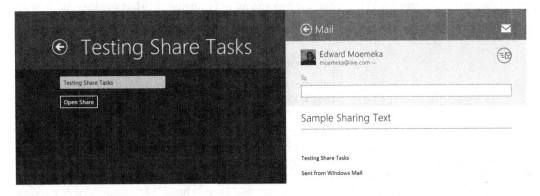

Figure 5-11. *Sharing with Windows Mail*

What you can see in Listing 5-7 is that sharing follows an event subscription model to connect. This is because, as stated, sharing happens exclusively through the Windows 8 share experience. The event handler `ondatarequested` is called any time the user exposes the share pane (whether through the Share charm or through `showShareUI()`). It gives the application an opportunity to load any information into the sharing context.

The giving end of the share relationship is accomplished via three main classes: `DataTransferManager`, `DataRequest`, and `DataPackage`. `DataTransferManager` is used to hook into the sharing context to listen for the click of the Share button. `DataRequest` encapsulate the request for data initiated by Windows 8 in response to the user starting the share experience—exposed through the `args.request` property. It's passed in to the application through the event handler for the `ondatarequested` event. `DataPackage` represents the conceptual package of data that is transferred between the sharing applications; hence it controls the actual reading and writing of data. It's exposed through the `args.request.data` property. Table 5-4 lists some of the methods of the `DataPackage` class.

Table 5-4. *DataPackage Methods*

Name	Description
getView	Returns a DataPackageView object. This object is a read-only copy of the DataPackage object.
setBitmap	Sets the bitmap image contained in the DataPackage.
setData	Sets the data contained in the DataPackage in a RandomAccessStream format.
setDataProvider	Sets a delegate to handle requests from the target app.
setHtmlFormat	Adds HTML content to the DataPackage.
setRtf	Sets the Rich Text Format (RTF) content that is contained in a DataPackage.
setStorageItems(IIterable(IStorageItem))	Sets the files and folders contained in a DataPackage.
setStorageItems(IIterable(IStorageItem), Boolean)	Adds files and folders to a DataPackage.
setText	Sets the text that a DataPackage contains.
setUri	Sets the Uniform Resource Identifier (URI) that is contained in the DataPackage.

DataPackage also exposes a property of type DataPackagePropertySet through its properties property, which you can use to apply metadata to the content being shared. It contains title and description properties but is also a property bag that can be used to store additional properties in name/value format.

Listing 5-8 sends data between applications using one of the standard formats provided through the data package classes: text. As you saw from Table 5-4, in addition to this you can also send images, RTF content, HTML content, and even raw data (using setData) across applications. Listing 5-7 shows how an image might be added to the DataPackage between two applications.

Listing 5-8. Sharing Images

```
(function ()
{
    "use strict";

    WinJS.UI.Pages.define("/samples/SharingSample/TestSharing.html", {

        ready: function (element, options)
        {
            var transfer = Windows.ApplicationModel.DataTransfer. ↵
                DataTransferManager;
            var share = transfer.getForCurrentView();
            share.ondatarequested = function (args)
            {
                args.request.data.properties.title = "Sample Sharing Text";
                args.request.data.properties. ↵
                    description = "Description of the text being sent";
```

```
            //set text
            args.request.data.setText(txt_content.value);

            //set image
            var file = Windows.Storage.ApplicationData.current ↵
                .localFolder.getFileAsync("image_file.bmp");
            var stream = Windows.Storage.Streams ↵
                .RandomAccessStreamReference.createFromFile(file);
            args.request.data.setBitmap(stream);

        };

        btn_openshare.onclick = function ()
        {
            transfer.showShareUI();
        };
    },
  });
})();
```

Sharing as a Target

Each application has a set of content types that it supports (some public and some private). The Windows Mail application, for instance, can accept HTML for use in rendering a message being generated from a "giving" application. For the content to render properly, the message must follow a specific format (controlled by Microsoft, in this case). The moral of the story is that content structure is less of a concern than specific application requirements as defined by documentation received directly from the application authors.

Receiving content through the share contract is far more involved than sending. For starters, unlike sending content to other applications, receiving content requires an application to be registered as a target for the type of content being shared. This makes sense because you wouldn't want every application that is shared presented in the listing of share targets when the user wishes to transfer content between applications. Instead, Windows 8 filters the list of applications that appear when the user clicks the Share button to include only those applications that can consume content in the format being shared. It isn't difficult to see why applications that want to register as share targets need to declare the type of content they can handle.

Not surprisingly, the pattern for doing this is similar to the manner in which search is registered and processed. First, you must add the Share Target capability to the application's manifest. Figure 5-12 shows this capability's node.

In the image, I've added some data formats that the application supports. You add data formats by specifying the format moniker for the format type. In this case, I'm saying the application can handle text of any kind. (For more

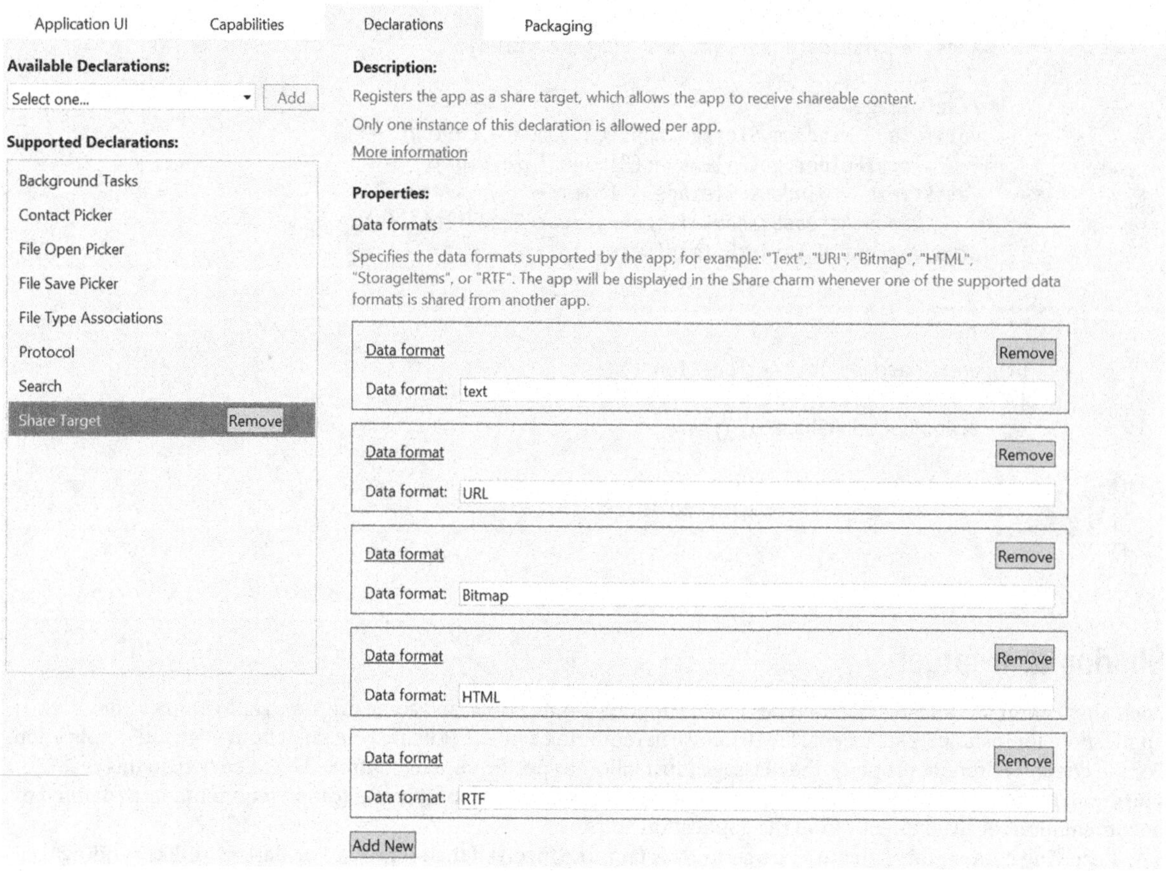

Figure 5-12. *Share Target configuration*

specific formats, I suggest using the setData method with a format name that can be used to identify the layout and structure of documents of this type, beyond just by MIME type.) Let's expand the simple sharing example to support receiving content in text format.

If you remember from the search example, when an application is activated, its activation kind is registered by Windows and passed as a launch argument so the application can chose which page to display for a given scenario. You can also use file-type associations to enable sharing. Doing so allows the application to use nonstandard formats to share data through the StorageItems property. If a file format is used that matches the data formats specified, it's treated as such; otherwise the share source must use the args.Request.Data.SetStorageItems method to add the nonstandard format (as a storage file) to the sharing context. Figure 5-13 shows a larger view of the Share Target configuration page with both data-format and file-type associations included.

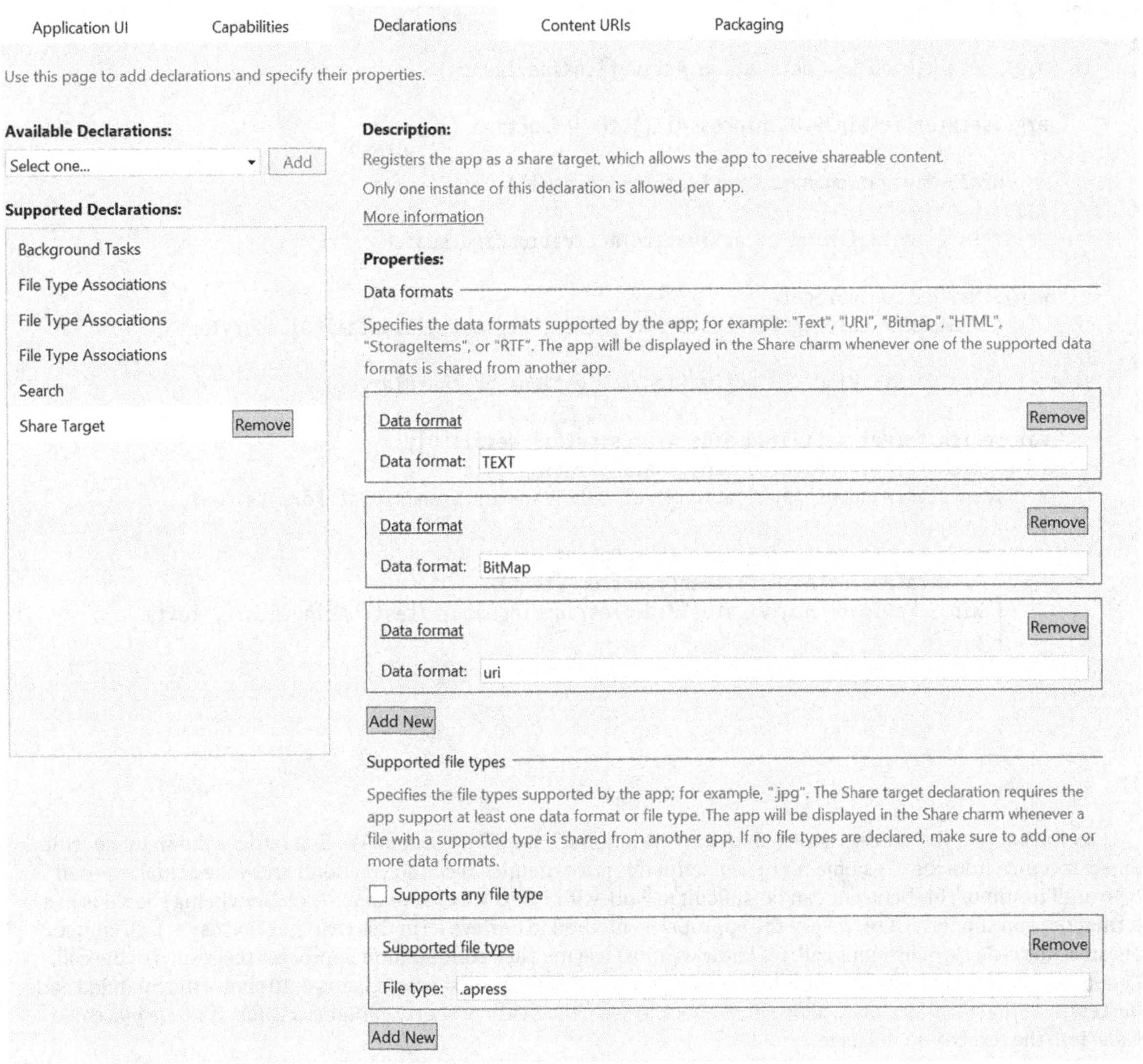

Application UI	Capabilities	Declarations	Content URIs	Packaging

Use this page to add declarations and specify their properties.

Available Declarations:

Select one... ▼ [Add]

Supported Declarations:

Background Tasks

File Type Associations

File Type Associations

File Type Associations

Search

Share Target [Remove]

Description:

Registers the app as a share target, which allows the app to receive shareable content.

Only one instance of this declaration is allowed per app.

More information

Properties:

Data formats ─────────────────────────────

Specifies the data formats supported by the app; for example: "Text", "URI", "Bitmap", "HTML", "StorageItems", or "RTF". The app will be displayed in the Share charm whenever one of the supported data formats is shared from another app.

Data format [Remove]

Data format: TEXT

Data format [Remove]

Data format: BitMap

Data format [Remove]

Data format: uri

[Add New]

Supported file types ─────────────────────

Specifies the file types supported by the app; for example, ".jpg". The Share target declaration requires the app support at least one data format or file type. The app will be displayed in the Share charm whenever a file with a supported type is shared from another app. If no file types are declared, make sure to add one or more data formats.

☐ Supports any file type

Supported file type [Remove]

File type: .apress

[Add New]

Figure 5-13. *Share Target configuration with file-type association*

Listing 5-5 used the activation kind parameter passed to it from Windows 8 to point the application directly to the TestSearch page when it was launched from the Search charm. Listing 5-9 modifies Listing 5-5 by adding a new else-if block that filters out application startups where ActivationKind is shareTarget.

Listing 5-9. shareTarget Activation Kind at Work

```
"use strict";

var app = WinJS.Application;
var activation = Windows.ApplicationModel.Activation;
```

```
app.onactivated = function (args)
{
    if (args.detail.kind === activation.ActivationKind.launch)
    {
        args.setPromise(WinJS.UI.processAll().then(function ()
        {
            WinJS.Navigation.navigate("samplelist.html");
        }));
    } else if (args.detail.kind == activation.ActivationKind.search)
    {
        WinJS.Navigation.navigate ↲
            ("/samples/searchsample/testsearch.html", args.detail.detail[0].queryText);
    }
    else if (args.detail.kind === activation.ActivationKind.shareTarget)
    {
        var search_target_activated_args = args.detail.detail[0];
        if (search_target_activated_args.shareOperation.data ↲
            .contains(Windows.ApplicationModel.DataTransfer.StandardDataFormats.text))
        {
            search_target_activated_args.shareOperation ↲
                .data.getTextAsync().then(function (text)
            { WinJS.Navigation.navigate("/samples/sharingsample/testsharing.html", text)
            });
        }
    }

};
```

As you can see, the process is very similar to the approach used with search. We first retrieve the share-specific object instance from the args object. (In JavaScript this is a dynamic object, so you don't know the actual exposed type until runtime. This behavior can be difficult to work with.) Next we ensure that the content being shared is in a format the app supports; if so, we use the appropriate method to retrieve it (in this case, getTextAsync). Of course, because this is an asynchronous call, we know we must use the then continuation to process the results of the call. Finally, we navigate to testsharing.html, passing the content that was shared. Listing 5-10 shows the modified code for testsharing.html. Basically, all we do is check to see if the state property contains a value; if so, we place that value into the text box on the page.

Listing 5-10. Presenting Shared Content

```
"use strict";

    WinJS.UI.Pages.define("/samples/SharingSample/TestSharing.html", {

        ready: function (element, options)
        {
            var transfer = Windows.ApplicationModel.DataTransfer.DataTransferManager;
            var share = transfer.getForCurrentView();
            var state = WinJS.Navigation.state;
            if (state != null)
```

```
        {
            txt_content.value = state;
        }

        share.ondatarequested = function (args)
        {
            args.request.data.properties.title = "Sample Sharing Text";
            args.request.data.properties ↵
                .description = "Description of the text being sent";

            //set text
            args.request.data.setText(txt_content.value);

        };

        btn_openshare.onclick = function ()
        {
            transfer.showShareUI();
        };
    },
```

To test this, I went to google.com and did a search for this book. When I copied the contents in the Google search text box and then clicked Share, this application appeared as one of the possible share targets. Clicking it displayed the view shown in Figure 5-14.

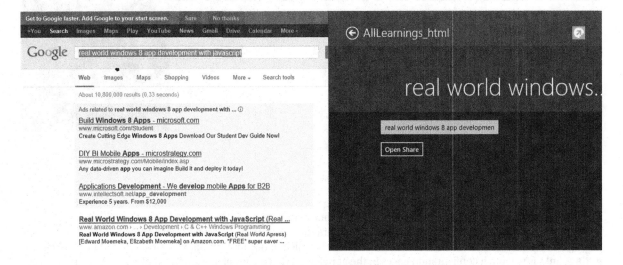

Figure 5-14. *Sharing between IE and the example application*

One thing to note is that share targets don't have the same width as normal applications. The layout of the share view must account for this, or the user experience suffers. Navigating the user to a standard page with normal dimensions (which is pixel or margin positioned) may make sharing impossible for the user.

Start Charm

The Start charm isn't an extensibility point but is listed here for completeness. It functions like the hardware Windows key on the keyboard (not all keyboards have a Windows key). Clicking this button toggles the user between the new Start screen and the currently running application or, depending on the context, the Windows desktop.

Devices Charm

Any functionality built in to an application that uses external devices is surfaced through the Devices charm slide-out menu. If an application subscribes to the appropriate Windows 8 mechanisms (discussed momentarily), clicking the Devices charm surfaces target devices to which functionality and content can be exported.

A great example is video playback and Digital Living Network Alliance (DLNA) devices. While playing back video in an application, you can opt to have video streamed to any screen that is DLNA compatible (for instance, Xbox- or DLNA-compatible televisions). Another good example—one that is the basis for Chapter 6—is printing. When printing is enabled in an application screen, the user can see potential printing devices in the slide-out property page for the Devices charm. The interesting thing about the latter case is that it functions somewhat indirectly. Unlike the Share charm, which triggers an event on the focused application as a result of the charm being clicked, the Devices menu surfaces a set of devices that map specifically to the type of behavior the current application view is surfacing. In the case of the printing example, the use of the printing functionality (via the `PrintManager` class) exposes to Windows the appropriate set of devices to show in the list: printers. Much as with sharing, the list is filtered to devices that make sense to be listed. Figure 5-15 shows the Internet Explorer app (not the desktop version) when I clicked the Devices charm.

Figure 5-15. *Devices pane when IE is the running app*

Settings Charm

The Settings charm rounds out the charm menu extensibility story. Not surprisingly, it provides an extension point to which you can attach application settings and configuration user interfaces. These hooks appear as links in the Settings menu; when clicked, they fire events that can be handled in the application. The most common use of the settings links is to launch configuration pages in the application that are otherwise unnavigable. Listing 5-11 is a basic example of hooking into the Windows 8 Settings charm.

Listing 5-11. Connecting to the Settings Charm

```
(function () {
    "use strict";

    WinJS.UI.Pages.define("/samples/SettingsSample/TestSettings.html", {

        ready: function (element, options) {
            var settings = Windows.UI.ApplicationSettings ↵
                .SettingsPane.getForCurrentView();
            settings.oncommandsrequested = function (args)
            {
                var privacy_command = new Windows.UI.ApplicationSettings ↵
                    .SettingsCommand("privacy_statement", "Privacy Policy", function (command)
                {
                    var msg = new Windows.UI.Popups ↵
                        .MessageDialog("This app does nothing so there is no policy.");
                    msg.showAsync();
                });

                var help_command = new Windows.UI.ApplicationSettings ↵
                    .SettingsCommand("helo", "Help", function (command)
                {
                    var msg = new Windows.UI.Popups ↵
                        .MessageDialog("This app does nothing so there is need for help.");
                    msg.showAsync();
                });

                var about_command = new Windows.UI.ApplicationSettings ↵
                    .SettingsCommand("about", "About", function (command)
                {
                    var msg = new Windows.UI.Popups ↵
                        .MessageDialog("This app was developed by the collective we.");
                    msg.showAsync();
                });

                var options_command = new Windows.UI.ApplicationSettings ↵
                    .SettingsCommand("options", "Options", function (command)
                {
                    var msg = new Windows.UI.Popups ↵
                        .MessageDialog("This app does nothing so there are no options.");
                    msg.showAsync();
                });

                args.request.applicationCommands.clear();
                args.request.applicationCommands.append(options_command);
                args.request.applicationCommands.append(about_command);
                args.request.applicationCommands.append(help_command);
                args.request.applicationCommands.append(privacy_command);

            };
        },

    });
```

```
btn_settings.onclick = function ()
            {
                Windows.UI.ApplicationSettings.SettingsPane.show();
            };
})();
```

Each command added to the applicationCommands property essentially contains a label, unique name, and a handler function that is called when the link for the command is clicked. Figure 5-16 shows how this application looks when run.

Figure 5-16. *Settings pane with additional settings added*

Implicit Contracts

Like charms-driven contracts, implicit contracts extend the Windows 8 out-of-the-box experience by allowing new combinations of usage patterns with each additional app install. Unlike their counterparts, however, the point of integration with implicit contracts is much more seamless: an application may even subvert the user-centric permissions model previously described. An app can, for instance, declare that it handles files of a certain type by specifying in its application manifest the file extension of the file type it handles. Activating a file of that type from anywhere on Windows (even in another application) immediately launches the declaring application (or provides an interface in which the user can select the appropriate application to use in instances where multiple applications declare that they can handle a specified file type).

Implicit contracts include contracts that extend the built-in pickers: FileSavePicker, FileOpenPicker, and ContactPicker. Like the search contract and share target contract, pickers like these rely on reading the activation kind. Table 5-5 lists all possible activation kinds available to applications.

Table 5-5. *ActivationKind Members*

Member Name	Declaration Type	Description
launch	N/A	The user launched the app or tapped a content tile.
search	Search	The user wants to search with the app.
shareTarget	Share Target	The app is activated as a target for share operations.
file	File Type Association	An app launched a file whose file type this app is registered to handle.
protocol	Protocol	An app launched a URL whose protocol this app is registered to handle.

(*continued*)

Table 5-5. (*continued*)

Member Name	Declaration Type	Description
fileOpenPicker	File Open Picker	The user wants to pick files that are provided by the app.
fileSavePicker	File Save Picker	The user wants to save a file and selected the app as the location.
cachedFileUpdater	Cached File Uploader	The user wants to save a file for which the app provides content management.
contactPicker	Contact Picker	The user wants to pick contacts.
device	Autoplay Device	The app handles AutoPlay.
printTaskSettings	Print Task Settings	The app handles print tasks.
cameraSettings	Camera Setting	The app captures photos or video from an attached camera.

Listing 5-12 illustrates the strategy of using the activation kind to determine how the application should present itself.

Listing 5-12. More Contracts

```
(function ()
{
    "use strict";


    var activation = Windows.ApplicationModel.Activation;
    var stack = new Stack();


    app.onactivated = function (args)
    {
        if (args.detail.kind === activation.ActivationKind.launch)
        {
            args.setPromise(WinJS.UI.processAll().then(function ()
            {
                WinJS.Navigation.navigate("samplelist.html");
            }));
        } else if (args.detail.kind == activation.ActivationKind.search)
        {
            //TODO: target the page you want here
        }
        else if (args.detail.kind === activation.ActivationKind.shareTarget)
        {
            //TODO: target the page you want here
        }
        else if (args.detail.kind === activation.ActivationKind.fileOpenPicker)
        {
            //TODO: target the page you want here
        }
```

```
        else if (args.detail.kind === activation.ActivationKind.fileSavePicker)
        {
            //TODO: target the page you want here
        }
        else if (args.detail.kind === activation.ActivationKind.contactPicker)
        {
            //TODO: target the page you want here
        }
        else if (args.detail.kind === activation.ActivationKind.file)
        {
            //TODO: target the page you want here
        }
        else if (args.detail.kind === activation.ActivationKind.cameraSettings)
        {
            //TODO: target the page you want here
        }

    };

})();
```

Summary

With the close of this chapter, you should feel well on your way toward gaining more in-depth knowledge of the Windows 8 ethos and environment to serve you as you forge ahead into JavaScript development for Windows 8. Charms grant the user the ability to search across the entire device as well as in applications, send content to other applications or devices, and access settings in a standardized manner. Through the use of contracts, interoperability between applications can be enhanced further. Five charms are accessed in the Windows 8 platform. These include Start and the four covered in this chapter: Search, Share, Devices, and Settings. Following are some key points about these charms:

- The Search charm can be used to perform system-wide searches across all applications, files, and settings.

- The Share charm is the most prominent means of sharing between applications. When an application subscribes to the sharing experience, it can send and receive content in various forms ranging from simple to complex structures.

- Functionality built in to an application that uses external devices is surfaced through the Devices charm. The Devices charm surfaces target devices to which functionality and content can be exported.

- The Settings charm provides an extension point for which application settings and configuration user interfaces can be attached to. Its most common use is launching otherwise unnavigable configuration pages in the application.

- Implicit contracts extend the Windows 8 out-of-the-box experience by allowing new combinations of usage patterns with each additional app install.

■ ■ ■

CHAPTER 6

Solving the Printing Problem

Now that you know all about charms and their usages and functions, you can get into the specifics of their real-world use. Chapter 5 discussed the Devices charm. This chapter delves into greater detail on using this charm for one specific scenario: printing. As stated in the previous chapter, when printing is enabled in an application screen, the user can see potential printing devices in the fly-out property page for the Devices charm. This chapter also compares and contrasts printing in Windows 8 with printing in Windows legacy applications. And you review samples in which a print task is created. Let's get started.

Pre–Windows 8 Printing

Windows applications of old—desktop applications, as they're now called—used the menu paradigm for application commands. This meant that typically, an application had a content area and an area where the user could control the content through commands. This command area was the *menu*, which began as just a top-level menu and evolved into context menus, toolbars, and floating windows dedicated to issuing commands.

Menus are great for a number of reasons, not the least of which is that they give you up front and outright a full list of all the actions an application can perform. Although they're context aware, menus use an enable/disable mechanism to train users about what can and can't be done at any given time. The benefit is that you know that at some point, you can perform an action.

In contrast, features like context menus and ribbons follow a different approach. As the number of actions an application can perform increases, it becomes prohibitive to list them all in a top menu. A large percentage of actions are disabled during most normal interaction with the application. In such instances, using a context menu displays only the appropriate commands—the ones relevant to the specific context. The downside is that this method doesn't advertise functionality to the user.

Printing has historically been presented to users through the mechanism of menus and commands. The user's approach to printing is simple: click the File menu, and select Print if the menu option exists. Figure 6-1 shows the File menu for Internet Explorer 10 on a Windows 8 machine just before I printed an article by my favorite blogger, Ed Bott (CNET).

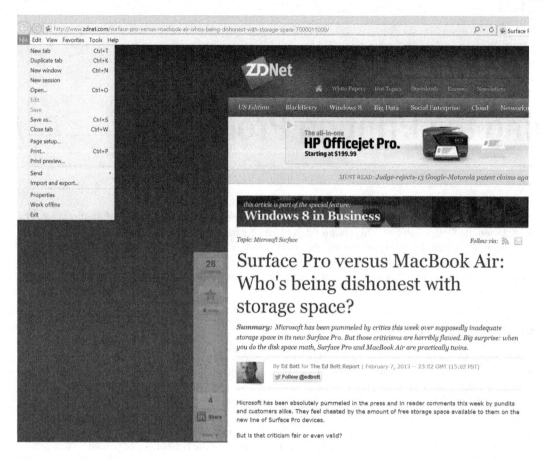

Figure 6-1. *The File menu with printing enabled*

As a developer building a desktop .NET application, for instance, it's up to you to decide which screens contain printable content and need the print function enabled, and which screens don't. Although IE10 isn't a .NET application, the same rule applies. Figure 6-2 shows the launch screen for IE10: because it has no actual content, there is nothing to print, and thus the print function is disabled in the File menu.

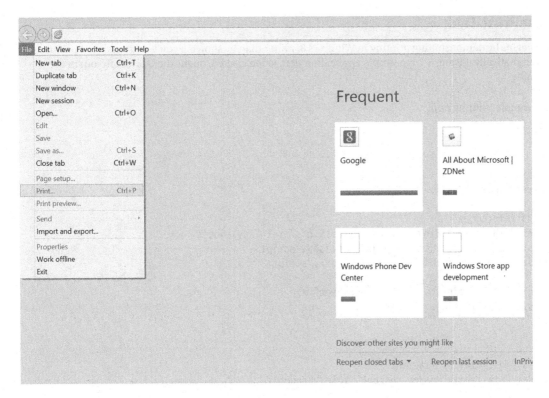

Figure 6-2. *The File menu with printing disabled*

Unlike standard desktop applications, web-based applications (the kinds of apps that a JavaScript developer might have previously worked on) exist as content in the context of the overarching application (the browser). Although menus can be built to mimic the functionality of their desktop counterparts, the convention has been, for the most part to embed commands in the content in the form of links and buttons. In JavaScript you can only programmatically invoke the Print dialog through the `window.print()` function; you can't initiate an actual print action (that is, printing a document separate from what the user sees). Thus the usual approach is to redirected to a "print ready" page where the user can initiate the printing action. Of course, because the commands are embedded front and center in the content where the user can see them, the problem of advertising functionality is solved.

The Windows 8 Printing Story

As you transition into Windows 8 apps, the printing story starts to lose focus from the user's standpoint. First, menus are gone, so there is no standardized control mechanism to speak of (app bars do fill this role to some extent). Second, there is no print command or charm that is recognizable to the user—printing takes place through the Devices charm, which, in my opinion, isn't remotely intuitive.

You might think that, given this fact, taking the web application approach of embedding commands into the content is viable, but you would be wrong (at least, according to the style guidelines published by Microsoft). Instead, the idea is to use the bottom app bar—the area dedicated to commands (by convention) for Windows 8 apps—and programmatically invoke the printing experience from within your app rather than expect the user to click the Devices charm to determine whether the page they're presently can be printed.

Creating a Print Task

This example begins by demonstrating printing in Windows 8, rather than by showing you how to start the printing process programmatically. Listing 6-1 is a simple application that, when clicked, opens the Devices fly-out in the context of printing.

Listing 6-1. A Simple Printing App

```
<!DOCTYPE html>
<html>
<head>
    <meta charset="utf-8" />
    <title>TestPrinting</title>

    <!-- WinJS references -->
    <link href="//Microsoft.WinJS.1.0/css/ui-dark.css" rel="stylesheet" />
    <script src="//Microsoft.WinJS.1.0/js/base.js"></script>
    <script src="//Microsoft.WinJS.1.0/js/ui.js"></script>

    <link href="TestPrinting.css" rel="stylesheet" />
    <script src="TestPrinting.js"></script>

</head>
<body>
    <div class="TestPrinting fragment">
        <header aria-label="Header content" role="banner">

        </header>
        <section aria-label="Main content" role="main">
            <p>
                <input id="btn_start" type="button" value="Start Printing" />
            </p>
        </section>

    </div>
</body>
</html>
```

The relevant JavaScript for this file is shown in Listing 6-2.

Listing 6-2. Print Experience JavaScript Handler

```
btn_start.onclick = function (e)
{
    Windows.Graphics.Printing.PrintManager.showPrintUIAsync();
};
```

The listing asks Windows to display the printing user interface when the specified button is clicked. The first view of this interface always displays the list of available printers for the user to choose from. In order for this list to appear, printing must be enabled.

Enabling printing for an application means handling the `printtaskrequested` method of the `PrintManager` class and making a call to the `createPrintTask` function (see Listing 6-3).

Listing 6-3. Creating a Print Task

```
<!DOCTYPE html>
<html>
<head>
    <meta charset="utf-8" />
    <title>TestPrinting</title>

    <!-- WinJS references -->
    <link href="//Microsoft.WinJS.1.0/css/ui-dark.css" rel="stylesheet" />
    <script src="//Microsoft.WinJS.1.0/js/base.js"></script>
    <script src="//Microsoft.WinJS.1.0/js/ui.js"></script>

    <link href="TestPrinting.css" rel="stylesheet" />
    <script src="TestPrinting.js"></script>
</head>
<body>
    <div class="TestPrinting fragment">
        <header aria-label="Header content" role="banner">
            <button class="win-backbutton" aria-label="Back" disabled type="button"></button>
            <h1 class="titlearea win-type-ellipsis">
                <span class="pagetitle">Welcome to TestPrinting</span>
            </h1>
        </header>
        <section aria-label="Main content" role="main">
            <p><input id="btn_print" type="button" value="Enable Printing" /></p>
        </section>
    </div>
</body>
</html>
```

The JavaScript code behind for this is shown in Listing 6-4.

Listing 6-4. Handling a Print Request from Windows

```
(function () {
    "use strict";

    WinJS.UI.Pages.define("/samples/PrintingSample/TestPrinting.html", {

        ready: function (element, options) {
            btn_print.onclick = function (e)
            {
                var print_manager = Windows.Graphics.Printing ↩
                    .PrintManager.getForCurrentView();
```

```
            print_manager.onprinttaskrequested = function (print_event)
            {

                print_event.request ↩
                    .createPrintTask("Sample Print Task", function (args)
                    {

                    });
                };
            };
        },


    });
})();
```

Placing the code for creating a print task into the button click event is impractical for everyday use. In normal situations, the code that enables printing is at the page level and not invoked by a button. That way, clicking the Devices charm immediately displays the app's printing options. In this case, it illustrates the way printing is enabled in the Devices charm and Devices fly-out. If you run the sample and then click the Devices charm, your screen should look like Figure 6-3.

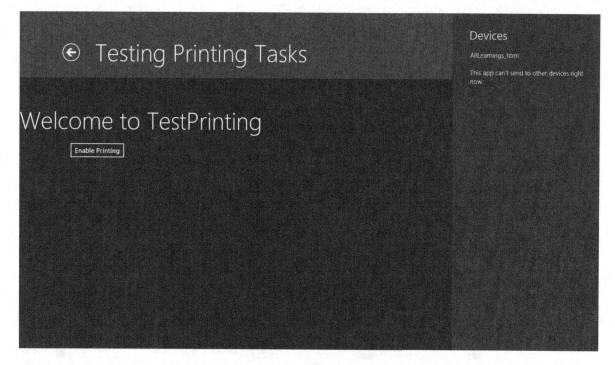

Figure 6-3. *The Devices charm fly-out before printing is enabled by the application*

Clicking the Enable Printing button hooks the application into printing. Now, when the Devices charm is clicked, onprinttaskrequested is called, and a list of print targets is revealed as shown in Figure 6-4.

Figure 6-4. *Devices charm fly-out after printing is enabled by the application*

Because the particular machine I'm using (the Windows 8 emulator) doesn't have a printer attached to it, no printers appear on the list. OneNote and Microsoft's XPS Writer function as printers, so they appear as the defaults.

Note that the application can also initialize the printing experience through the `PrintManager` class by calling `showPrintUIAsync`. This function does nothing but automate the activity of the user clicking the Devices charm. You can modify the code sample to try this: first add a new button to the user interface (see Listing 6-5).

Listing 6-5. Adding a Button to Invoke the Printing Pane

```
<section aria-label="Main content" role="main">
    <p>
        <input id="btn_start" type="button" value="Start Printing" />
    </p>
</section>
```

Then handle the `click` event of that button, as shown in Listing 6-6.

Listing 6-6. Displaying the Printing Pane from Code

```
btn_start.onclick = function (e)
{
    Windows.Graphics.Printing.PrintManager.showPrintUIAsync();
};
```

Printing with WinJS

To complete the process and provide an actual document to print, you need to create a print document. For XAML applications, print documents must be instantiated using a distinct PrintDocument class. HTML applications using WinJS don't need this. WinJS provides a utility object (MSApp) that you can use to convert the document object that represents the application's HTML to a print document; the utility method is getHtmlPrintDocumentSource. Using this method, as shown in Listing 6-7, you can format the print source to be used for printing to the targets discussed earlier.

Listing 6-7. Setting the Print Source for a Document

```
btn_print.onclick = function (e)
{
    var print_manager = Windows.Graphics.Printing.PrintManager.getForCurrentView();
    print_manager.onprinttaskrequested = function (print_event)
    {

        print_event.request.createPrintTask("Sample Print Task", function (args)
        {
            args.setSource(MSApp.getHtmlPrintDocumentSource(document));
        });
    };
};

btn_start.onclick = function (e)
{
    Windows.Graphics.Printing.PrintManager.showPrintUIAsync();
};
```

With the print source set, clicking the Enable Printing button and then the Start Printing button takes you to the same Devices fly-out. But there is now more. Clicking any of the print targets displays the fly-out shown in Figure 6-5. You should see a preview of the first page of the document, with paging controls that allow you to quickly navigate to other pages as needed. The fly-out also lets you specify the orientation of the document to be printed and apply additional options (through the More Settings link) like page layout and paper quality.

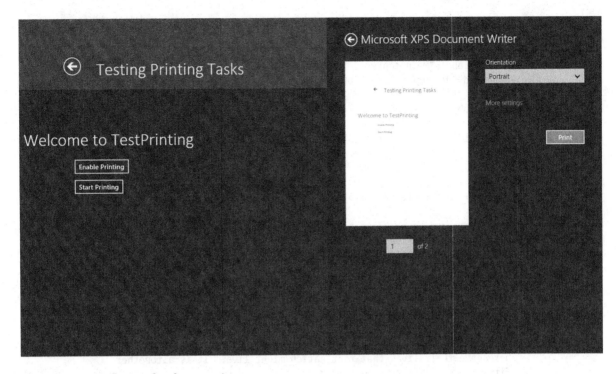

Figure 6-5. *Print fly-out after the source is set*

The great thing about the WinJS implementation of printing is that it automates paging. In standard WinRT printing, an application developer typically has to determine what constitutes a "page" of the print document. Because WinJS uses HTML, much of this functionality is built in. Let's modify the document to illustrate (see Listing 6-8).

Listing 6-8. Multipage Document

```
<!DOCTYPE html>
<html>
<head>
    <meta charset="utf-8" />
    <title>TestPrinting</title>

    <!-- WinJS references -->
    <link href="//Microsoft.WinJS.1.0/css/ui-dark.css" rel="stylesheet" />
    <script src="//Microsoft.WinJS.1.0/js/base.js"></script>
    <script src="//Microsoft.WinJS.1.0/js/ui.js"></script>

    <link href="TestPrinting.css" rel="stylesheet" />
    <script src="TestPrinting.js"></script>
</head>
<body>
    <div class="TestPrinting fragment">
        <header aria-label="Header content" role="banner">
            <button class="win-backbutton" aria-label="Back" disabled type="button"></button>
            <h1 class="titlearea win-type-ellipsis">
```

```
            <span class="pagetitle">Welcome to TestPrinting</span>
        </h1>
    </header>
     <section aria-label="Main content" role="main">
        <p><input id="btn_print" type="button" value="Enable Printing" /></p>
    </section>
    <section aria-label="Main content" role="main">
        <p>
            <input id="btn_start" type="button" value="Start Printing" />
        </p>
    </section>

    <div aria-label="Main content" role="main" style="width:200px;">
        <p>
            Four score and seven years ago our fathers brought forth on this continent
            a new nation conceived in liberty and dedicated to the
            proposition that all men are created equal.
        </p>
        <p>
            Now we are engaged in a great civil war testing whether that nation,
            or any nation so conceived and so dedicated, can long endure.
            We are met on a great battlefield of that war.  We have come to dedicate
            a portion of that field as a final resting place for those who
            here gave their lives that that nation might live.  It is altogether
            fitting and proper that we should do this.
        </p>
        <p>
            But in a larger sense we can not dedicate - we can not consecrate -
            we can not hallow - this ground.  The brave men living and dead who
            struggled here, have consecrated it far above our poor power to add
            or detract.
        </p>

    </div>
    </div>
</body>
</html>
```

Depending on the device, if you run this sample, you should see that the document is now two pages (this may vary slightly depending on the user's page size); see Figure 6-6.

■ **Note**   If this doesn't display as two pages on your PC, add more text to the body of the Main content div until it runs over.

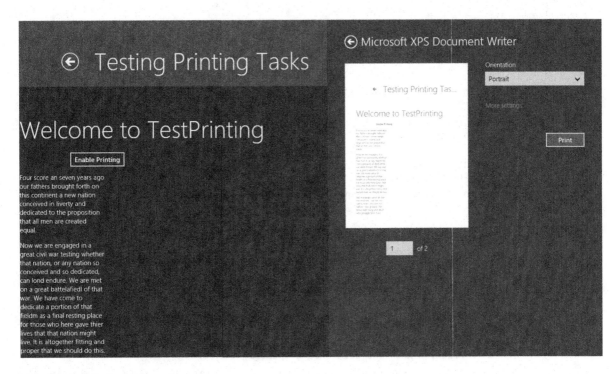

Figure 6-6. *Printing with paging*

Elements of Printing

An application can subscribe to events that are fired once printing is complete. To do so, you handle the `oncompleted` event of the `PrintTask` object. Table 6-1 provides a full list of the events that can be subscribed to on the `PrintTask` class.

Table 6-1. *PrintTask Events*

Event	Description
`completed`	Raised when the print task is completed
`previewing`	Raised when the print system initializes print preview mode
`progressing`	Raised to provide progress information about how much of the printed content has been submitted to the print subsystem for printing
`submitting`	Raised when a print task begins submitting content to the print subsystem to be printed

Listing 6-9 is the same JavaScript, subscribed to the events listed in Table 6-1.

Listing 6-9. PrintTask Events Handled

```
(function () {
    "use strict";

    WinJS.UI.Pages.define("/samples/PrintingSample/TestPrinting.html", {

        ready: function (element, options) {
            btn_print.onclick = function (e)
            {
                var print_manager = Windows.Graphics.Printing.PrintManager ↵
                    .getForCurrentView();
                print_manager.onprinttaskrequested = function (print_event)
                {

                    var print_task = print_event.request ↵
                        .createPrintTask("Sample Print Task", function (args)
                    {
                        args.setSource(MSApp.getHtmlPrintDocumentSource(document));
                    });

                    print_task.oncompleted = function (e)
                    {
                        //called when the print has completed
                    };

                    print_task.onsubmitting = function (e)
                    {
                        //called when the actual print button is hit.
                        //The print activity has been submitted.
                    };

                    print_task.onprogressing = function (e)
                    {
                        //called to give feedback on the progress of the print job
                    };

                    print_task.onpreviewing = function (e)
                    {
                        //called when the print document is being previewed
                    };
                };
            };

            btn_start.onclick = function (e)
            {
                Windows.Graphics.Printing.PrintManager.showPrintUIAsync();
            };
        },
    });
})();
```

PrintTask also contains a number of properties that are useful for manipulating the source after the fact or configuring the user's print experience (see Table 6-2).

Table 6-2. *PrintTask Properties*

Property	Access Type	Description
Options	Read-only	Retrieves PrintTaskOptions for the print task that defines how the content is to be formatted for printing.
Properties	Read-only	Retrieves a set of properties associated with PrintTask.
Source	Read-only	Returns a pointer to the app-provided object that represents the content to be printed. This object must support the IPrintDocumentSource interface.

Using the Options property (which exposes the PrintTaskOptions object), the application can modify various aspects of the printing experience's formatting. Table 6-3 highlights the key properties of this class. As you can see, these map to printer options that can be set programmatically.

Table 6-3. *PrintTaskOptions Properties*

Property	Access Type	Description
Binding	Read/write	Gets or sets the binding option of the print task
Collation	Read/write	Gets or sets the collation option of the print task
ColorMode	Read/write	Gets or sets the color mode option of the print task
DisplayedOptions	Read-only	Gets the list of options displayed for the print experience
Duplex	Read/write	Gets or sets the duplex option of the print task
HolePunch	Read/write	Gets or sets the hole punch option of the print task
MaxCopies	Read-only	Gets the maximum number of copies supported for the print task
MediaSize	Read/write	Gets or sets the media size option of the print task
MediaType	Read/write	Gets or sets the media type option for the print task
MinCopies	Read-only	Gets the minimum number of copies allowed for the print task
NumberOfCopies	Read/write	Gets or sets the value for the number of copies for the print task
Orientation	Read/write	Gets or sets the orientation option for the print task
PrintQuality	Read/write	Gets or sets the print quality option for the print task
Staple	Read/write	Gets or sets the staple option for the print task

Most of the objects returned by the properties highlighted are contained in the Windows.Graphics.Printing namespace. When it comes to printing, this is ground zero for hooking into what the Windows 8 APIs expose to developers. Table 6-4 shows the full list of the types this namespace contains.

Table 6-4. *Windows.Graphics.Printing Namespace Classes*

Class	Description
PrintManager	Informs Windows that an application wishes to participate in printing. The PrintManager class is also used to programmatically initiate printing.
PrintTask	Represents a printing operation, including the content to be printed, and provides access to information describing how the content is to be printed.
PrintTaskCompletedEventArgs	Reports on the completion of the print task.
PrintTaskOptions	Represents a collection of methods and properties for managing the options that define how the content is to be printed.
PrintTaskProgressingEventArgs	Event arguments for the PrintTask.Progressing event. This event is raised during the submitting phase (not to be confused with the submitting event) of the PrintTask. During the submitting of a document, the content is sent to the printing subsystem. The progress of that effort is what is tracked here.
PrintTaskRequest	Contains the request from the system to create a print task. In Listing 6-9, you made a call to the request property of the print_event object that was returned as part of handling onprinttaskrequested. The exact code was print_event.request.createPrintTask("Sample Print Task", function (args). The request property here returns an instance of this class.
PrintTaskRequestedEventArgs	Event arguments associated with PrintTaskRequest.
PrintTaskSourceRequestedArgs	Arguments associated with the PrintTaskSourceRequestedHandler delegate. Provides a method for handing the content to be printed to PrintTask.

Summary

Congratulations! You now have specific working knowledge of how printing functions for Windows Store applications. After reading this chapter and examining the samples, you've gained exposure to

- Using the Devices charm for printing

- How you can use a utility object provided by WinJS to convert the actual document object that represents the HTML of the application to a print document

- The fly-out that is displayed by clicking a print target

- How the WinJS implementation of printing automates paging

- How an application can subscribe to events that are fired after printing is previewed, progressing, or complete

- PrintTask, which contains properties that are useful for manipulating the source after the fact or configuring the user's print experience

- Using the Options property to modify various formatting aspects of an app's printing experience

CHAPTER 7

■ ■ ■

Providing Clear Notifications

The discussion in the previous chapter ended with a walkthrough of the Windows 8 lock screen, including an example of using the notification mechanisms built in to the Windows Store APIs to send messages to the user in one form or another. This leads into a discussion of two key types of notifications: toasts and tiles. This chapter examines these notifications, the purposes they serve, and how you as a developer can engineer them to most effectively serve your app and your users.

The Notification Process

Let's start by defining what notifications are in the context of Modern Windows 8 applications. A *notification* is a message that goes out to your app's end user and provides meaningful information about the use of your application. It could be letting the user know that their password is invalid, that they don't have access to certain content in your application, that they have been idle for some time and their session is about to time out, or that there was an error in the application. This type of general-purpose notification isn't what this chapter discusses. Rather, you focus on a class of notifications that have previously had no distinct representation in the API landscape of Windows development: notifications that occur while an application is out of focus.

Take Microsoft Office's Outlook mail client, for example. If you have toast notifications enabled in Outlook, a small borderless window appears above the system tray area every time you receive a new email message. Clicking this toast window immediately launches the full Outlook client and allows you to view the message.

A pattern like this isn't baked into legacy Windows application development. Each developer must create a distinct implementation of this functionality using hidden windows and system-tray icons. Most important, because the operating system doesn't provide any mechanisms to support it, any application wishing to use this mechanism must project the illusion of not running by either hiding itself when closed or having a separate executable (a *daemon*) that owns the notification process and also is in charge of launching the primary app when a user interacts with the toast window. Windows 8 takes the notion of notification and bakes it into the operating system so that all Windows 8 apps use the same mechanism—one that is instantly recognizable to all users and uniform across all applications.

As a Windows 8 developer building applications that target the Modern app platform, you can use four key mechanisms to provide notifications to your users: toast notifications, tile notifications, badge notifications, and push notifications. Toast, tile, and badge notifications typically require the application to be running (if not in focus), whereas push notifications represent a new class of notification in which the app doesn't need to be running on the client.

As stated earlier, part of the problem statement of notifications that Windows 8 attempts to solve is that of uniformity. If every application had to create its own notification framework, as legacy applications do, it would be difficult for a user to easily ascertain not just whether a user interface element is a notification but also what type of notification it is and what interaction patterns it exposes. Internet Explorer 10, for example, uses notifications. When a download is complete, the taskbar icon flashes to notify the user. To a trained eye, this makes sense. But a novice user might not understand the implication—particularly because not every application functions this way. It was important when designing the Windows 8 API landscape to create a stronger sense of uniformity with regard to notifications. Toward that end, rather than just expose a user interface surface in which applications present their notifications, the Windows API designers chose to use a predefined set of templates. These templates ensure that all notifications follow a standardized presentation format that remains consistent across applications, preventing a fractured or inconsistent experience for the user. The following sections talk more about these templates during the discussion of the toast and tile notification types.

Toast Notifications

Toast notifications function similarly to the notifications discussed in the previous section. Whereas legacy Windows toast notifications are an interaction pattern that applications follow, the toast notification mechanism exposed to Modern Windows 8 apps are baked into the operating system and API surface area. This means all Modern applications can use them through a common set of APIs and that the user is presented with an interaction pattern that is similar regardless of the notifier. This is consistent with the overarching Windows 8 paradigm: the primary differentiating factor between applications is the content. Of course, applications can differ in design, but generally speaking content is king and takes precedence over chrome in with Modern Windows 8 applications.

Figure 7-1 shows how a toast notification looks when displayed while the user is on the Windows 8 Start screen. It appears, as you can see, in the upper-right corner of the screen.

Figure 7-1. *Example of a toast notification*

No matter where you are or what you're doing in the operating system, a toast notification always appears in the upper-right corner and gradually fades when the user doesn't interact with it. In scenarios where multiple toasts are received, subsequent toasts are displayed beneath the previously presented toast. Figure 7-2 shows how multiple toast notifications appear on a user's screen.

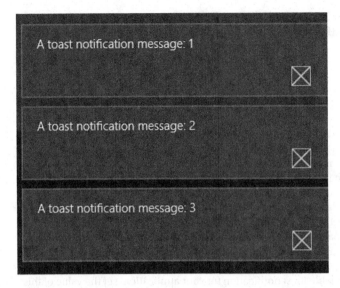

Figure 7-2. Multiple toast notifications on screen (unlike the example in Figure 7-1, these notifications have no icon associated with them)

Generating Toast Notifications

Toasts can be sent locally or via push notification. A user can select the toast by touching or clicking it in order to launch the associated app. Because these notifications are designed to be context aware, the context of the toast notification can be handled in the launched application such that it presents a detailed view of the notification content.

Listing 7-1 shows a very simple example of a local toast notification. The user clicks a button (btn_toast), and in the event handler you present a toast notification using a call to the show method.

Listing 7-1. Local Toast Notification

```
(function ()
{
    "use strict";

    WinJS.UI.Pages.define("/samples/NotificationSample/TestNotification.html", {

        ready: function (element, options)
        {
            var count = 0;
            btn_toast.onclick = function ()
            {
                count++;
                var toast_xml = Windows.UI.Notifications.ToastNotificationManager↵
                    .getTemplateContent(Windows.UI.Notifications↵
                    .ToastTemplateType.toastText01);
                var text_node = toast_xml.documentElement.getElementsByTagName("text")[0];
                text_node.appendChild(toast_xml.createTextNode("A toast notification ↵
                    message: " + count));
```

```
            var toast = new Windows.UI.Notifications.ToastNotification(toast_xml);
            var toast_notifier = Windows.UI.Notifications.ToastNotificationManager. ⏎
                createToastNotifier();
            toast_notifier.show(toast);
        };
    },
  });
})();
```

The example is relatively straightforward. First you establish a variable count that represents the number of times the toast button is clicked. Each time btn_toast is clicked, you increment count and then generate a new toast notification that incorporates the new count into its message. As you can see from the listing, generating a toast is as simple as getting access to an XML document, manipulating the content in this document, and then passing the completed document as an argument into an instance of the ToastNotificationManager class. ToastNotificationManager then uses this to construct the appropriate ToastNotifier.

The example in Listing 7-1 is the very one that created the list of toast notifications in Figure 7-2. To get it to work, you must open your package.appmanifest file and enable toast notifications for the application. The setting to do this can be found on the Application UI tab. In the All Image Assets tree, select Badge Logo, and you see the Notifications section with a drop-down labeled Toast Capable. To enable toast notification for your application, set the value of this drop-down to Try.

This XML document used to start the process is referred to as a *template* and is exposed through the enumeration ToastTemplateType. You were introduced to templates at the beginning of this chapter. Templates let you present toast notifications in a variety of ways. In the example, you present a text-only notification. Windows 8 provides eight templates: four that are text only and four that use both images and text.

The following section walks through the various toast notification formats in greater detail. Note that for all instances, overrun text is trimmed and invalid images are treated as though no image was specified.

ToastText01

This is the most basic form of text toast. This template presents a single string wrapped across a maximum of three lines of text. Listing 7-2 shows the XML for this template type. The node in bold represents the area to be targeted based on the pattern illustrated in Listing 7-1.

Listing 7-2. ToastText01 Template Definition

```
<toast>
    <visual>
        <binding template="ToastText01">
            <text id="1">bodyText</text>
        </binding>
    </visual>
</toast>
```

ToastText02

This template presents one string in bold text on the first line and one string of regular text wrapped across the second and third lines. Listing 7-3 shows the XML for this template type. The node in bold represents the area to be targeted based on the pattern illustrated in Listing 7-1.

Listing 7-3. ToastText02 Template Definition

```xml
<toast>
    <visual>
        <binding template="ToastText02">
            <text id="1">headlineText</text>
            <text id="2">bodyText</text>
        </binding>
    </visual>
</toast>
```

ToastText03

A variation of the design from ToastText02, this template presents one string in bold text across the first and second lines with one string of regular text on the third line. Listing 7-4 shows the XML for this template type. Notice that the only distinction between this and Listing 7-3 is the template name. The node in bold represents the area to be targeted based on the pattern illustrated in Listing 7-1.

Listing 7-4. ToastText03 Template Definition

```xml
<toast>
    <visual>
        <binding template="ToastText03">
            <text id="1">headlineText</text>
            <text id="2">bodyText</text>
        </binding>
    </visual>
</toast>
```

ToastText04

This template presents one string in bold text on the first line and one string of regular text on each subsequent line (note that there is no wrapping; each line has its own unique string). Listing 7-5 shows the XML for this template type. The node in bold represents the area to be targeted based on the pattern illustrated in Listing 7-1.

Listing 7-5. ToastText04 Template Definition

```xml
<toast>
    <visual>
        <binding template="ToastText04">
            <text id="1">headlineText</text>
            <text id="2">bodyText1</text>
            <text id="3">bodyText2</text>
        </binding>
    </visual>
</toast>
```

Adding Images to Toasts

Toast notifications may also include images. Figure 7-3 shows the modified toast notification, now programmed to support an image.

Figure 7-3. *Toast notification with an image*

To accomplish this, you only need to change the template being used and insert the appropriate content into the appropriate node of the underlying document. Listing 7-6 shows the code used to generate the toast notification in Figure 7-3. The bolded text is the changed part.

Listing 7-6. Toast Notification with an Image

```
(function ()
{
    "use strict";

    WinJS.UI.Pages.define("/samples/NotificationSample/TestNotification.html", {

        ready: function (element, options)
        {
            var count = 0;
            btn_toast.onclick = function ()
            {
                count++;
                var toast_xml = Windows.UI.Notifications.ToastNotificationManager↵
                    .getTemplateContent(Windows.UI.Notifications.ToastTemplateType↵
                    .toastImageAndText01);

                //set text
                var text_node = toast_xml.documentElement.getElementsByTagName("text")[0];
                text_node.appendChild(toast_xml.createTextNode↵
                    ("A toast notification message: " + count));

                //set image
                var image_node = toast_xml.documentElement.getElementsByTagName("image")[0];
                image_node.setAttribute("src", "ms-appx:///images/hiredup_150150.png");

                var toast = new Windows.UI.Notifications.ToastNotification(toast_xml);
                var toast_notifier = Windows.UI.Notifications.ToastNotificationManager↵
                    .createToastNotifier();
                toast_notifier.show(toast);
            };
        },
    });
})();
```

Notice the use of the protocol ms-appx when specifying the source of the image to use. You can use this protocol to retrieve content from the application's deployment package. The API also supports http/https to retrieve web-based images and ms-appdata:///local/ to pull images from local storage.

Listing 7-7 shows all the document template types exposed for toast notifications with images. They mirror the same documents exposed for plain-text toast notifications (with the exception of the added image element), so there is no need for further explanation.

Listing 7-7. Image-Based Toast Notification Document Types

```
<toast>
    <visual>
        <binding template="ToastImageAndText01">
            <image id="1" src="image1" alt="image1"/>
            <text id="1">bodyText</text>
        </binding>
    </visual>
</toast>
<toast>
    <visual>
        <binding template="ToastImageAndText02">
            <image id="1" src="image1" alt="image1"/>
            <text id="1">headlineText</text>
            <text id="2">bodyText</text>
        </binding>
    </visual>
</toast>

<toast>
    <visual>
        <binding template="ToastImageAndText03">
            <image id="1" src="image1" alt="image1"/>
            <text id="1">headlineText</text>
            <text id="2">bodyText</text>
        </binding>
    </visual>
</toast>

<toast>
    <visual>
        <binding template="ToastImageAndText04">
            <image id="1" src="image1" alt="image1"/>
            <text id="1">headlineText</text>
            <text id="2">bodyText1</text>
            <text id="3">bodyText2</text>
        </binding>
    </visual>
</toast>
```

Adding Sound to Toasts

Toast notifications may also have sounds associated with them. Imagine a scenario in which a VoIP-style application like Skype is receiving an incoming call. Just popping up a notification might not be enough (particularly if the user isn't presently working on the computer!). In this area, the API designers again chose uniformity over ultimate flexibility by allowing only a prescribed set of sounds to be used in concert with toast notifications. Windows 8 provides eight sounds in all: four that can be looped (like a phone call sound) and four that can't. Additionally, you can specify that a toast notification be silent. Listing 7-8 shows the audio node in full.

Listing 7-8. Audio Node

```
<audio src="ms-winsoundevent:Notification.Mail" loop="false" silent="false"/>
```

You can add toast notification audio to any of the aforementioned templates by adding the audio tag as a direct child of the top-level toast element. (Remember that everything else you've looked at thus far has been tied to the visual representation of the toast. It wouldn't make much sense for the audio element to be a child of the visual node.) In Listing 7-9, you add a looping call sound to the existing example.

Listing 7-9. Toast Notification with Audio

```
(function ()
{
    "use strict";

    WinJS.UI.Pages.define("/samples/NotificationSample/TestNotification.html", {

        ready: function (element, options)
        {
            var count = 0;
            btn_toast.onclick = function ()
            {
                count++;
                var toast_xml = Windows.UI.Notifications.ToastNotificationManager↩
                    .getTemplateContent(Windows.UI.Notifications.ToastTemplateType↩
                    .toastImageAndText01);
                toast_xml.documentElement.setAttribute("duration", "long");

                //set text
                var text_node = toast_xml.documentElement.getElementsByTagName("text")[0];
                text_node.appendChild(toast_xml.createTextNode↩
                    ("A toast notification message: " + count));

                //set image
                var image_node = toast_xml.documentElement.getElementsByTagName("image")[0];
                image_node.setAttribute("src", "ms-appx:///images/hiredup_150150.png");

                //add audio to the notification
                var audio_node = toast_xml.createElement("audio");
                audio_node.setAttribute("src", "ms-winsoundevent:Notification.Looping.Call");
                audio_node.setAttribute("loop", "true");

                toast_xml.documentElement.appendChild(audio_node);
```

```
        var toast = new Windows.UI.Notifications.ToastNotification(toast_xml);
        var toast_notifier = Windows.UI.Notifications.ToastNotificationManager↵
            .createToastNotifier();
        toast_notifier.show(toast);
    };
  },
 });
})();
```

As you can see, to add sound to a toast notification you create the audio node, populate the appropriate attributes, and add it to the XML document the template represents, and you're done. Notice, however, that something else has changed in the example. Your top-level document now has a duration attribute, which is set to long. This is required specifically for looping notifications but can be used in all toast notifications to create persistent toasts. Persistent toasts remain visible longer.

■ **Note** When you use the values from Table 7-1 in the src attribute of the audio tag, be sure to qualify them with the ms-winsoundevent namespace. Hence Notification.Looping.Alarm2 becomes ms-winsoundevent:Notification. Looping.Alarm2. Although omitting this doesn't cause an error, the audio notifications won't work.

Table 7-1. *Looping and Non-Looping Sounds that Can Be Attached to Toast Notifications*

Non Looping	Looping
Notification.Default	Notification.Looping.Alarm
Notification.IM	Notification.Looping.Alarm2
Notification.Mail	Notification.Looping.Call
Notification.Reminder	Notification.Looping.Call2
Notification.SMS	

Scheduling Toasts

In certain scenarios, it might be more appropriate to schedule a toast to happen at some point in the future (or perhaps happen in a recurring manner) than to have the notification fired off as soon as the command to show it is executed. In such scenarios, you can use a specialized class called ScheduledToastNotification. ScheduledToastNotification provides a constructor that accepts not only the XML template for the notification but also a date when the notification should be displayed, a sleep time for the notification (in scenarios where the notification repeats over a period of time), and a number that indicates the maximum number of times the notification will sleep before finally terminating. Listing 7-10 shows the use of this type of toast notification. When the user clicks the toast button, you schedule a notification for December 20, 2012, one day before the end of the world according to the Mayans!

Listing 7-10. Toasting the End of the World

```
(function ()
{
  // "use strict";

  WinJS.UI.Pages.define("/samples/NotificationSample/TestNotification.html", {
```

```
        ready: function (element, options)
        {
            var count = 0;
            btn_toast.onclick = function ()
            {
                count++;
                var toast_xml = Windows.UI.Notifications.ToastNotificationManager↵
                    .getTemplateContent(Windows.UI.Notifications.ToastTemplateType↵
                    .toastImageAndText01);
                toast_xml.documentElement.setAttribute("duration", "long");

                //set text
                var text_node = toast_xml.documentElement.getElementsByTagName("text")[0];
                text_node.appendChild(toast_xml.createTextNode↵
                    ("A toast notification message: " + count));

                //set image
                var image_node = toast_xml.documentElement.getElementsByTagName("image")[0];
                image_node.setAttribute("src", "ms-appx:///images/hiredup_150150.png");

                //add audio to the notification
                var audio_node = toast_xml.createElement("audio");
                audio_node.setAttribute("src", "ms-winsoundevent:Notification.Looping.Call");
                audio_node.setAttribute("loop", "true");

                toast_xml.documentElement.appendChild(audio_node);

                var stoast = new Windows.UI.Notifications.ScheduledToastNotification↵
                    (toast_xml, new Date("12/20/2012"),(60 * 1000) * 60,5);
                stoast.id = "the_end";

                var toast_notifier = Windows.UI.Notifications.ToastNotificationManager↵
                    .createToastNotifier();
                toast_notifier.addToSchedule(stoast);
            };
        },
    });
})();
```

Note the use of addToSchedule instead of show. As the name implies addToSchedule will enque the toast notification request and, at the point when the date specified is hit, display the toast.

Responding to Toast Notification Events

Earlier, you learned that one of the cool things about toast notifications—something that makes them different from the other types of notifications discussed in this chapter—is that they're context aware. This means your application can react in unique and context-specific ways to toast notifications activated or dismissed by the user. WinJS exposes events on the ToastNotification class to handle this scenario. See Listing 7-11.

Listing 7-11. Using the Events of the ToastNotification Class

```
(function ()
{
    // "use strict";

    WinJS.UI.Pages.define("/samples/NotificationSample/TestNotification.html", {

        ready: function (element, options)
        {
            var count = 0;
            btn_toast.onclick = function ()
            {
                count++;
                var toast_xml = Windows.UI.Notifications.ToastNotificationManager⏎
                    .getTemplateContent(Windows.UI.Notifications.ToastTemplateType⏎
                    .toastImageAndText01
                    );
                toast_xml.documentElement.setAttribute("duration", "long");

                //set text
                var text_node = toast_xml.documentElement.getElementsByTagName("text")[0];
                text_node.appendChild(toast_xml.createTextNode⏎
                    ("A toast notification message: " + count));

                //set image
                var image_node = toast_xml.documentElement.getElementsByTagName("image")[0];
                image_node.setAttribute("src", "ms-appx:///images/hiredup_150150.png");

                //add audio to the notification
                var audio_node = toast_xml.createElement("audio");
                audio_node.setAttribute("src", "ms-winsoundevent:Notification.Looping.Call");
                audio_node.setAttribute("loop", "true");
                audio_node.setAttribute("silent", "false");
                toast_xml.documentElement.appendChild(audio_node);

                var toast = new Windows.UI.Notifications.ToastNotification(toast_xml);

                //lift the value of count so that it is always the value at the
                //time when the button is clicked that is used when the toast
                //is activated or deactivated
                var indicator = count;

                toast.onactivated = function ()
                {
                    txt_display.innerText = "you activated toast for: " + indicator;

                };
                toast.ondismissed = function ()
                {
                    txt_display.innerText = "you dismissed toast for: " + indicator;
                };
```

```
            var toast_notifier = Windows.UI.Notifications.ToastNotificationManager↵
               .createToastNotifier();
            toast_notifier.show(toast);
         };
      },
   });
})();
```

In this example, you add a new user interface element, txt_display, which you use to record the disposition of your toast notifications by the user. If the user activates a toast by clicking or tapping, you record it as an activation; if the user cancels it, you record it as a dismissal. (Because these are long toast notifications, they appear for longer.) You additionally indicate which specific toast was dismissed or cancelled by displaying the value of count that was used to generate it.

Figure 7-4 shows the application in action. Note that the figure contains additional buttons that aren't included in the code example's user interface HTML.

Figure 7-4. *Toast notification handling events*

■ **Note** In Listing 7-11, you set count to a local variable in the onclick event handler. Doing this ensures that the value of count used when any of the toast event handlers are called is the same value used when the button was initially clicked. Each unique value of indicator is said to be *lifted* in a unique global state so it can each be used when the appropriate version of onactivated/ondismissed is called.

Tile Notifications

Remember the overview discussion of Windows 8 from Chapter 1? It talked about the rectangular shapes on the Start screen that combine the functionality of the quick launch area with an application's launch shortcut, with the representation of an application on the taskbar. As mentioned in Chapter 1, these rectangular shapes are known as *live tiles*. The great thing about their "live-ness" is that it turns these tiles into yet another surface with which applications can present notifications to users. Tile notifications differ from toast notifications in many ways.

First, they're really a pattern of application behavior layered on top of the notion of live tiles. You could argue that they aren't notifications at all. Many applications, such as Travel, employ the live-tile functionality without informing the user of anything (Travel shows pictures of different places in the world, which is markedly different that the Mail app's use of tiles). Second, because this style of notification uses a given application's tile, it can be limited in a number of ways. For one thing, if the tile isn't on the Windows Start screen, there is no notification (and no indication to the application that a notification hasn't happened). Yet another problem is that this type of notification is localized to the Windows Start screen; depending on where the tile sits on a user's Start screen, it may not be visible. Finally and most important, the application's live tile is primarily designed for non-intrusive glance-and-go information. It isn't meant to be a dialog or message box; it's meant to present quick tidbits of information to the user that might entice them to click the tile and get more information.

Let's keep this functionality in perspective as you work through this section. Because the use of the term *notification* here is somewhat misleading (particularly when juxtaposed against its counterparts in this section), you might be tempted to limit your use of live tiles to presenting messages to the user. Doing so would grossly underuse the power of this technology. Figure 7-5 shows the live tiles of a number of popular Windows 8 apps.

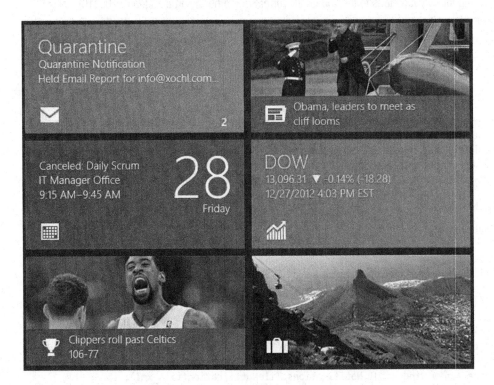

Figure 7-5. *Live tiles for some Modern Windows 8 apps*

Tile notifications can be text only, text with an image, all image, or a combination of images, or they can encompass another class of notifications called *badge notifications*. Unlike toast notifications, which as mentioned earlier should mainly be used to alert the user about actions or information they need to act on relatively quickly, tile notifications focus on presenting notification content that is more persistent and less intrusive. A general approach you can take to the distinction between toast notifications and tile notifications (as far as the content they should present) is that live tiles present content and represent events the user *could* be interested in, whereas toast notifications present content and represent events the user *should* be interested in.

Leaving aside what a powerful notification mechanism an app's live tile is, there are benefits to using the live-tile infrastructure to present notifications to the user. For one thing, because a live tile is about enticing the user, it can be used as an alert or update—something to grab the user's attention. You can find a comprehensive list of all tile templates, complete with images of the final tile layout, on the Microsoft MSDN site at http://msdn.microsoft.com/en-us/library/windows/apps/hh761491.aspx. This can be used as a reference to get a sense of what you can and can't do with live tiles.

■ **Note** Windows 8.1 adds two new tile sized to make a total of 4 possible sizes that a user can configure an app start screen tile to. These tile sizes are a 50x50 square, a 150x150 pixel square, a 310x150 rectangle, and the giant 310x310 square. When Microsoft first conceived of the notion of tiles in Windows 8 they naturally thought that the aforementioned "Small" and "Wide" tile sizes would be sufficient for users from now until the end of eternity so the tile names used for identifying templates had the general form "tileSquare" and "tileWide". As of Windows 8.1 Microsoft has thankfully renamed these templates to allow for more tile sizes. Now in addition to the generic names, the templates also incorporate the actual dimensions of the tile. Hence the "tileSquare" portion of the template name now becomes "tileSquare150x150", allowing for two variations to the square tile format (the other being tileSquare310x310). The following section uses the Windows 8 convention, bear in mind however that once a user upgrades to Windows 8.1 your tile notifications will cease to function if your app is not recompiled and republished with the new template names updated.

Generating Tile Notifications

Like toast notifications, tile notifications can be sent locally or via push notification (as discussed in the next chapter). Unlike toasts, there is no separate interaction pattern for the notifications that target an application's tile. They're simply presented on the tile, and it's left to the user to decide whether to launch the application or not.

Listing 7-12 shows a very simple example of local tile notification. It extends the notification example from the previous section with a new button btn_tile that the user can click to generate a basic tile notification.

Listing 7-12. Simple Tile Notification

```
btn_tile.onclick = function ()
        {
            count++;
            var tile_xml = Windows.UI.Notifications.TileUpdateManager⏎
                .getTemplateContent(Windows.UI.Notifications.TileTemplateType⏎
                .tileWideText01
                );
            var text_nodes = tile_xml.documentElement.getElementsByTagName("text");
            text_nodes[0].appendChild(tile_xml.createTextNode("Message : " + count));

            var tile = new Windows.UI.Notifications.TileNotification(tile_xml);

            var tile_updater = Windows.UI.Notifications.TileUpdateManager⏎
                .createTileUpdaterForApplication();
            tile_updater.update(tile);

        };
```

If you read the entire previous section, then you should notice something here. The development pattern for creating tile notifications is similar to the approach used for creating toast notifications. It starts with selecting an appropriate template (which maps to an XML document). Once you retrieve the template, you find the sections of the document in which you need to place content. You then place content in those elements/attributes, use the created document to generate the appropriate tile-notification object, and pass the object to the TileUpdateManager. It's the job of the TileUpdateManager to update the actual tile. What you can surmise from this is that once again, Microsoft has chosen uniformity and a template-driven approach to provide a surface on which developers can place one-off presentations of application-specific notifications. The example in Listing 7-12 produces the result shown in Figure 7-6 when btn_tile is clicked ten times (as long as a wide logo image has been specified for the application).

Figure 7-6. *Updated live tile*

Because tile presentation is significantly more complex than the simple examples you saw when working with toast notifications, it follows that the templates exposed to tiles are also different and varied. In all, there are 45 templates to choose from! They range from simple text, as shown in Listing 7-12, to arrays of images with no text. The templates also encompass the two possible tile sizes available to Modern Windows 8 applications: square tiles and wide (rectangular) tiles. You saw rectangular tiles in Figures 7-5 and 7-6. Square tiles function in a similar manner but take up less space on the Windows 8 Start screen.

■ **Note**   Square tiles can't be used to present the full spectrum of template formats afforded to Modern Windows 8 applications. In all, they can use only ten templates: five text-only, one image-only, and four with peeking images and text. Peeking image tiles are tiles configured with images that emerge from the bottom of the tile and then slide back down as if peeking in from somewhere underneath the tile display area. Also note that the application is only in charge of the type of tile it presents when you don't include a wide tile logo in the app's manifest (effectively forcing your app to exist only in a square tile on the Start screen). When an app tile is in the square tile state, notifications are limited to those that are targeted at square tiles alone. If you include a wide tile logo, you need to perform tile updates to both the square and wide tiles at the same time because you don't know which version of your tile is presently on the Start screen.

In general, tile templates take six forms: text only, image only, image and text, peeking images and text, peeking images, and peeking image collection. You might have seen the peeking phenomena on your windows Start screen with the People app. The tile update appears from the bottom of the tile as if peeking and then slides back down. Within a few seconds, it slides up and overlays the previous tile content.

This discussion focuses exclusively on wide tile templates. The development and interaction patterns for both are the same, so it should be no trouble to apply the same concepts outlined in the following sections to square app tiles. Also, rather than discuss all the wide template types, this chapter focuses on a few interesting ones that you may find helpful in presenting content to the user.

Presenting Text Content with a Heading

TileWideText09 is the mainstay for presenting simple text content to the user. It uses the first text element as the header and a second element wrapped across the remaining four lines as text content. Listing 7-13 shows the template definition for this template type.

Listing 7-13. TileWideText09 Template Definition

```
<tile>
  <visual>
    <binding template="TileWideText09">
      <text id="1">Text Header Field 1</text>
      <text id="2">Text Field 2</text>
    </binding>
  </visual>
</tile>
```

This is a great template for presenting text because it allows you to wrap the content area across multiple lines. Almost all the other template types require you to enter text into each line separately, which forces you to monitor the length of your notification strings. If you don't need line breaks in your content area, this approach is recommended. Listing 7-14 modifies the example from Listing 7-12 to use TileWideText09 instead of TileWideText01. Figure 7-7 shows what the tile renders when the btn_tile button is clicked a single time.

Listing 7-14. Using TileWideText09 to Display Text Content

```
btn_tile.onclick = function ()
          {
                count++;
                var tile_xml = Windows.UI.Notifications.TileUpdateManager↵
                    .getTemplateContent(Windows.UI.Notifications.TileTemplateType↵
                    .tileWideText09
                    );
                var text_nodes = tile_xml.documentElement.getElementsByTagName("text");
                text_nodes[0].appendChild(tile_xml.createTextNode("Message : " + count));
                text_nodes[1].appendChild(tile_xml.createTextNode↵
                    (count + " quick brown fox jumped over a lazy dog!"));

                var tile = new Windows.UI.Notifications.TileNotification(tile_xml);

                var tile_updater = Windows.UI.Notifications.TileUpdateManager↵
                    .createTileUpdaterForApplication();
                tile_updater.update(tile);

          };
```

Figure 7-7. *What the tile renders when the btn_tile button is clicked once*

Text-Only Content

In situations where you need to present text-only content with no heading (for instance, headlines for news-type applications), `TileWideText04` is a great template. It removes the heading and gives the application one line of text wrapped across all five lines of the tile. Listing 7-15 shows the template definition for this template.

Listing 7-15. Template Definition for `TileWideText04`

```
<tile>
  <visual>
    <binding template="TileWideText04">
      <text id="1">Text Field 1</text>
    </binding>
  </visual>
</tile>
```

Templates for Summaries

Finally, if an application needs to present summary information in a text-only list format, `TileWideText02` and `TileWideText01` are good templates to use. Listing 7-12 used `TileWideText01` to present some simple text on screen. It lists text lines individually with a header above them, as you saw in Figure 7-6. `TileWideText02` follows this same format, with one key distinction: the text is displays in two columns, each containing four rows of text. Listing 7-16 shows the template definition for `TileWideText02`.

Listing 7-16. Template Definition for `TileWideText02`

```
<tile>
  <visual>
    <binding template="TileWideText02">
      <text id="1">Text Header Field 1</text>
      <text id="2">Text Field 2</text>
      <text id="3">Text Field 3</text>
      <text id="4">Text Field 4</text>
      <text id="5">Text Field 5</text>
      <text id="6">Text Field 6</text>
      <text id="7">Text Field 7</text>
      <text id="8">Text Field 8</text>
      <text id="9">Text Field 9</text>
    </binding>
  </visual>
</tile>
```

Listing 7-17 modifies the tile-notification example to use `TileWideText02`.

Listing 7-17. Using `TileWideText02` to Update an Application Tile

```
btn_tile.onclick = function ()
            {
                count++;
                var tile_xml = Windows.UI.Notifications.TileUpdateManager
                    .getTemplateContent(
                    Windows.UI.Notifications.TileTemplateType.tileWideText02
                    );
```

```
        var text_nodes = tile_xml.documentElement.getElementsByTagName("text");
        text_nodes[0].appendChild(tile_xml.createTextNode("Message : " + count));
        text_nodes[1].appendChild(tile_xml.createTextNode(count.toString()));
        text_nodes[3].appendChild(tile_xml.createTextNode((count + 1).toString()));
        text_nodes[5].appendChild(tile_xml.createTextNode((count + 2).toString()));
        text_nodes[7].appendChild(tile_xml.createTextNode((count + 3).toString()));
        text_nodes[2].appendChild(tile_xml.createTextNode("Dogs"));
        text_nodes[4].appendChild(tile_xml.createTextNode("Cats"));
        text_nodes[6].appendChild(tile_xml.createTextNode("Bunnies"));
        text_nodes[8].appendChild(tile_xml.createTextNode("Fish"));

        var tile = new Windows.UI.Notifications.TileNotification(tile_xml);

        var tile_updater = Windows.UI.Notifications.TileUpdateManager↵
            .createTileUpdaterForApplication();
        tile_updater.update(tile);

    };
```

When this application runs and the user clicks btn_tile, the tile looks like Figure 7-8.

Figure 7-8. *Using TileWideText02*

Creating a Cleaner Template

TileWideText02 does a good job but suffers from a disjointed aesthetic in my opinion. If the notification's look and feel are of paramount importance, then you can use a cleaner template like TileWideBlockAndText01. This template renders as four strings of unwrapped text on the left and a large block of text over a single short string of bold text on the right. You lose the columns but can use the free text on the left to display both numbers and text, as shown in Figure 7-9.

Figure 7-9. *Using* `TileWideBlockAndText01`

This notification was achieved by applying the template definition outlined in Listing 7-18.

Listing 7-18. `TileWideBlockAndText01` Template Definition

```
<tile>
  <visual>
    <binding template="TileWideBlockAndText01">
      <text id="1">1 dogs</text>
      <text id="2">2 cats</text>
      <text id="3">3 bunnies</text>
      <text id="4">4 fish</text>
      <text id="5">10</text>
      <text id="6">House Pets</text>
    </binding>
  </visual>
</tile>
```

Adding Images to Tile Notifications

As with toast notifications, images can be applied to tile notifications to improve the overall aesthetic of the tile. In extreme scenarios where you're unsatisfied with any of the 45 possible template types provided by Microsoft, you can use one of the image-only notification templates and generate your own notification layout through dynamic image generation. At present, WinJS doesn't provide a means to create images from user interface elements, but in future releases this may become a possibility. Also, nothing prevents you from doing this through a web service call. The various forms of tile notifications as they relate to images are too many and too similar in utilization to go into further in this book.

Scheduling Tile Notifications

Like toast notifications, tile notifications can be scheduled to run at a predetermined time. As stated previously, in certain scenarios it's more appropriate to schedule a tile update to happen at some point in the future rather than have the notification fired off as soon as the command to do so is executed. In such scenarios, you can use `ScheduledTileNotification`. Its constructor accepts not only the XML template for the notification but also a date when the notification should be displayed.

Listing 7-19 shows how easy it is to schedule a tile notification. When the user clicks the tile-notification button, you schedule a notification for December 20, 2012, one day before what should have been the end of the world according to the Mayans.

Listing 7-19. Summary of Equipment for the End of the World

```
btn_tile.onclick = function ()
            {
                count++;
                var tile_xml = Windows.UI.Notifications.TileUpdateManager↵
                    .getTemplateContent(Windows.UI.Notifications.TileTemplateType↵
                    .tileWideBlockAndText01
                    );

                var text_nodes = tile_xml.documentElement.getElementsByTagName("text");
                text_nodes[0].appendChild(tile_xml.createTextNode(count + " food"));
                text_nodes[1].appendChild(tile_xml.createTextNode↵
                    ((count + 1).toString() + " drink"));
                text_nodes[2].appendChild(tile_xml.createTextNode↵
                    ((count + 2).toString() + " maps"));
                text_nodes[3].appendChild(tile_xml.createTextNode↵
                    ((count + 3).toString() + " tools"));
                text_nodes[4].appendChild(tile_xml.createTextNode↵
                    (count + (count + 1) + (count + 2) + (count + 3)));
                text_nodes[5].appendChild(tile_xml.createTextNode("World End List"));

                //var tile = new Windows.UI.Notifications.TileNotification(tile_xml);
                var stile = new Windows.UI.Notifications.ScheduledTileNotification↵
                    (tile_xml, new Date("12/20/2012"));

                var tile_updater = Windows.UI.Notifications.TileUpdateManager↵
                    .createTileUpdaterForApplication();
                tile_updater.addToSchedule(stile);

            };
```

Summary

I hope you've found this thorough explanation of toast and tile notifications informative and beneficial for your future app development. To review, the discussion included generating toast and tile notifications, adding images and sound, scheduling, and responding to notifications. With the rules and forms covered in this chapter, Windows 8 again creates uniformity for the user—in this case, through notifications. As a Windows 8 developer, you now have the tools and real-world examples to use these notifications for tile design and lock-screen interaction. Following are some points to remember from this chapter:

- Toast and tile notifications can be sent locally.

- Toast notifications are context aware. An application can react uniquely and in contextually specific manner to toast notifications that are activated or dismissed by the user.

- Tile notifications are essentially a pattern above the notion of live tiles. If a tile isn't on the Windows Start screen, there is no notification.

- Tile notifications can be text-only, text with images, all images, or a combination of images. Toast notifications can be text-only or text with images.

- Toast and tile notifications can serve as dynamic tools for grabbing the user's attention in a variety of ways.

■ ■ ■

CHAPTER 8

Keeping Apps Running in the Background

It should come as no surprise to anyone that the term *Windows* as defined, coined, and trademarked by Microsoft relates to the computing feature whereby the functioning area of an application can be partitioned to a corner of the screen, moved around, and maximized to take up the entire screen surface area. In short, Windows allows you a "window" into a running application. Through the years, that ability to display an application evolved into being able to run and use multiple applications, complete with window overlap, fast task switching, and many more delightful features we have all come to know, love, and expect from a self-respecting operating environment like Windows, Mac OS, and even Linux and Unix trees of products.

It should therefore come as a *complete* surprise to everyone who begins working with Windows 8 that all the beautiful innovations you've come to love, and that have naturally evolved over years of user feedback, trial and error, and functional adjustment, are all but gone in this re-invention of the window. How do you provide the same experience—application switching, background processing, windowing, and so on—while maintaining the new paradigm, which allows Windows to run on anything from an ARM-based device (the type you might find on an iPhone) to the full-fledged Windows experience (such as a Core i7 über device)?

This chapter focuses on a tenet of Windows that has survived what I like to call the "great purge": *background processing* in its many forms. In previous versions of Windows, applications ran in the background through a myriad of mechanisms. Simply switching away from one application to another essentially put the first app into the background (although in previous versions of Windows, it continued to run as though in the foreground). This provided ultimate flexibility for both the user and developer but, as a downside, introduced incredible complexity into their work streams. As a user, it was difficult to know exactly what was running on your machine at any given time without breaking out all the superuser tools. As a developer, it was nearly impossible to predict how other applications would react to and treat yours, and compatibility issues between your application and another were invariably tied to your application as bugs. I remember once writing a little invisible console application that periodically monitored for a certain word-processing software's executable and shut it down with a `process -kill` command. (Before you call the FBI, please understand that this was a joke between CS roommates.)

Because Windows 8 introduces a new approach to application behavior, one in which the app user interface always takes up the entire screen surface area—meaning the user is expected to interact with one app (or two, if the user has *snapped* a secondary application)—the foreground app is assumed to be the most important to the user.

■ **Note** The snapping feature is available only on screens that have enough horizontal real estate to support it. In the present incarnation of Windows 8, such a screen must support 1366 x 768 resolution. In future versions of Windows 8, rumor has it that many more snap widths will be allowed.

Chapter 1 talked about this to some extent. Because the foreground application receives all the system resources, apps that aren't visible to the user enter into a suspended state in which they're no longer executing. An app suspended in this way remains so until it's resumed by the user through app switching, relaunching, or initialization via the contract mechanisms. One of the benefits of this approach is that the system isn't adversely impacted by applications running in the background that the user can't see.

■ **Note**   In the current implementation of Windows 8, the vision for this groundbreaking operating system isn't yet fully realized. On the WinRT version of the operating system, which runs on ARM-based processors like the NVIDIA Tegra 3, you can't install legacy applications like Skype for desktop (which runs in the background at all times). However, on the full versions of Windows 8, a user can install applications while in desktop mode that have a persistent and continuous performance impact on the system. So while a batch job is running on the SQL Server instance in desktop mode, the Start menu may experience lags and delays.

Running in the Background

Windows 8 apps use background tasks to provide functionality that runs regardless of whether the underlying app is presently running. When registered, background tasks are initiated by external events called *triggers* and are allowed to start based on a number of criteria called *conditions*, all of which must be true in order for the background task to run. This is true even if the trigger event is fired. A triggering event for background tasks might be time, or some system event like the completion of a software installation or system update.

Because of the requirements around speed and fluidity, it's important that background tasks don't run rampant, slowing down the system without the user's knowledge. So, such tasks are executed through a resource-managed environment that provides only a limited amount of time to the background task to be used to run its arbitrary code.

Given that Modern Windows 8 apps function in this manner, the question is what an app can do while not in the foreground. Windows 8 provides a number of features to give an app the opportunity to execute from a not-running state, execute from the background, or continue to execute when switched from the foreground. The execution mechanisms, even though they aren't in the foreground, are optimized for system performance and longer battery life (another reason multiple applications aren't allowed to run in the background). Some scenarios where Windows 8 allows this are as follows:

- To perform a task at a timed interval

- To continue background transfer of data even after an app is closed

- To continue playback of audio even after an app is closed

- To perform a task when a system event occurs

Background Tasks

The introduction to this section said that background tasks use an external event called a trigger. Triggers indicate when the task should run and provide a set of conditions that must be true for the task to run. When a trigger is fired, the underlying task infrastructure launches the class or calls the method associated with the trigger. This is done whether the app is presently running, suspended, or completely removed from memory. Note that background tasks never shift into the foreground or use any foreground-related features, such as presenting a user interface. (They can launch tile and toast notifications, though.)

The example in Listing 8-1 creates a time-based background task that wakes and executes every 15 minutes. You might be tempted to reduce this interval to a minute so you can see your background task at work; but be warned, background tasks of this type can't be run in anything less than 15-minute increments (the next section discusses this further). This should underscore the attention Microsoft is paying to performance. Better or worse, the idea is to provide a consistent experience for the user regardless of whether they're on a low-power machine or a high-powered behemoth. Unfortunately, this usually translates to exposing the lowest common denominator to the API landscape.

Listing 8-1. Timer-Triggered Background Task

```
function GetTask(task_name) {
    var iter = Windows.ApplicationModel.Background.BackgroundTaskRegistration.allTasks.first();
    var hascur = iter.hasCurrent;
    while (hascur) {
        var cur = iter.current.value;
        if (cur.name === task_name) {
            return cur;
        }
        hascur = iter.moveNext();
    }
    return null;
}


(function () {
    "use strict";
    var Background = Windows.ApplicationModel.Background;
    WinJS.UI.Pages.define("/samples/BGTaskSample/TestBGTasks.html", {
        ready: function (element, options) {
            var timer_id = -1;
            var task_name = "timer task";
            var can_run = false;
            var background_task = null;
            //request the background task
            Background.BackgroundExecutionManager.requestAccessAsync().then(
                function (access_status) {
                    if (access_status != Background.BackgroundAccessStatus.Denied
                            && access_status != Background .BackgroundAccessStatus.Unspecified) {
                        can_run = true;
                        background_task = GetTask(task_name);
                        if (background_task != null) {
                            btn_timer.innerText = "Unregister Background Task";
                        } else {
                            btn_timer.innerText = "Register Background Task";
                        }
                    }
                });

            btn_timer.onclick = function () {

                if (!can_run) {
                    var v = new Windows.UI.Popups.MessageDialog("Application ↵
                        cannot run in the background/");
                    v.showAsync();
                    return;
                }
```

211

```
            //if this has not been created, do so
            if (background_task == null) {
                btn_timer.innerText = "Unregister Background Task";
                var task = new Background.BackgroundTaskBuilder();
                var timer = new Background.TimeTrigger(15, false);
                task.setTrigger(timer);
                task.taskEntryPoint = "BackgroundTaskHost.TestTimerTask";
                task.name = task_name;
                background_task = task.register();
                if (background_task != null) {
                    background_task.oncompleted = function (evt) {
                        try {
                            var complete_date = new Date();
                            txt_display.textContent = txt_display.textContent + ↵
                                "_done at " + complete_date.getHours() + " : " + ↵
                                complete_date.getMinutes();
                        } catch (e) {


                        }
                    };


                    background_task.onprogress = function (evt) {
                        try {
                            txt_display.Text = txt_display.Text + "_" ↵
                                + evt.progress.toString();
                        } catch (e) {
                        }
                    };


                    //countdown to the trigger being fired
                    var minutes_count = 0;
                    var seconds_count = 0;
                    timer_id = setInterval(function () {
                        try {
                            seconds_count++;

                            if (seconds_count == 60) {
                                seconds_count = 0;
                                minutes_count++;
                            }
                            txt_display.value = minutes_count + " mins, " ↵
                                + seconds_count + " secs";
                        } catch (e) {
                        }

                    }, 1000);
                }

            } else {
                //unregister the created task
                background_task.unregister(true);
```

```
                    if (background_task != null) {

                    }
                    btn_timer.innerText = "Register Background Task";
                     clearInterval(timer_id);
                }
            };
        },

    });
})();
```

Listing 8-1 first requests access to the background execution engine through the requestAccessAsync method. As with all things Windows 8, this action prompts the user to grant the application permission to run as a background task. Figure 8-1 shows the permissions dialog for the app you just created. When you run the app on your computer, this is what you should see.

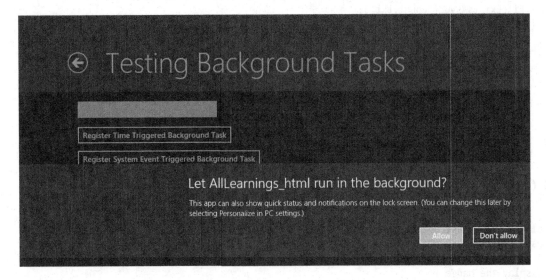

Figure 8-1. *Permissions dialog box for background tasks*

If the user grants access, you record the answer as a true value in can_run. Notice the global method getTask, which returns a previously scheduled task given its name. Scheduled tasks are stored outside an application in a structure keyed by the task name. This allows you to reference tasks you previously created in order to unregister them. In Listing 8-1, you use this functionality to search for the task name first: if it doesn't exist, you create it; and if it does exist, you unregister it.

To register a timed task with the background task infrastructure, you use BackgroundTaskBuilder. In the example, you're registering a task defined in the type BackgroundTaskHost.TestTimerTask. In this case, this is a type created using another Windows 8 programming language (C#). As a result, some additional rules must be applied to registering the code you want executed as a background task. Whereas in JavaScript you merely have to create a simple JavaScript file called a *dedicated worker*, in C# you must use the strongly typed system to identify a piece of code as a background task. First you create a new class whose type, which must implement IBackgroundTask, is passed as a string into the TaskEntryPoint property of BackgroundTaskBuilder.

Note that you don't have to wait for trigger conditions to be met in order to debug your background task code. Visual Studio 2012 provides a nifty debugging tool that lets you run against the code in your actual background task class.

213

Back in the JavaScript world, you can now create a time trigger and pass that as an argument into the setTrigger method of BackgroundTaskBuilder. *Time triggers* are a type of triggering mechanism that make background tasks run. Unlike the approach for traditional Win32 applications, background tasks can't be started by their host app; instead, a particular set of conditions must be met, which then trigger the launch of the background task. The next section talks more about this; for now, let's look at the task that is run when the trigger conditions for this example are met. An excerpt of the background task is shown (in C#) in Listing 8-2.

Listing 8-2. Run Example for the Background Task

```
async public void Run(IBackgroundTaskInstance taskInstance)
{
    var def = taskInstance.GetDeferral();
    try
    {

        //create the state for the application
        var has_count = await Windows.Storage.ApplicationData.Current.LocalFolder ↵
            .FileExistsAsync("count.txt");
        if (!has_count)
        {
            await Windows.Storage.ApplicationData.Current.LocalFolder ↵
                .CreateFileAsync("count.txt");

        }

        //read the count from the local state
        var text = await Windows.Storage.ApplicationData.Current.LocalFolder ↵
            .ReadTextAsync("count.txt");
        int count;
        if (!int.TryParse(text, out count))
            count = 0;

        //display the toast notification
        Toast("toast " + count);

        //display the badge
        var badge_type = count % 6;
        Badge((BadgeType)badge_type);

        //display the tile notification
        Tile("Tile notification " + count);

        count++;
        await Windows.Storage.ApplicationData.Current ↵
            .LocalFolder.WriteAllTextAsync("count.txt",count.ToString());
    }
    catch (Exception ex)
    {
    }
    def.Complete();

}
```

I'll preface the walkthrough of this code by saying that you aren't expected to understand C# in order to build background tasks. This example uses a C# background task to illustrate the seamless language integration that WinRT provides. Don't freak out if you don't know what it does or if it seems overly complicated. Part of the charm and power of JavaScript is that it can mask many of these complexities from you (or at least provide them through a less cryptic API). This background task implementation reads a count from a text file and fires off toast, tile, and badge notifications that display the count, increment the count, and save the value back to the text file—so that the next time the task is triggered, it displays a higher number.

As stated, the great thing about WinRT is that it extends evenly to all languages (for the most part), meaning no language is treated as a second cousin requiring closer relatives to get in the door. This is a roundabout way of saying that you can also use JavaScript to build background tasks, using specialized JavaScript files called *workers*. (The following sections go into more detail about how workers operate and can be hooked into the background task engine.) To implement a background task using a JavaScript worker, you add a dedicated worker to your project and reference the worker's file name (instead of a fully qualified type name of the C# class) in the TaskEntryPoint property of BackgroundTaskBuilder. So in Listing 8-1, instead of the call task.taskEntryPoint = "BackgroundTaskHost. TestTimerTask"; you use the call task.taskEntryPoint = "/samples/bgtasksample/timerworker.js", assuming of course that you've added the timerworker.js dedicated worker file to your project. Again, the following sections discuss this further. Figure 8-2 shows the project item picker with the dedicated worker template selected.

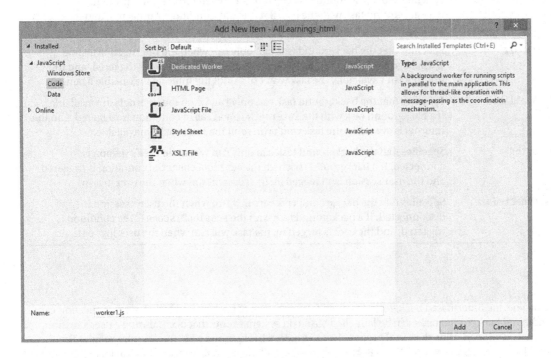

Figure 8-2. *Selecting the background worker project item type*

Conditions

Background tasks can also have conditions associated with them. You can add these using the addCondition method of BackgroundTaskBuilder. Conditions applied to a background task must all evaluate to true for the task to execute. For example, if you want the background task you created in Listing 8-1 to execute only if an Internet connection is available, adding the snippet from Listing 8-3 after the call to setTrigger activates the condition.

Listing 8-3. Adding Conditions to a Background Task

```
...
task.setTrigger(timer);
task.addCondition(new Background.SystemCondition ↵
    (Background.SystemConditionType.internetAvailable));
...
```

Table 8-1 lists the possible condition types.

Table 8-1. *Conditions Types*

Member	Description
userPresent	Specifies that the background task can only run when the user is present. If a background task with the userPresent condition is triggered, and the user is away, the task won't run until the user is present.
userNotPresent	Specifies that background task can only run when the user isn't present. If a background task with the UserNotPresent condition is triggered, and the user is present, the task won't run until the user becomes inactive.
internetAvailable	Specifies that the background task can only run when the Internet is available. If a background task with the internetAvailable condition is triggered, and the Internet isn't available, the task won't run until the Internet is available again.
internetNotAvailable	Specifies that the background task can only run when the Internet isn't available. If a background task with the internetNotAvailable condition is triggered, and the Internet is available, the task won't run until the Internet is unavailable.
sessionConnected	Specifies that the background task can only run when the user's session is connected. If a background task with the sessionConnected condition is triggered, and the user session isn't logged in, the task will run when the user logs in.
sessionDisconnected	Specifies that the background task can only run when the user's session is disconnected. If a background task with the sessionDisconnected condition is triggered, and the user is logged in, the task will run when the user logs out.

Triggers

As you can imagine, the timer-based background task isn't the only type of background task that an application can use. Like conditions, background tasks can be launched based on system events that occur during a user's session. Up to this point, you've been using the TimeTrigger class to trigger a background task; this trigger executes the background task at a given time interval. Table 8-2 provides a list of all the possible triggers that can be used to initiate background tasks. Many trigger types follow a similar pattern, so this section focuses on common maintenance and system triggers.

Table 8-2. *Background Task Trigger Types*

Trigger Name	Description
Time trigger	`Windows.ApplicationModel.Background.TimeTrigger` represents a time event that triggers a background task to run.
System trigger	`Windows.ApplicationModel.Background.SystemTrigger` represents a system event that triggers a background task to run. Examples of system events are network loss, network access, and the user signing in or signing out.
Push notification trigger	`Windows.ApplicationModel.Background.PushNotificationTrigger` represents an object that invokes a background work item on the app in response to the receipt of a raw notification. Push notification is beyond the scope of this book; for more information on setting up push notification services for your Windows 8 app, go to the Windows 8 App Dev Center.
Maintenance trigger	`Windows.ApplicationModel.Background.MaintenanceTrigger` represents a maintenance trigger. Like `TimeTrigger`, `MaintenanceTrigger` is executed at the end of a time interval (it can be configured to execute only once), but the device must be connected to power for tasks that specify the trigger be valid.

For applications that require code to execute when a system event beyond the scope of time and AC power occurs, the `SystemTrigger` class is the catch-all alternative. `SystemTrigger` is instantiated with an enumeration that identifies which system event triggers the underlying background task. Listing 8-4 creates a system trigger that is fired when the device gains Internet connectivity.

Listing 8-4. System Trigger

```
var task = new Background.BackgroundTaskBuilder();
var internet_available = new
Background.SystemTrigger(Background.SystemTriggerType.internetAvailable, false);

            task.taskEntryPoint = "/samples/bgtasksample/timerworker.js";
            task.setTrigger(internet_available);
            background_task = task.register();
```

Table 8-3 lists the available system trigger types.

Table 8-3. System Trigger Types

Trigger Type	Description
smsReceived	The background task is triggered when a new SMS message is received by an installed mobile broadband device.
userPresent	The background task is triggered when the user becomes present. Note: An app must be placed on the lock screen before it can successfully register background tasks using this trigger type.
userAway	The background task is triggered when the user becomes absent. Note: An app must be placed on the lock screen before it can successfully register background tasks using this trigger type.
networkStateChange	The background task is triggered when a network change occurs, such as a change in cost or connectivity.
internetAvailable	The background task is triggered when the Internet becomes available.
sessionConnected	The background task is triggered when the session is connected. Note: An app must be placed on the lock screen before it can successfully register background tasks using this trigger type.
servicingComplete	The background task is triggered when the system has finished updating an app.
lockScreenApplicationAdded	The background task is triggered when a tile is added to the lock screen.
lockScreenApplicationRemoved	The background task is triggered when a tile is removed from the lock screen.
timeZoneChange	The background task is triggered when the time zone changes on the device (for example, when the system adjusts the clock for daylight saving time).
onlineIdConnectedStateChange	The background task is triggered when the Microsoft account connected to the account changes.

■ **Note**   Some system triggers need the app to be on the lock screen: SessionConnected, UserPresent, UserAway, and ControlChannelReset. If you use these triggers without the app being on the lock screen, the register call on BackgroundTaskBuilder will fail.

Host Process

Background tasks execute either in a system-provided host executable (called backgroundtaskhost.exe) or in the app process. Listing 8-1 used a background task from a separate library as the background task. In that scenario, backgroundtaskhost.exe is used, and the task is launched independently of the state of the app. This means the background task can be started and run without the associated application being started. In Listing 8-4, the background task points to a JavaScript worker located at /samples/bgtasksample/timerworker.js. This is an example of a background task that executes in the app process. Because the application is hosting this type of background task, it follows that it might need to be started in order to run the underlying task. If the app is already running when such a task is triggered, it's launched in the context of the app. If the app is suspended when the task is triggered, its threads are unfrozen and the task is then launched. Finally, if the application is in a terminated state at the point at which the background task is triggered, the app is launched and the task is then executed.

Reporting Progress

To report progress to the app (when the app is running in the foreground while the background task is executing), BackgroundTaskRegistration provides the progress event handlers. For WinJS applications, WebUIBackgroundTaskInstance is passed to the Run method to communicate progress to the foreground app. The interface has an optional Progress property that can be updated by the background task.

BackgroundTaskRegistration also provides a completed event that apps can use to be notified when the background task has completed. The completion status or any exception thrown while the task ran is passed to any completion handlers in the foreground app as an input parameter of the event handler. If the app is suspended when the task is completed, it receives the completion notification the next time it's resumed. In cases where the app is terminated, it doesn't receive the completion notification. In such cases, it's up to the app developer to persist any completion state information in a store that can also be accessed by the foreground app.

A JavaScript background task must call close after it has completed its work so the task can be shut down. Be sure to make this call, because it indicates to the background task infrastructure that the task has completed (without it, the JavaScript host will remain active).

You saw an example of a C#-based background worker back in Listing 8-2. Listing 8-5 creates a simple background task in JavaScript. Note the use of the close function before the method returns.

Listing 8-5. JavaScript Background Worker

```
onmessage = function (event) {

    var task_instance = Windows.UI.WebUIBackgroundTaskInstance.current;
    var count= 0;

    for (int i = 0; i < 10; i++)
    {
        count += 10;
        backgroundTask.progress = count;
    }

    backgroundTask.succeeded = true;

    close();
}
```

Declaring Background Tasks

This chapter began by talking about some of the disadvantages of traditional applications as they relate to the use of system resources. Again, given that legacy applications can run in the background without user notification or involvement (beyond starting them), the system as a whole may suffer from perceived lagginess. It's not that there is anything inherently wrong with running applications in the background; but the impact of such activity is scarcely communicated to the user. You would be surprised how many foreground applications on your system have one or more background tasks running, even when the app isn't running! Following the overarching theme of Windows 8, decisions like this aren't left to the application developer but are delegated to the user. It's up to the user to pick which applications should run in the background.

To help facilitate this, Modern Windows 8 apps seeking to use background tasks must explicitly declare themselves as such and specifically indicate which types of background tasks they expose. Figure 8-3 shows where in the Visual Studio 2012 IDE this declaration is made (package.appmanifest). It's in the same Declarations tab that has been used time and again to clearly outline to the user what features an application exposes. This is great because the user is ultimately responsible for making a choice to use one app versus another.

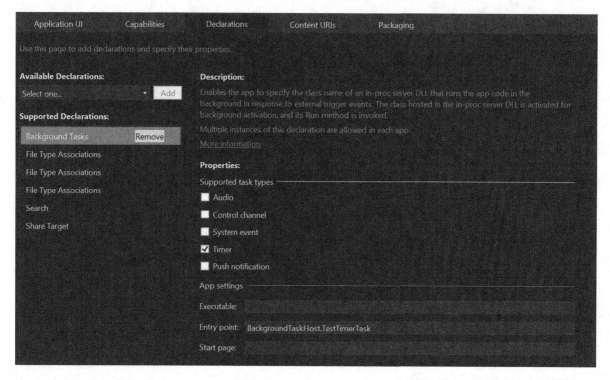

Figure 8-3. *Background task declaration*

In the figure, Entry Point represents the fully qualified type name of the class that contains an implementation of the background task. It should be used in scenarios where your background task has been developed using C# or C++/Cx. If the background task is defined in the hosting JavaScript application, Start Page should be populated with the path to the dedicated worker file.

■ **Note** Because many background tasks require lock-screen access to function, you need to also specify badge information on the Application UI tab in order for the declaration to be correct. Figure 8-4 shows the Visual Assets section of the Application UI tab of an app's manifest. The application must have a valid badge logo and must enable some form of lock-screen notification in order for the declaration in Figure 8-1 to be valid. As you can see in the figure, the application won't build correctly if these elements aren't properly configured.

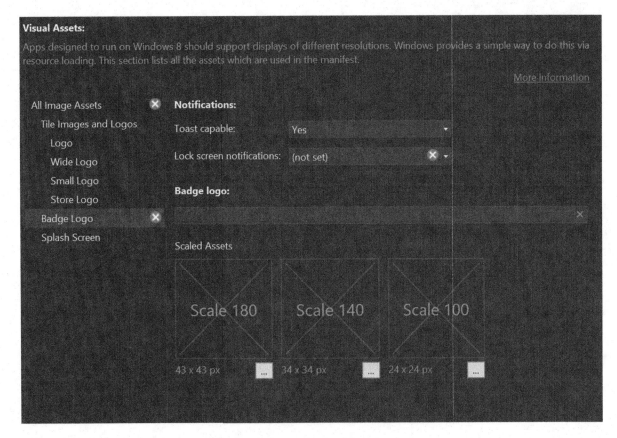

Figure 8-4. *Visual Assets section of the Application UI tab in an app's manifest*

Resource Constraints

Because background tasks are meant to be quick-in-and-out, short-lived work units that consume very little system resources, it should come as no surprise that CPU and network usage constraints are applied to them. Specifically, each app on the lock screen receives 2 seconds of CPU time every 15 minutes for use by all of the app's background tasks. At the end of 15 minutes, each app on the lock screen receives another 2 seconds of CPU time for use by its background tasks. (Each app not on the lock screen receives 1 second of CPU time every 2 hours.)

On the networking side, data throughput is used to constrain background tasks. These metrics vary based on phone, network interface, battery life available, and of course CPU usage. In general, with 10Mbps average throughput available on the device, an app might be allowed about 4.69MB every 15 minutes (450MB per day).

There are some caveats; for instance, if the app also happens to be the foreground app, then these CPU and networking constraints no longer apply. In addition, network constraints don't apply if the device isn't connected to a power source.

Finally, in the case of control-channel and push-notification background tasks, constraints exist but are applied per task instead of for all tasks, as with the other background task types.

Background Transfers

Moving files over a network is a common activity in this modern age of computing. Whether you're uploading video, audio, or images to a social networking site or downloading movies from a media catalog, there is a fundamental need for this functionality. If the target file is very small, this is usually as simple as making a connection to the content provider and pulling down (or pushing up) the desired content. But what happens when the content is very large? Given that Windows 8 has been designed to be fast and fluid, allowing users to quickly and seamlessly switch between applications, how do applications handle situations where long-running network data-transfer activities are in progress, and the user moves the app out of the foreground state? Surely the solution isn't to tell the user, "Warning: don't leave the app until the download is complete!"

The folks at Microsoft have this use case covered with the BackgroundTransfer functionality. Using BackgroundDownloader, an application can schedule the download (or upload, using BackgroundUploader) of content such that even if the application is suspended or terminated by the user, the download/upload continues in the background. Listing 8-6 shows a simple example of using the BackgroundDownloader class to pull down a large file from a remote resource.

Listing 8-6. BackgroundDownloader at Work

```
btn_transfer.onclick = function ()
        {
                var known_folders = Windows.Storage.KnownFolders;
                var foundation = Windows.Foundation;
                var downloader = new Windows.Networking.BackgroundTransfer ↵
                    .BackgroundDownloader();
                var file = known_folders.videosLibrary.createFileAsync("kinectnui_ch9.wmv") ↵
                    .then(function (file)
                {

                    var download_operation = downloader.createDownload(

                        new foundation.Uri↵
                            ("http://www.xochl.com/media/videos/KinectNui_ch9.wmv"), file);
                    download_operation.startAsync();
                });

        };
```

Listing 8-6 shows the event handler for a btn_transfer button that, when clicked, initiates the download of a large file from a remote resource. For this example to run, you must add the Video Library capability to the target application's manifest, because that is the location to which the remote file is downloaded. Once the button is clicked and the download begins, the user can switch away from the target app or even stop it, and the download will still complete.

Summary

Now that you've completed your exploration of the ways in which to keep apps running in the background in the Windows 8 ethos, let's review some key points this chapter covered:

- You learned about the various types of triggers. For applications that require code to execute even when a system is beyond the scope of time and AC power, the SystemTrigger class is the catch-all alternative.

- Background tasks are meant to be quick-in-and-out, short-lived work units that consume very little system resources. CPU and network usage constraints apply to them.

- Using the BackgroundTransfer functionality, BackgroundDownloader is a class that can schedule a download (or upload, using BackgroundUploader) of content so that even if the application is suspended or terminated by the user, the download/upload will continue in the background.

- Background tasks execute in either a system-provided host executable or in the app process.

■ ■ ■

CHAPTER 9

Monetizing Your App: The Lowdown

When all is said and done, most developers aren't in it just for the sake of creative expression. In most cases, you want some financial gain from the work you've done—even if it's only enough to cover the expenses of building an application. And to be sure, building and maintaining modern apps can get very expensive very quickly. For one thing, because of the sandboxed nature of Windows 8 apps, many features—specifically of those applications built to target the legacy desktop—aren't available in the Windows 8 app world. Windows 8 apps are of course sandboxed for a reason—to minimize the damage a misbehaving application can do to a device—but the side effect of these well-deserved limitations is a need for apps to generally include a cloud component. This cloud-resident part of the application functions like a traditional application with full access to the cloud server's environment. Hosting such a solution quickly turns your fixed-cost app (the sweat equity used to build the application has a onetime price tied to it) into a recurring-cost app.

The market adds to this problem. Consumers of apps are generally accustomed to the ease and frequency with which apps can be and are updated. This means an underlying expectation of ongoing development is extended to any app in the marketplace, whether it's created by a billion-dollar organization like Facebook or by you. When you publish an app into the market, you must also consider the cost of the time required to support it.

For these and many more reasons, digital marketplaces such as the Windows Store, Windows Phone Store, and Google Play all let you monetize applications through direct sales, with the marketplaces acting as merchants. Using this marketplace mode, prospective Windows 8 users can discover and purchase apps from the Windows Store. A percentage of the profits goes to the developer who built the target app, and the rest goes to Microsoft to help offset the cost of maintaining the Windows Store. Figure 9-1 shows the landing screen of the Windows Store.

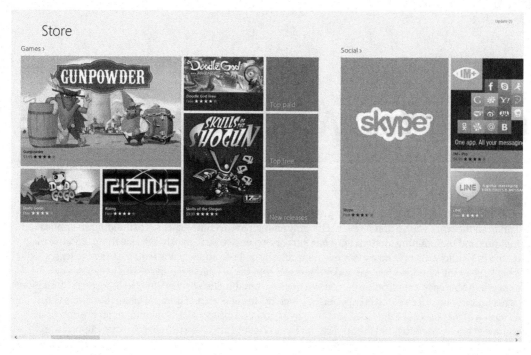

Figure 9-1. *Windows Store landing page*

This chapter discusses two common ways to make money through your app: selling the app and selling within the app. Many apps also generate revenue through in-app advertising, but the nuances of that approach are outside of the scope of this book.

Selling Your App

If you've had the opportunity to own an iPhone and walk through Apple's App Store purchasing process, you might have noticed that many non-free/for cost applications have two versions: a free "demo" version that's used to show what the application can do, and an accompanying full-featured version. The demo version either has limited functionality or is totally open but ad supported. The accompanying full-featured version typically isn't ad supported. Users can get used to a convention like this, but on the development side it can lead to headaches because features must essentially be managed across two code bases: one for the demo version of the application and one for the full version.

Microsoft's Windows Store helps resolve this issue by letting you publish paid apps as trials. This allows developers to maintain one version of an application to serve as both the trial version and the full version, and specify the conditions under which the app can be migrated from one version to the other. From the standpoint of the Windows Store, this prevents needless repetition like that in the Apple App Store. From the perspective of the end user, it provides a simple and easy way to try an application and purchase it if you like it. Figure 9-2 shows a Windows Store paid application page with a trial mode available for the user.

Figure 9-2. *Application with trial mode*

From the developer's perspective, the workflow for building an application that will be for sale but include a trial component is relatively straightforward:

1. Build the application as a full-featured application without worrying about which pieces of functionality are trial bits and which aren't.

2. After the application is built and tested and you're sure everything works as intended, determine which features you want available to trial-version users and which bits you want to make visible only to paid-version users.

3. Use the Microsoft-provided classes to gate the sections of the application that a trial user can't access.

Each application has its own means of gating trial users. For some applications, such as games, you might want to show everything the app can do, but time-restrict the advanced features (or usage of the app as a whole).

The idea of the trial isn't just to give a test drive of the application; it's also to market the app's goodies. When you're building apps for the purpose of monetization, keep this core concept in mind: upsell, upsell, upsell!

Next, let's look at sample trial application.

Example of a Trial Application

With the three steps from the previous section in mind, Listing 9-1 presents a very simple application at the end of step 1.

Listing 9-1. Simple Application with Two Features and a Buy App Button

```
<!DOCTYPE html>
<html>
<head>
    <meta charset="utf-8" />
    <title>Listing1</title>
```

```
        <!-- WinJS references -->
        <link href="//Microsoft.WinJS.1.0/css/ui-dark.css" rel="stylesheet" />
        <script src="//Microsoft.WinJS.1.0/js/base.js"></script>
        <script src="//Microsoft.WinJS.1.0/js/ui.js"></script>

        <link href="Listing1.css" rel="stylesheet" />
        <script src="Listing1.js"></script>
</head>
<body>
    <div class="Listing1 fragment">
        <section aria-label="Main content" role="main">
            <header aria-label="Header content" role="banner">
                <button class="win-backbutton" aria-label="Back" disabled type="button"></button>
                <h1 class="titlearea win-type-ellipsis">
                    <span class="pagetitle">Trial Mode Sample</span>
                </h1>
            </header>
        </section>
        <section aria-label="Main content" role="main">
            <input type="button" id="btn_buyapp" value="buy app" />
        </section>
        <section aria-label="Main content" role="main">
            <input type="button" id="btn_coolfeature" value="cool feature" />
        </section>
        <section aria-label="Main content" role="main">
            <input type="button" id="btn_coolerfeature" value="even cooler feature" />
        </section>
    </div>
</body>
</html>
```

App Trial Mode

The trial-mode application presents two features to the user: one that is cool and one that is even cooler. Presumably, you want to allow users of this app to be able to use the cool feature but only see the even cooler feature. Also, when the app is in trial mode, you want the Buy App button to be visible, but after the app has been purchased, you want the button to disappear—otherwise the user may become confused and think their purchase wasn't registered or that the application is defective.

For Windows 8 apps, purchases are managed through the Windows Store APIs available via the `Windows.ApplicationModel.Store` namespace. This is your entry point to all relevant information about whether the user is using a trial version and, if so, how much time is left in that trial. Unfortunately, these classes work solely against the actual production Windows Store data, meaning they expect that your app is in the store and live. This of course poses a problem, because an unpublished app has no information available, making it impossible to test the trial-mode workflow. To help with this quagmire, the Windows Store API includes a simulator API set that mimics the live-version functionality but works against an XML file that you provide. Working on a Windows Store app that uses the Windows Store commerce infrastructure this way requires you to build and manage this XML file, which is called `WindowsStoreProxy.xml` and is always located in the `%userprofile%\appdata\local\packages\<package-moniker>\localstate\microsoft\Windows Store\Apidata` folder. It's up to you, the developer, to place/modify this file to fit the scenario in which you intend to test in your application (in this case, testing to see how the application behaves in trial mode and in purchased mode). Listing 9-2 shows a sample of this file's format.

Listing 9-2. `WindowsStoreProxy.xml`

```xml
<?xml version="1.0" encoding="utf-16" ?>
<CurrentApp>
  <ListingInformation>
    <App>
      <AppId>2B14D306-D8F8-4066-A45B-0FB3464C67F2</AppId>
      <LinkUri>http://apps.microsoft.com/app/2B14D306-D8F8-4066-A45B-0FB3464C67F2</LinkUri>
      <CurrentMarket>en-us</CurrentMarket>
      <AgeRating>6</AgeRating>
      <MarketData xml:lang="en-us">
        <Name>Trial management full license</Name>
        <Description>Sample app for demonstrating trial license management</Description>
        <Price>4.99</Price>
        <CurrencySymbol>$</CurrencySymbol>
      </MarketData>
    </App>
  </ListingInformation>
  <LicenseInformation>
    <App>
      <IsActive>true</IsActive>
      <IsTrial>true</IsTrial>
      <ExpirationDate>2011-01-01T00:00:00.00Z</ExpirationDate>
    </App>
  </LicenseInformation>
</CurrentApp>
```

Licensing Your App

The next section goes into more detail about the various elements of the `WindowsStoreProxy.xml` file. For now, let's focus on the `LicenseInformation` section, with an emphasis on the `IsTrial` node—which in this document is set to `true`.

You interact with the Windows Store primarily through one class: `CurrentApp`. (Due to the aforementioned reasons, in this example you use another class—the one that uses `WindowsStoreProxy.xml`—called `CurrentAppSimulator`. It mimics the API surface area of `CurrentApp`.) `CurrentApp` exposes a `LicenseInformation` property of type `LicenseInformation`, which you can use to read the license data associated with an application. The bolded section of the `WindowsStoreProxy.xml` file in Listing 9-2 corresponds to this section. `LicenseInformation` provides properties like `IsActive`, `IsTrial`, and `ExpirationDate`. In normal circumstances (when your app has been published to the Windows Store and is public), calling `Windows.ApplicationModel.Store.CurrentApp.licenseInformation` returns the `LicenseInformation` instance for the application. In this case, because your app isn't published yet, you have to use `CurrentAppSimulator`, which expects the `WindowsStoreProxy.xml` fileto be in the previously discussed location when the property is invoked; otherwise an error occurs.

In this example, rather than digging through the Windows Store folders looking for the location where this file should be placed and manually copying it there, you create a temporary version of the file that you can edit as needed. You place it in the application's install directory; then, each time the app is started, you dynamically create the appropriate Windows Store folder, create the `WindowsStoreProxy.xml` file in that folder, and copy the contents of the temporary proxy file to that final location. This way, you can work with a local copy without much hassle.

In your example project, add the `storeproxy` folder; within it, add the file `TrialManagement.xml`, which is a copy of the default `WindowsStoreProxy.xml` file. Listing 9-3 shows the JavaScript for the sample app with the functionality just described.

Listing 9-3. JavaScript for Example App

```javascript
(function ()
{
    "use strict";
    var _listing_information = null;
    var _license = null;

    WinJS.UI.Pages.define("/Listing1/Listing1.html", {
        // This function is called whenever a user navigates to this page. It
        // populates the page elements with the app's data.
        ready: function (element, options)
        {
            initializePurchaseState();
        },

    });

    function initializePurchaseState()
    {
        var proxy_folder = null;
        var install_location = null;
        var temp_proxy_file = null;



        Windows.Storage.ApplicationData.current.localFolder.
            createFolderAsync("Microsoft\\Windows Store\\ApiData", ↵
                Windows.Storage.CreationCollisionOption.replaceExisting)

            .then(
            function (folder)
            {
                proxy_folder = folder;

                return Windows.ApplicationModel.Package.current.installedLocation ↵
                    .getFolderAsync("storeproxy");
            })

            .then(function (location)
            {
                install_location = location;
                return install_location.getFileAsync("trialmanagement.xml");
            })

            .then(function (temp)
            {
                temp_proxy_file = temp;
                return proxy_folder.createFileAsync("WindowsStoreProxy.xml", ↵
                    Windows.Storage.CreationCollisionOption.replaceExisting);
            })
```

```
        .then(function (proxy_file)
        {
            temp_proxy_file.copyAndReplaceAsync(proxy_file);
        })

        .done(function ()
        {
            _license = Windows.ApplicationModel.Store↵
                .CurrentAppSimulator.licenseInformation;
        });

    }
})();
```

Listing 9-3 starts with a call to initializePurchaseState. Regardless of whether you're using a proxy file or going to the Windows Store for information about the application's license, it makes sense to do this up front. After all, you use this information to determine what functionality to expose to the user and what functionality to hide. initializePurchaseState is fairly straightforward; you open or create the target folder where the proxy file should be, create the official proxy file there, and then copy the contents of your temporary proxy file (the one you work with and modify) to the official WindowsStoreProxy.xml file. Notice the use of promises when working with file I/O. In this case, because this is solely for development purposes, and all parameters and file names are under your control, you omit the second parameter of each then function, which is a handler for error conditions. In normal situations, this should be included!

At the end of the async chain is the done function, where you finally read the LicenseInformation. Again, because you're using CurrentAppSimulator, this reads from your WindowsStoreProxy.xml file and not the actual Windows Store. Figure 9-3 shows the look and feel of the application at this point.

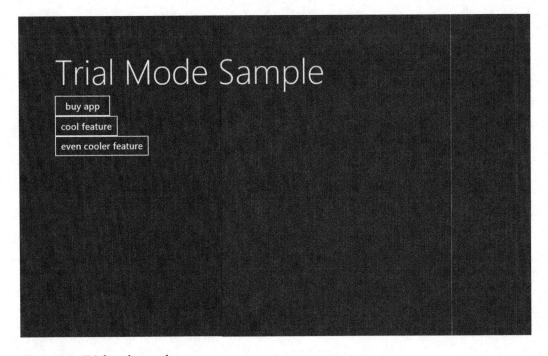

Figure 9-3. *Trial mode sample app*

Now that you have the details of the application's license, you can begin showing and hiding functionality as needed. In this case, all you need to do is read the value of IsTrial and, based on that, toggle the visibility of the Buy App button and the interactability of the Even Cooler Feature button. Listing 9-4 updates the app accordingly.

Listing 9-4. Trial App Updated with IsTrial Logic

```
(function ()
{
    "use strict";
    var _listing_information = null;
    var _license = null;

    WinJS.UI.Pages.define("/Listing1/Listing1.html", {
        // This function is called whenever a user navigates to this page. It
        // populates the page elements with the app's data.
        ready: function (element, options)
        {
            initializePurchaseState();

            btn_coolfeature.onclick = function ()
            {
                var v = new Windows.UI.Popups
                        .MessageDialog("This feature available to ALL customers");
                v.showAsync();
            };

            btn_coolerfeature.onclick = function ()
            {
                if (_license.isTrial)
                {
                    var v = new Windows.UI.Popups
                        .MessageDialog("This feature is only available to PAYING customers");
                    v.showAsync();
                } else
                {
                    var v = new Windows.UI.Popups
                        .MessageDialog("PAYING customer feature");
                    v.showAsync();
                }
            };
        },

    });

    function initializePurchaseState()
    {
        var proxy_folder = null;
        var install_location = null;
        var temp_proxy_file = null;
```

```
        Windows.Storage.ApplicationData.current.localFolder.
            createFolderAsync("Microsoft\\Windows Store\\ApiData", ↵
                Windows.Storage.CreationCollisionOption.replaceExisting)

        .then(
        function (folder)
        {
            proxy_folder = folder;

            return Windows.ApplicationModel.Package.current.installedLocation↵
                .getFolderAsync("storeproxy");
        })

        .then(function (location)
        {
            install_location = location;
            return install_location.getFileAsync("trialmanagement.xml");
        })

        .then(function (temp)
        {
            temp_proxy_file = temp;
            return proxy_folder.createFileAsync("WindowsStoreProxy.xml",↵
                Windows.Storage.CreationCollisionOption.replaceExisting);
        })

        .then(function (proxy_file)
        {

            temp_proxy_file.copyAndReplaceAsync(proxy_file);
        })

        .done(function ()
        {
            _license = Windows.ApplicationModel.Store.CurrentAppSimulator↵
                .licenseInformation;
            loadAppPurchaseStateUI();
        });
    }

    function loadAppPurchaseStateUI()
    {
        if (_license.isTrial)
        {
            btn_buyapp.style.visibility = "visible";
        } else
        {
            btn_buyapp.style.visibility = "hidden";
        }
    }

})();
```

The changes in bold are straightforward. You essentially toggle the behavior based on the IsTrial flag when the application starts and when the user clicks the Even Cooler Feature button. Figures 9-4, 9-5, 9-6, and 9-7 show the various states of the application based on what the user clicks.

Figure 9-4. *App main screen when* IsTrial *is false*

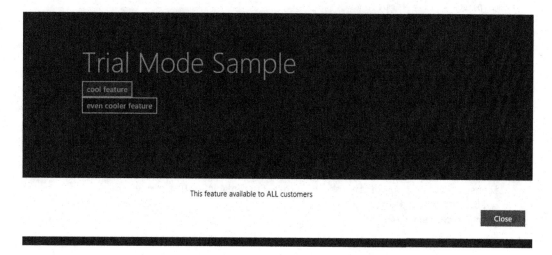

Figure 9-5. *Prompt when Cool Feature is clicked*

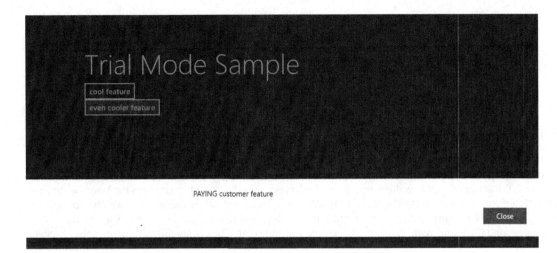

Figure 9-6. *App view when Even Cooler Feature is clicked (IsTrial is false)*

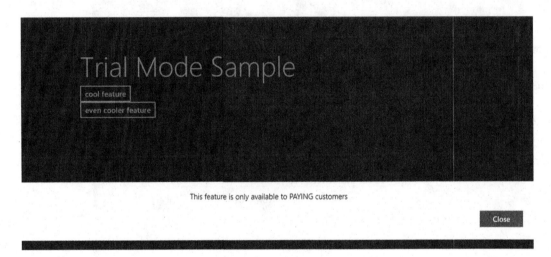

Figure 9-7. *App view when Even Cooler Feature is clicked (IsTrial is true)*

Adding the Code to the App

The final component of the flow is adding the code necessary to perform the actual purchase of the application. Once the app is activated, you refresh the user interface by again calling loadAppPurchaseStateUI. Listing 9-5 shows the function callback for the onclick event of the Buy App button.

Listing 9-5. Simulating the User Purchasing the Application

```
btn_buyapp.onclick = function ()
        {
            Windows.ApplicationModel.Store.CurrentAppSimulator
                .requestAppPurchaseAsync(true)
            .then(function (receipt)
```

```
        {
            _license = Windows.ApplicationModel.Store.CurrentAppSimulator↵
                .licenseInformation;
            loadAppPurchaseStateUI();
        });
    };
```

Application Purchase Requests

An application can make a purchase request on behalf of the user (this must be done via a user-driven event like a mouse click) by invoking the requestAppPurchaseAsync method of CurrentApp or CurrentAppSimulator. Although the API is the same, the actions that follow differ based on which class is used. CurrentApp invokes the Windows Store purchasing user interface, whereas CurrentAppSimulator launches a legacy Windows dialog box in which you can select the type of response you want the simulator to return to your app. You can use this functionality to simulate various use cases beyond the happy path. Figure 9-8 shows the resulting dialog box when the Buy App button is clicked.

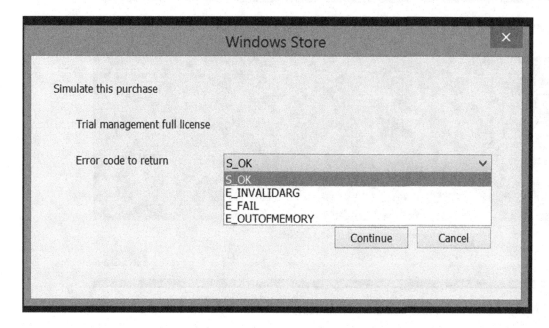

Figure 9-8. CurrentAppSimulator *purchasing dialog for testing purchasing scenarios*

Your code should be able to handle these scenarios so your application doesn't crash. To do so, you need to incorporate the error-handler function from Listing 9-5. Recall from Chapter 1 that the then promise you use can accept three functions: the normal completed handler, an error handler for when an error occurs during asynchronous processing, and a progress handler that provides insight into the operation's progress. The value selected in the dialog in Figure 9-8 is passed as a parameter into the error event handler. You can use this value to present an appropriate message to the user.

Selling Within an App

You've looked at how to build out an application so it supports trials. This approach is predicated on publishing your application as a paid app. Paid apps represent the principle way of monetizing your application through the Windows Store but only scratch the surface of the overarching model.

Offering a trial is a good way to get potential customers to download your app and give it a dry run before committing to the cost, but this approach suffers from some distinct disadvantages when it comes to competing with free counterparts. Statistics show beyond a reasonable doubt (and across all major app stores) that free apps are downloaded far more than paid apps and also have more activity and dialogue tied to them. Although a trial application is technically free, it's still listed in the Windows Store in the paid category, making discovery of your app an issue. Furthermore, as you saw from the previous example, the paid/trial model has limited flexibility.

As a developer, you really have only two products that you're presenting to the end user: the free version of the app and the full version of the app. The binary nature of the implementation restricts the opportunities for commerce that naturally exist within the application. For instance, in the example, suppose you created a "coolest feature" piece of functionality that you valued at an extra dollar. That would raise the cost of the application to $5.99 (based on the WindowsStoreProxy.xml file, the product presently costs $4.99). Not only might the high price point be hard to digest, but it also removes the option of the user just paying for that one feature for the dollar. With in-app purchases, you can shift the pressure of purchasing away from the app as a whole and into specific features within the app. This kills two birds with one stone. On one hand, you shift your app to the higher-traffic free side of the world, making it easier to discover. On the other hand, you continue to monetize your app, this time with finer-grained control over which pieces of the app you provide for free.

A category of app that stands out in regard to in-app purchasing is gaming. Users often stumble on free games, which they're quick to download due to the nonexistent price tag. Once engaged (*addicted* is a common term), users are more apt to pay for additional features.

Adding In-App Purchasing to an App

Let's modify the example application to use in-app purchasing. Listing 9-6 starts by slightly modifying the app's user interface.

Listing 9-6. Modified User Interface for the Trial App

```
<section aria-label="Main content" role="main">
        <input type="button" id="btn_buyapp" value="buy app" />
    </section>
    <section aria-label="Main content" role="main">
        <input type="button" id="btn_coolfeature" value="cool feature" />
    </section>
    <section aria-label="Main content" role="main">
        <input type="button" id="btn_coolerfeature" value="please wait..." />
    </section>
    <section aria-label="Main content" role="main">
        <input type="button" id="btn_coolestfeature" value="please wait..." />
    </section>
```

So far you've added a new button btn_coolestfeature and also modified the contents of btn_coolerfeature to indicate to the user that their content is loading. As you see in a moment, you do this to take advantage of one of the benefits of using in-app purchases: the fact that you can define your catalog of products outside the app. You no longer need to hard-code the names of the features you're selling; you read them directly from the Windows Store.

Chapter 10 goes into more detail about setting up your app in the store. To help with this, in-app purchasing introduces some new element types to the `WindowsStoreProxy.xml` file. Listing 9-7 updates your local copy to include all the elements necessary to represent the in-app purchasing functionality.

Listing 9-7. `WindowsStoreProxy.xml` with Product Listing Information Included

```xml
<?xml version="1.0" encoding="utf-16" ?>
<CurrentApp>
  <ListingInformation>
    <App>
      <AppId>2B14D306-D8F8-4066-A45B-0FB3464C67F2</AppId>
      <LinkUri>http://apps.microsoft.com/app/2B14D306-D8F8-4066-A45B-0FB3464C67F2</LinkUri>
      <CurrentMarket>en-us</CurrentMarket>
      <AgeRating>6</AgeRating>
      <MarketData xml:lang="en-us">
        <Name>Trial management full license</Name>
        <Description>Sample app for demonstrating trial license management</Description>
        <Price>0.00</Price>
        <CurrencySymbol>$</CurrencySymbol>
      </MarketData>
    </App>
    <Product ProductId="coolerfeature">
      <MarketData xml:lang="en-us">
        <Name>Cooler Feature</Name>
        <Price>1.99</Price>
        <CurrencySymbol>$</CurrencySymbol>
      </MarketData>
    </Product>
    <Product ProductId="coolestfeature">
      <MarketData xml:lang="en-us">
        <Name>Coolest Feature</Name>
        <Price>2.99</Price>
        <CurrencySymbol>$</CurrencySymbol>
      </MarketData>
    </Product>
  </ListingInformation>
  <LicenseInformation>
    <App>
      <IsActive>true</IsActive>
      <IsTrial>false</IsTrial>
    </App>
    <Product ProductId="coolerfeature">
      <IsActive>false</IsActive>
    </Product>
    <Product ProductId="coolestfeature">
      <IsActive>false</IsActive>
    </Product>
  </LicenseInformation>
</CurrentApp>
```

Implementing In-App Purchasing

Implementing in-app purchasing changes an application in numerous ways. In the previous approach, you let the user click the Even Cooler Feature button and then prompted them with a message that to use the feature, they would have to purchase the application. Now that you're transitioning the application to a commerce-style app, you should provide the user up front with information to help them make a purchase decision. Toward that end, you need to access product-listing information to identify the name of each feature and how much the feature costs.

Listing 9-6 modified the two target buttons to display the text Please Wait. Let's move to the next step now and populate each button with the appropriate content pulled directly from the WindowsStoreProxy.xml file. Listing 9-8 shows the modifications to the loading process that support in-app purchasing.

Listing 9-8. Loading Content from the Windows Store

```
function initializePurchaseState()
    {
        var proxy_folder = null;
        var install_location = null;
        var temp_proxy_file = null;



        Windows.Storage.ApplicationData.current.localFolder.
            createFolderAsync("Microsoft\\Windows Store\\ApiData", ↵
                Windows.Storage.CreationCollisionOption.replaceExisting)

            .then(
            function (folder)
            {
                proxy_folder = folder;

                return Windows.ApplicationModel.Package.current.installedLocation↵
                    .getFolderAsync("storeproxy");
            })

            .then(function (location)
            {
                install_location = location;
                return install_location.getFileAsync("trialmanagement.xml");
            })

            .then(function (temp)
            {
                temp_proxy_file = temp;
                return proxy_folder.createFileAsync("WindowsStoreProxy.xml",
                    Windows.Storage.CreationCollisionOption.replaceExisting);
            })

            .then(function (proxy_file)
            {
                temp_proxy_file.copyAndReplaceAsync(proxy_file);
            })
```

```
            .then(function ()
            {
                _license = Windows.ApplicationModel.Store.CurrentAppSimulator↵
                    .licenseInformation;
                return Windows.ApplicationModel.Store.CurrentAppSimulator↵
                    .loadListingInformationAsync();
            })

            .done(function (listing)
            {
                _listing_information = listing;
                loadAppUI();
            });

}

function loadAppUI()
{
    if (_listing_information.productListings["coolerfeature"] != null)
    {
        GenerateButtonUI(btn_coolerfeature, "coolerfeature");
    }

    if (_listing_information.productListings["coolestfeature"] != null)
    {
        GenerateButtonUI(btn_coolestfeature, "coolestfeature");
    }
}

function GenerateButtonUI(btn_target, feature_name)
{
    var feature = _listing_information.productListings[feature_name];
    var action_type = "Buy for " + feature.formattedPrice;

    var feature_license = _license.productLicenses[feature_name];
    if (feature_license.isActive)
    {
        action_type = "Use now";
    }

    btn_target.value = feature.name + " - " + action_type;
}
```

The first thing you do in Listing 9-8 is extend the async chain with a call to
Windows.ApplicationModel.Store.CurrentAppSimulator.loadListingInformationAsync. This call returns the listing information you need to present the feature name and price to the user. Running the application at this point results in a view like that shown in Figure 9-9.

Figure 9-9. *User interface elements populated from the Windows Store listing*

You now need to add the logic necessary to purchase or activate the respective feature when either button is clicked. Listing 9-9 shows the changes to each button's `onclick` event to enable this functionality.

Listing 9-9. Enabling In-App Commerce

```
btn_coolerfeature.onclick = function ()
        {
            var feature_license = _license.productLicenses["coolerfeature"];
            var feature_listing = _listing_information.productListings["coolerfeature"];
            if (feature_license.isActive)
            {
                var v = new Windows.UI.Popups ↵
                    .MessageDialog("Using " + feature_listing.name + "!");
                v.showAsync();
            }
            else
            {
                //buy the product
                Windows.ApplicationModel
                    .Store.CurrentAppSimulator
                    .requestProductPurchaseAsync(feature_license.productId, true)

                .then(function (receipt)
                {
                    //refresh after purchase
                    loadAppUI();
                });
            }
        };
```

```
btn_coolestfeature.onclick = function ()
{
    var feature_license = _license.productLicenses["coolestfeature"];
    var feature_listing = _listing_information.productListings["coolestfeature"];
    if (feature_license.isActive)
    {
        var v = new Windows.UI.Popups↵
            .MessageDialog("Using " + feature_listing.name + "!");
        v.showAsync();
    }
    else
    {
        //buy the product
        Windows.ApplicationModel
            .Store.CurrentAppSimulator
            .requestProductPurchaseAsync(feature_license.productId, true)

        .then(function (receipt)
        {
            //refresh after purchase
            loadAppUI();
        });
    }
};
```

The logic is simple: when the user clicks either button, you check to see if the product feature has an active license. If it does, the feature functionality is invoked. If it doesn't, a request to purchase the feature is initiated with the store. As with app purchasing, CurrentAppSimulator presents the dialog shown earlier in Figure 9-8. Once a feature is purchased, you call loadAppUI to reload the user interface. This time you shouldn't see a price tied to that particular feature, because it has been purchased and is now active. Figure 9-10 illustrates.

Figure 9-10. *App after both features have been purchased*

Figure 9-11 shows what happens when one of these buttons is clicked—in this case, the Coolest Feature button.

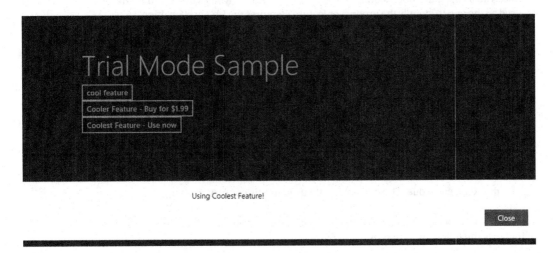

Figure 9-11. *Using a purchased feature in an app*

In-app purchasing and trial apps are powerful features to help you monetize applications, so ensuring proper functionality is critical. The last thing you want is for your app to function improperly in a purchasing scenario, considering how critical confidence in your app's stability is to the purchasing experience from a user's standpoint. Using CurrentAppSimulator in tandem with the WindowsStoreProxy.xml file is of paramount importance in testing these scenarios. The following section from the MSDN documentation (http://msdn.microsoft.com/en-us/library/windows/apps/hh779766.aspx) outlines in detail this file's various nodes. If you're interested in monetizing your app, be sure you understand how each of these nodes work:

1. ListingInformation: Represents data that would normally be found in the app's listing and includes these elements:

   a. App: Represents data about the app and contains these elements:

      i. AppId: The GUID that identifies the app in the store. This can be any GUID for testing.

      ii. LinkUri: The URI of the listing page in the store. This can be any valid URI for testing.

      iii. AgeRating: An integer that represents the minimum age rating of the app. This is the same value you would specify in the Dashboard when you submit the app. The values used by the Windows Store are: 3, 7, 12, and 16.

      iv. CurrentMarket: The customer's country/region. For each country/region in which the app is listed, there must be a MarketData element:

         1. MarketData: Info about the app for this country/region. Requires the xml:lang attribute, which specifies the country/region for which this info applies:

            a. Name: The name of the app in this country/region.

            b. Description: The description of the app for this country/region.

            c. Price: The price of the app in this country/region.

            d. CurrencySymbol: The currency symbol used in this country/region.

b.   Product: Describes a product or a feature in this app that is enabled when the customer makes an in-app purchase. Requires the ProductId attribute, which contains the string used by the app to identify the product or feature. Requires the LicenseDuration attribute, which contains the number of days the license will be valid after the purchase. The expiration date of the new license created by a product purchase is the purchase date plus the license duration:

    i.   MarketData: Info about the product or feature for this country/region. Requires the xml:lang attribute, which specifies the country/region for which this information applies:

       a.   Name: The name of the product or feature in this country/region.

       b.   Price: The price of the product or feature in this country/region.

       c.   CurrencySymbol: The currency symbol used in this country/region.

       d.   CurrencyCode: The currency code used in this country/region.

2.   LicenseInformation: Represents data that describes the licenses available for this app and includes the following elements:

a.   App: Describes the app's license:

    i.   IsActive: Describes the current license state of this app. true indicates the license is valid. Normally this value is true, whether the app has a trial mode or not. false indicates an invalid license. Set this value to false to test how your app behaves when it has an invalid license.

    ii.   IsTrial: Describes the current trial state of this app. true indicates the app is being used during the trial period. false indicates the app isn't in a trial, either because the app has been purchased or because the trial period has expired.

    iii.   ExpirationDate: The date the trial period for this app expires. The date must be express as: yyyy-mm-ddThh:mm:ss.ssZ. For example, 05:00 on January 19, 2012 is specified as 2012-01-19T05:00:00.00Z. This element is required when IsTrial is true. Otherwise, it isn't required.

    iv.   DefaultResponse: Describes the default error code returned by a given method. The MethodName attribute allows you to specify one of these methods: RequestAppPurchaseAsync_GetResult, RequestProductPurchaseAsync_GetResult, or LoadListingInformationAsync_GetResult. The HResult attribute allows you to specify the error code.

b.   Product: Describes the license status of a product or feature in the app:

    i.   IsActive: Describes the current license state of this product or feature. true indicates the product or feature can be used. false indicates the product or feature can't be used or has not been purchased.

    ii.   ExpirationDate: The date the product or feature expires. The date must be express as: yyyy-mm-ddThh:mm:ss.ssZ. For example, 05:00 on January 19, 2012 is specified as 2012-01-19T05:00:00.00Z. If this element is present, the product or feature has an expiration date. If this element isn't present, the product or feature doesn't expire.

Summary

Whether taking steps to monetize your app is a necessary evil or the icing on the cake, it's something you should know about and can benefit from in real-world app development. This chapter provided the steps to follow, as well as some useful insight to most effectively monetize your app. Key points covered in this chapter include the following:

- The Microsoft Windows Store can publish paid apps as trials, allowing you to create and maintain both a trial (free) and a full-functionality (paid) version of a single app, and to specify the conditions under which your application can be migrated from one version to the other.

- Implementing both trial and full-functionality versions of a single app is instrumental to upselling your app.

- It's important to use `CurrentAppSimulator` in tandem with the `WindowsStoreProxy.xml` file in testing scenarios.

- Monetizing your app via selling it is different than monetizing the app via selling within it.

- There are potential pros and cons to offering your app free, as a paid app, or as a paid app with a free trial option.

- Implementing in-app purchasing is a powerful methodology for monetizing the app.

■ ■ ■

Getting Your App on the Windows Store

The previous chapter dove in to monetization of your app. But you're not quite there yet. Some administrative duties await that mustn't be ignored in order for you to get your app published in the Windows Store. Pay attention: you're completing the final step toward sharing your Windows 8 app with the world.

As a developer, getting your app on the Windows Store may be the most tedious part of the journey. But rest assured that adherence to the guidelines set forth in previous chapters will make getting your app accepted for publication as seamless as possible. This chapter discusses setting up a developer account, app submission, app tracking, and app management. You learn about post-publication features including tools that provide a view of your sales data, downloads, activations, and telemetry. Hang on tight: you're almost—your app is almost—there!

Creating an App Package

Let's dive right in to the Windows Store submission process. You're familiar with the Developer Center and the developer dashboard. This is where the magic continues to happen—your portal into the Windows Store.

To create an app package, select the Create App Packages item in the Store submenu in Visual Studio 2012. If you select the option to build the app package for the Windows Store, you're prompted to sign in to the Store with your Windows Developer account, where you're directed to the Select an App Name screen. Figure 10-1 shows the Submit App menu and submenu selections in Visual Studio.

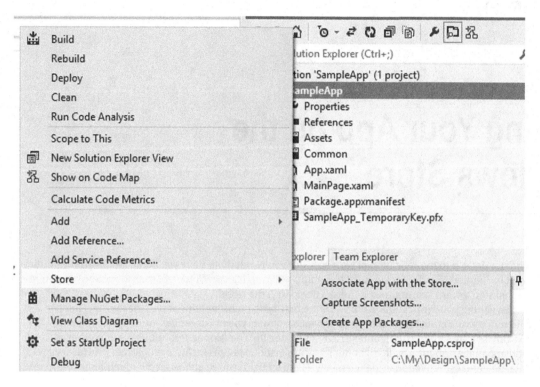

Figure 10-1. *Visual Studio Submit App drop-down menu and submenu selections*

Figure 10-2 shows the Select an App Name screen.

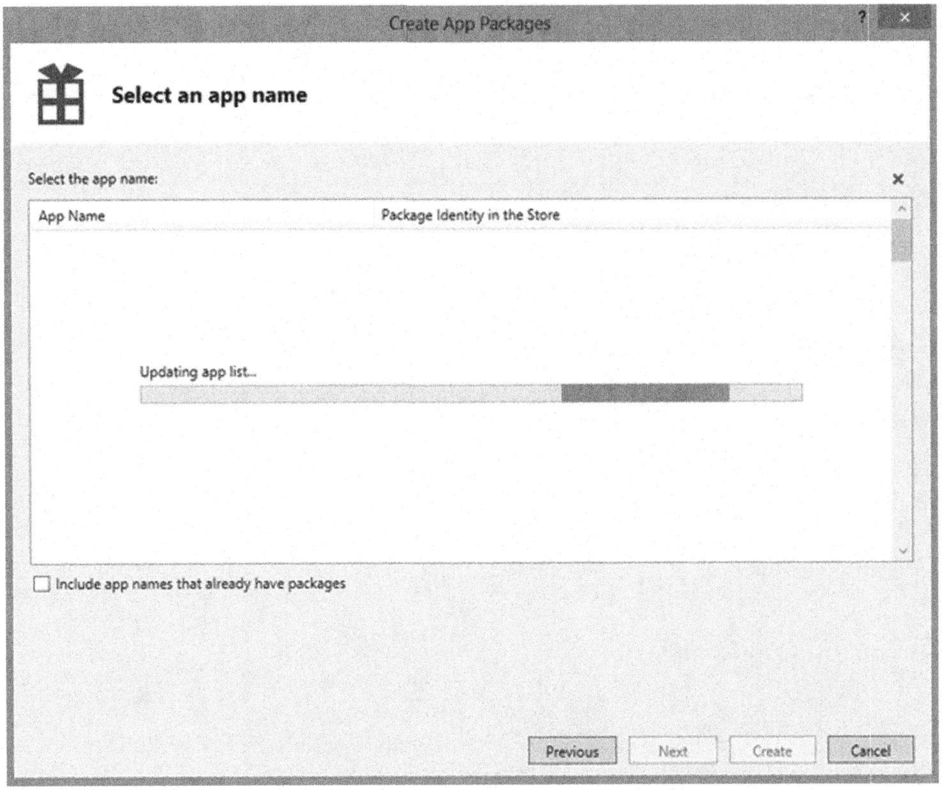

Figure 10-2. *Visual Studio Select an App Name screen*

The Windows Store app names listed in Figure 10-2 are names you must have previously registered through the Windows Store developer center. Selecting one of these names associates the project you're working on with that particular app. As of the time of this writing, you can't register app names through the Visual Studio 2012 interface. You learn more about registering app names later in this chapter; for now, let's focus on configuring your app so it's ready to publish to the Store.

If you choose not to create a Windows Store package, you don't have to sign in, but the resulting app package is installable only on developer machines or in an environment where side loading is supported. (*Side loading* is a process of installing a Windows 8 app directly on a PC, bypassing the Windows Store.) Click Next, and you're shown a package settings screen where you specify the package output location, the version number, and the build configuration (see Figure 10-3).

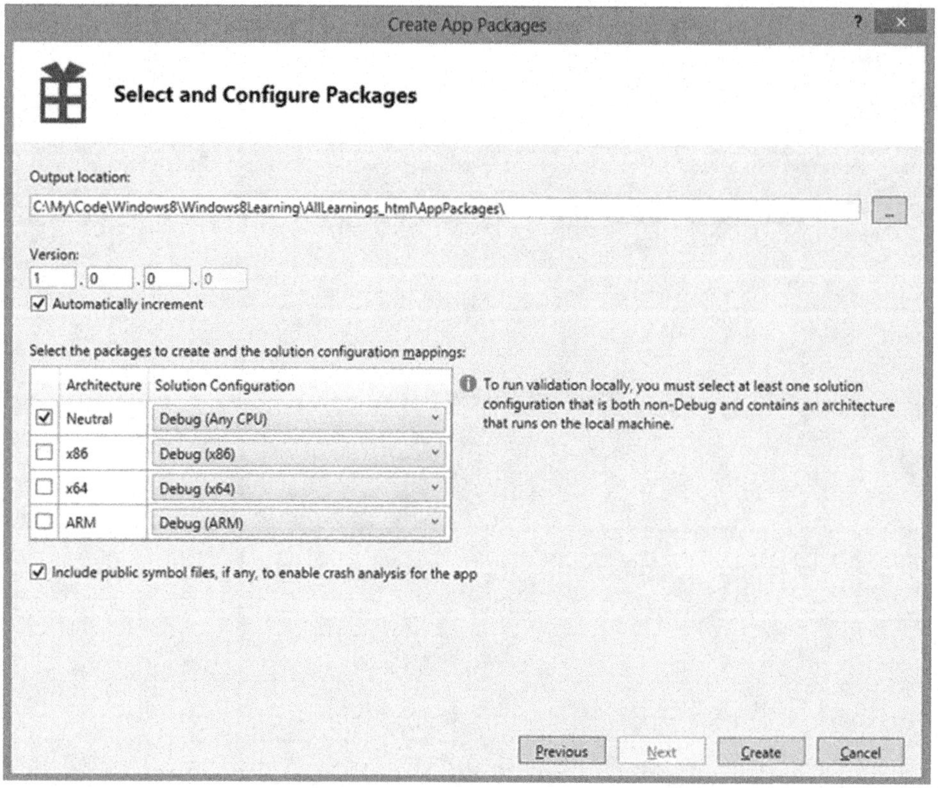

Figure 10-3. Package settings screen

App packages use the .zip-compliant APPX packaging format for Windows 8 app style guidelines. An APPX package is what is downloaded to your machine when you install an app from the Windows Store, and it's the format you use for submission to the Windows Store. APPX packages can be deployed as x86 (for 32-bit operating systems), x64 (for 64-bit Windows 8 versions), ARM (for ARM-based tablets and PCs like the Microsoft Surface and Asus VivoTab), or Neutral (a version that works on all platforms).

Once you're done configuring how you want your app package to be created, click the Create button to build the package. Visual Studio compiles your project into the appropriate executable format and packages it into an APPX (including certificates and a package manifest). At this point, the wizard is complete. It presents you with the location where you can find your created package. Figure 10-4 shows this final screen (showing the path to the All Learnings package on my machine).

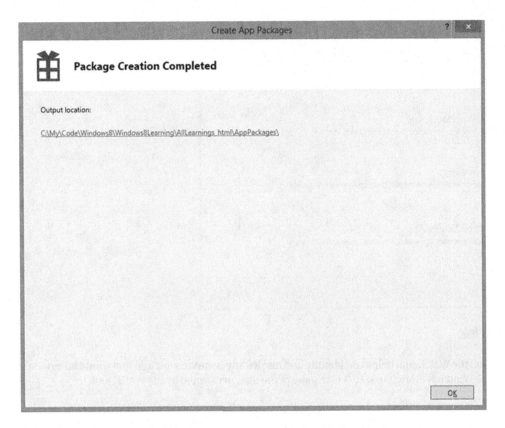

Figure 10-4. The wizard's final screen

Verifying Your App Package

In order for you to submit your app to the Windows Store, it must meet certain criteria identified by Microsoft. This ensures that apps in the Windows Store are safe for end users to install and work seamlessly on all platforms they target without exception. Microsoft expects your apps to utilize a standardized API surface area that is approved for use and to follow design, style, and content guidelines that match the theme of the Windows Store. Validating the content and style components requires human input; but as part of the app-submission process, the Windows Store automatically inspects the app package to determine which APIs and programming patterns you used. If the package doesn't meet the necessary requirements, it isn't accepted, and you can't continue the submission process.

Microsoft provides a useful certification tool called the Windows App Certification Kit (WACK) that runs your app locally and performs a series of tests designed to find common and easily detected app certification failures. To launch it, simply use the Search charm and enter its name. Figure 10-5 shows the WACK interface (pun intended).

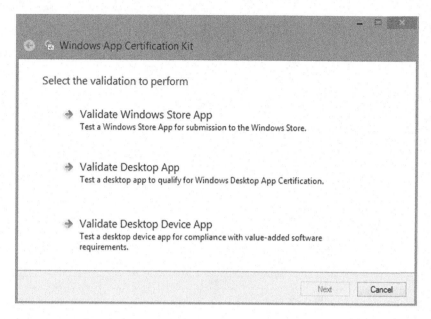

Figure 10-5. *WACK interface*

As you might imagine, the WACK tool helps you identify and resolve any issues in your app that would otherwise prevent submission to the Windows Store. Table 10-1 lists some of the tests performed by the WACK tool.

Table 10-1. *WACK App Tests*

Test	Description
Adherence to system restart messages	Tests whether your application exits as quickly as possible when notified of a system shutdown.
App manifest policy	Tests the contents of the app manifest to ensure that it's correct and formatted properly.
App manifest resources	Tests the resources defined in the app manifest to make sure they're present and valid. This includes having the appropriate images/strings to present the application in its various states.
Clean reversible install	Ensures that the app installs and uninstalls properly with no residual files or registry entries.
Compatibility and resiliency	Verifies that the app doesn't use any Windows compatibility fixes.
Crashes and hangs	Checks the app for crashes or hang-ups by performing startup, run, and shutdown processes.
Debug configuration	Confirms that the app package was built with the release configuration.
Digital signed file	Verifies a valid digital signature.
Direct 3d feature level	Tests Microsoft Direct3D apps to ensure that they work on all Windows 8 graphics hardware.

(continued)

Table 10-1. (*continued*)

Test	Description
File encoding	Confirms that all files are encoded as UTF-8.
Installation and writing to the correct folder	Ensures that the apps writes program and data files to the correct folders.
Performance	Confirms performance speed by timing app launch and suspension.
Support for Windows 8 Store API	Confirms use of Windows 8–style supported APIs.
Windows security features	Confirms no tampering with default Windows security protections.

The WACK test runs either in the background or in a small application window, depending on how you launched the tool. You'll see your app appear and disappear several times over the few minutes WACK takes to run the complete set of tests. Whatever you do, don't attempt to interact with your app during the test, or your computer may overheat and explode. Well not quite, but your app will close and you will not be allowed to interact with it. Once the WACK tool completes its tests, a results screen appears. If the test fails, the WACK tool report relays the reasons for the fail. If the WACK test passes, you can either head right to the Windows Store to continue your app submission, or look at the detailed report linked from the results window.

Submitting Your App

You ended the previous section with a verified app that you're sure can be submitted to the App Store without issue. You're sure of this because before attempting to submit it, you used the WACK tool to verify that the app meets the minimum criteria necessary to be allowed in the Windows Store. This section covers using the developer dashboard to upload this verified app package to the Windows Store and completing the process by submitting your application for certification by the Store.

You can access the Windows Store Dev Center by navigating to http://msdn.microsoft.com/en-US/windows/apps. Once there, you sign in with your Windows Store account (typically a Hotmail/live/outlook.com e-mail address). Figure 10-6 shows the Dev Center landing page.

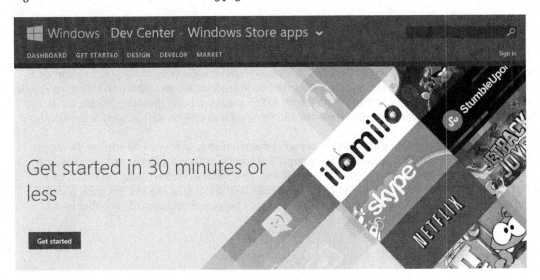

Figure 10-6. *Dev Center landing page*

Nothing you've done so far requires you to sign up for anything, but you need a developer account to reserve app names and submit applications to the Windows Store. You can begin the signup process at the following website: http://msdn.microsoft.com/en-us/library/windows/apps/jj193592.aspx.

Once you're signed up and signed in, clicking the Dashboard link (shown in Figure 10-6) takes you into your Windows Store dashboard for Windows 8 apps. Figure 10-7 shows the Windows Store dashboard. The sign-in name (which would typically appear in the upper-right corner of the screen) and the app list have been hidden for privacy reasons.

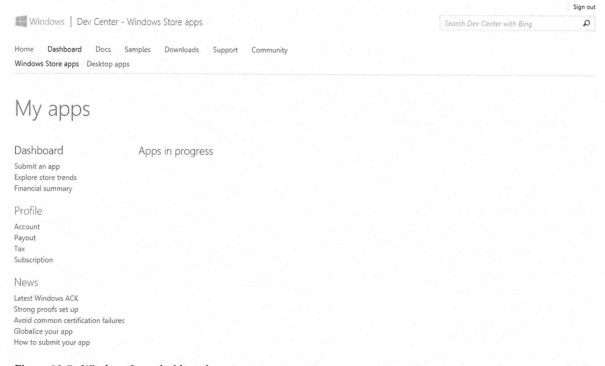

Figure 10-7. *Windows Store dashboard*

The primary means of submitting an app to the Windows Store is through the Submit an App link in the Dev Center dashboard. Clicking this link puts you in a workflow that takes you all the way from giving your application a name to providing a detailed description for it. As part of the submission process, you must also provide selling details for your application—tying in everything you learned in Chapter 9. This means not only providing pricing for the app as a whole but also providing pricing for features that exist within the app (in-app offers are included in the Advanced Features step of the process).

You also need to provide content rating information as part of the submission process. This ensures that apps published to the Store can be targeted to appropriate age groups. You specify any cryptography your app uses, and you go through a step where you upload your app to the Store. If your app has been verified using the WACK tool, then this should be a formality; otherwise it may turn out to be an extremely frustrating process, given the added upload time due to running the tool. (Note that app certification doesn't happen during upload but rather is run before anything else as part of the overall submission.)

The final step, providing your app description, may seem trivial, but it will most likely be the most engaging part of the processes (particularly if you don't have a graphic designer and well-defined iconography in place). In this step you must not only provide a textual description for your application but also include various screenshots of your running app, promotional images of varying resolutions, a privacy policy URL, e-mail address, and many more details. Figure 10-8 shows the Submit an App screen.

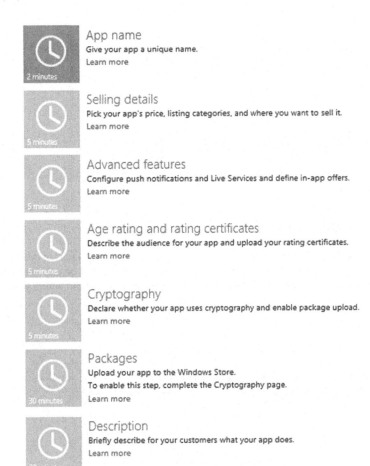

Figure 10-8. *App submission screen*

Naming Your App

The submission workflow starts with naming your app. As with web domains, app names are first-come, first-served. Luckily, in the world of apps, the real estate is prime for buying—in stark contrast to web domains these days.

When you click the App Name icon or link, you're taken to a simple screen with a single input box in which to enter the name of your app (see Figure 10-9). Enter the name of your choosing, and click Reserve App Name. If the name isn't available, you're presented with an error message.

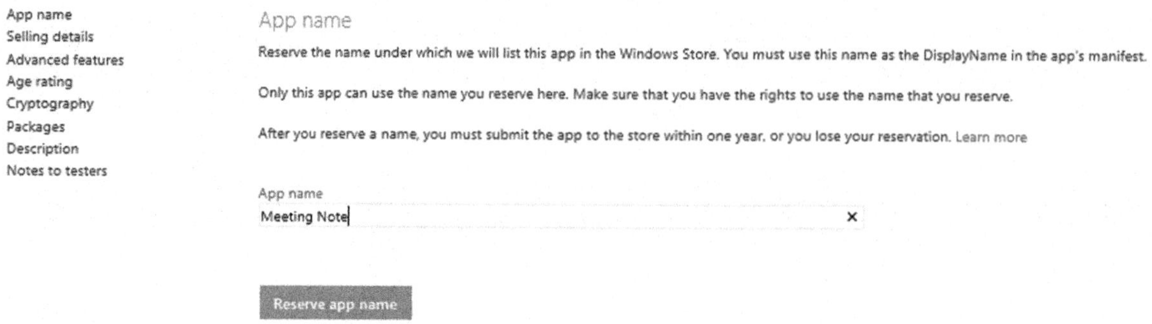

Figure 10-9. *Reserving an app name*

Once the selected name is reserved, you have a one-year deadline during which to submit your app. After that, the name goes back into the pool.

Selling Details

You're now directed to the Selling Details screen. Figure 10-10 shows the top part of the page, where you can choose whether you're listing your app as free or paid or using variety pricing based on app features/version, as discussed in depth in Chapter 9. You also provide free-trial details and information about where you want to sell your app.

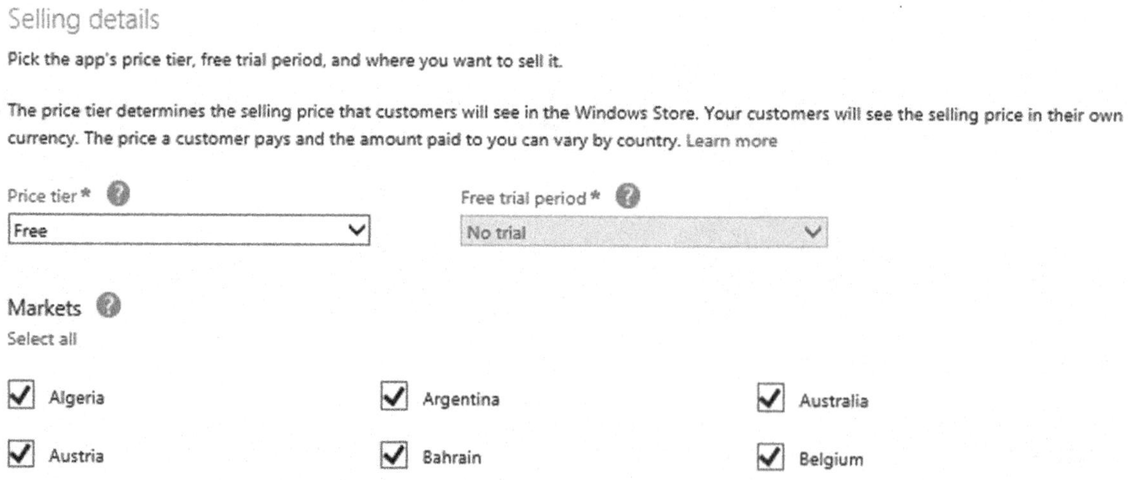

Figure 10-10. *Upper portion of the Selling Details screen*

Figure 10-11 shows the bottom part of the Selling Details screen. Here you indicate when your app is to be released. You're required to provide an app category and subcategory, and you also specify any hardware requirements and accessibility features.

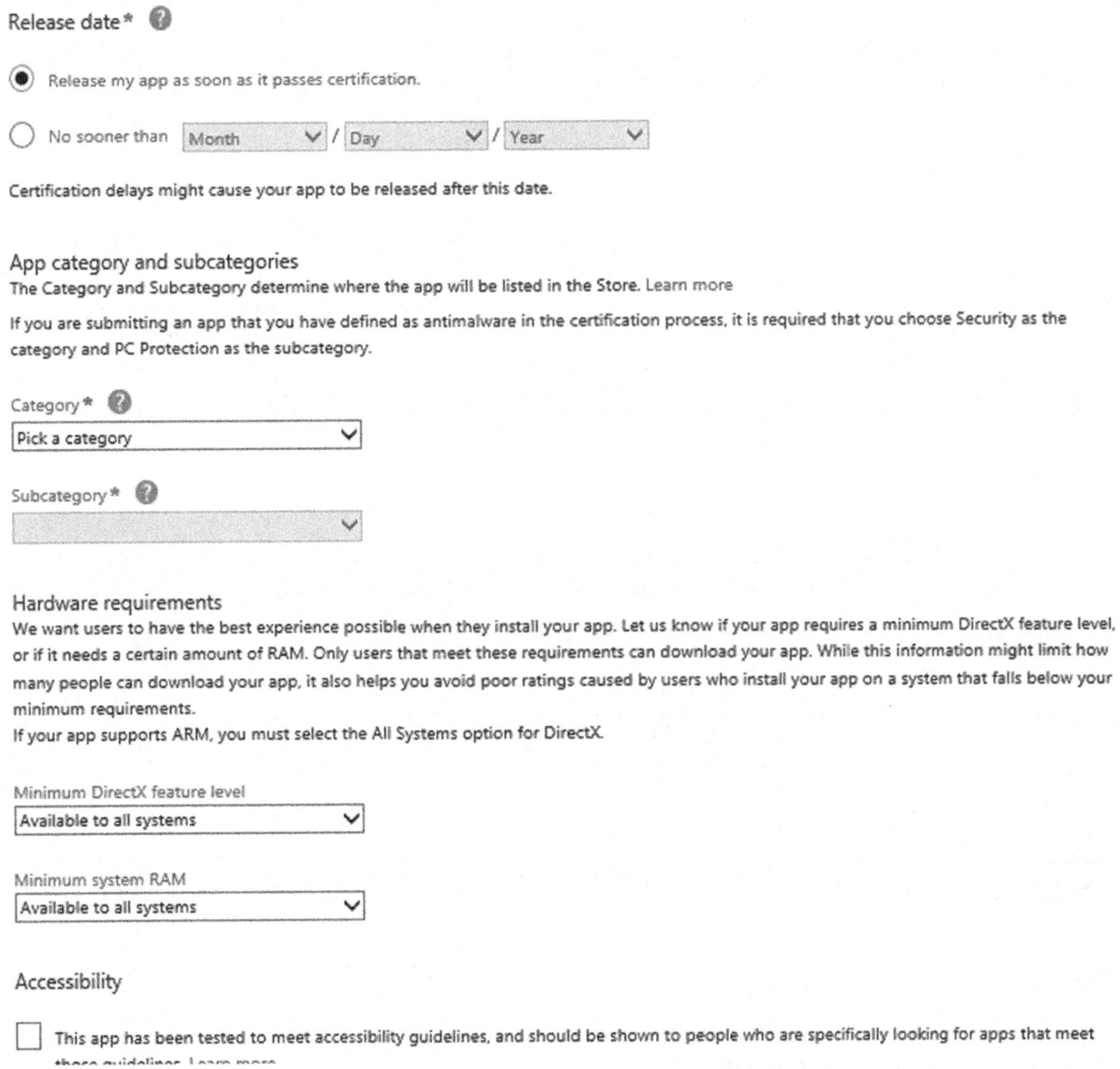

Release date* ❓

⦿ Release my app as soon as it passes certification.

◯ No sooner than [Month ⌄] / [Day ⌄] / [Year ⌄]

Certification delays might cause your app to be released after this date.

App category and subcategories
The Category and Subcategory determine where the app will be listed in the Store. Learn more

If you are submitting an app that you have defined as antimalware in the certification process, it is required that you choose Security as the category and PC Protection as the subcategory.

Category* ❓
[Pick a category ⌄]

Subcategory* ❓
[⌄]

Hardware requirements
We want users to have the best experience possible when they install your app. Let us know if your app requires a minimum DirectX feature level, or if it needs a certain amount of RAM. Only users that meet these requirements can download your app. While this information might limit how many people can download your app, it also helps you avoid poor ratings caused by users who install your app on a system that falls below your minimum requirements.
If your app supports ARM, you must select the All Systems option for DirectX.

Minimum DirectX feature level
[Available to all systems ⌄]

Minimum system RAM
[Available to all systems ⌄]

Accessibility

☐ This app has been tested to meet accessibility guidelines, and should be shown to people who are specifically looking for apps that meet these guidelines. Learn more

Figure 10-11. *Lower part of the Selling Details screen*

Advanced Features

Next you're prompted to specify any advanced features your app provides. These include push notifications for background tile updates, Live Connect services, and any in-app offers that will be offered through your Windows 8 app. If you've added products to your application (products are part of the in-app purchase functionality discussed in the previous chapter), you can specify these additions here; they let you offer pieces of functionality that the user can purchase while using your application. Figure 10-12 shows the Advanced Features screen from the Windows Store developer dashboard.

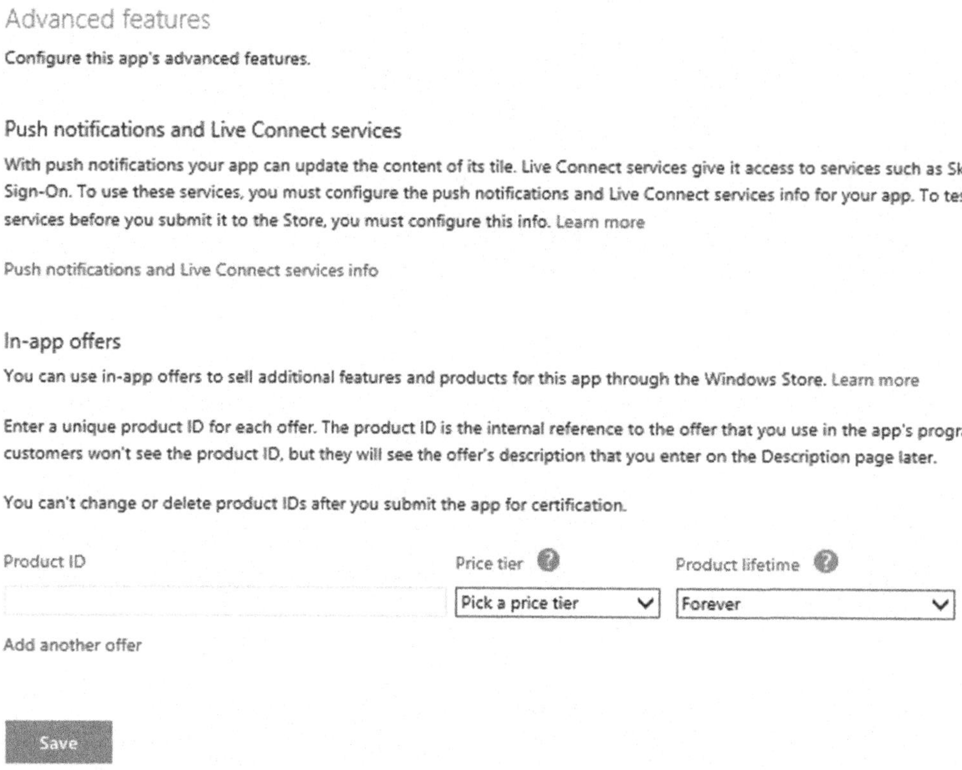

Advanced features

Configure this app's advanced features.

Push notifications and Live Connect services

With push notifications your app can update the content of its tile. Live Connect services give it access to services such as SkyDrive and Single Sign-On. To use these services, you must configure the push notifications and Live Connect services info for your app. To test your app with these services before you submit it to the Store, you must configure this info. Learn more

Push notifications and Live Connect services info

In-app offers

You can use in-app offers to sell additional features and products for this app through the Windows Store. Learn more

Enter a unique product ID for each offer. The product ID is the internal reference to the offer that you use in the app's program code. Your customers won't see the product ID, but they will see the offer's description that you enter on the Description page later.

You can't change or delete product IDs after you submit the app for certification.

Product ID   Price tier ?   Product lifetime ?

                                     Pick a price tier   ∨   Forever   ∨

Add another offer

Save

Figure 10-12. *Advanced Features screen*

Age Rating and Rating Certificates

Next you need to select an age rating for your app from among the choices listed in Table 10-2. These ratings are required for games. However, even if you app isn't a game, if contains adult content, it's best to stay on the cautious or conservative side and provide a rating. Doing so will help to ensure that you don't fail certification simply because of its absence. If you aren't sure how to rate the content you provide, I recommend using the highest age rating that makes sense for the provided content. (Again, it's beneficial to be conservative.)

Table 10-2. *Windows Store App Ratings*

Rating	Description
3+ Suitable for Young Children	These applications are considered appropriate for young children. There may be minimal comic violence in nonrealistic, cartoon form. Characters should not resemble or be associated with real-life characters. There should be no content that could be frightening, and there should be no nudity or references to sexual or criminal activity. Apps with this age rating also can't enable features that could access content or functionality unsuitable for young children. This includes, but is not limited to, access to online services, collection of personal information, or activating hardware such as microphones or webcams.
7+ Suitable for Ages 7 and Older	Apps with this age rating have the same criteria as the 3+ applications, except these apps can include content that might frighten a younger audience and can contain partial nudity, as long as the nudity doesn't refer to sexual activity.
12+ Suitable for Ages 12 and Older	Choose this rating if you aren't sure which age rating to select for your app. Apps with this age rating can contain increased nudity of a nonsexual nature, slightly graphic violence toward nonrealistic characters, or non-graphic violence toward realistic human or animal characters. This age rating might also include profanity, but not of a sexual nature. Also, apps with this age rating may include access to online services and enable features such as microphones and webcams.
16+ Suitable for Ages 16 and Older	Apps with this age rating can depict realistic violence with minimal blood, and they can depict sexual activity. They can also contain drug or tobacco use and criminal activities, and more profanity than would be allowed in a 12+ app, within the limits laid out in the certification requirements.
18+ Suitable for Adults Only.	Apps with this age rating may contain intense, gross, or specific violence, and blood or gore that is only appropriate for an adult audience, in addition to content that is appropriate for a 16+ app.

Also note that there are varying age requirements for things like gaming, online access, and online interaction that may not be immediately evident to you (and may vary by country). For instance, even though social-networking apps are inherently benign, they require higher ratings in general because there is no way to fully control the content that users ultimately view. If you're building such an application, it's important to present warnings that explicitly prohibit children if there is a potential for interactions between adults and minors. Having a higher rating allows parents and guardians to restrict access to such apps.

Provided your app is a game or, based on discretion, requires a rating, the next step is to submit and save your rating. The submitted app's content is evaluated against the rating you give it during the certification process. For Windows 8 apps classified as games, a rating board is presented in which there is a certificate for every geographic market in which the app is listed. Based on these geographic markets—specifically, Brazil, Korea, South Africa, and Taiwan—the listed certificates must be obtained should you plan to make the gaming app available worldwide. Naturally, you have the option to forego sales in certain markets, should obtaining the certificates prove problematic.

Cryptography

If your app uses any form of data-file encryption, uses a public key infrastructure, uses secure communication channels, or works with platform DRM features, you're asked to answer a set of questions and to verify that your use of encryption is limited to common cases like passwords, copy protection, digital signatures, or DRM. Figure 10-13 shows this page.

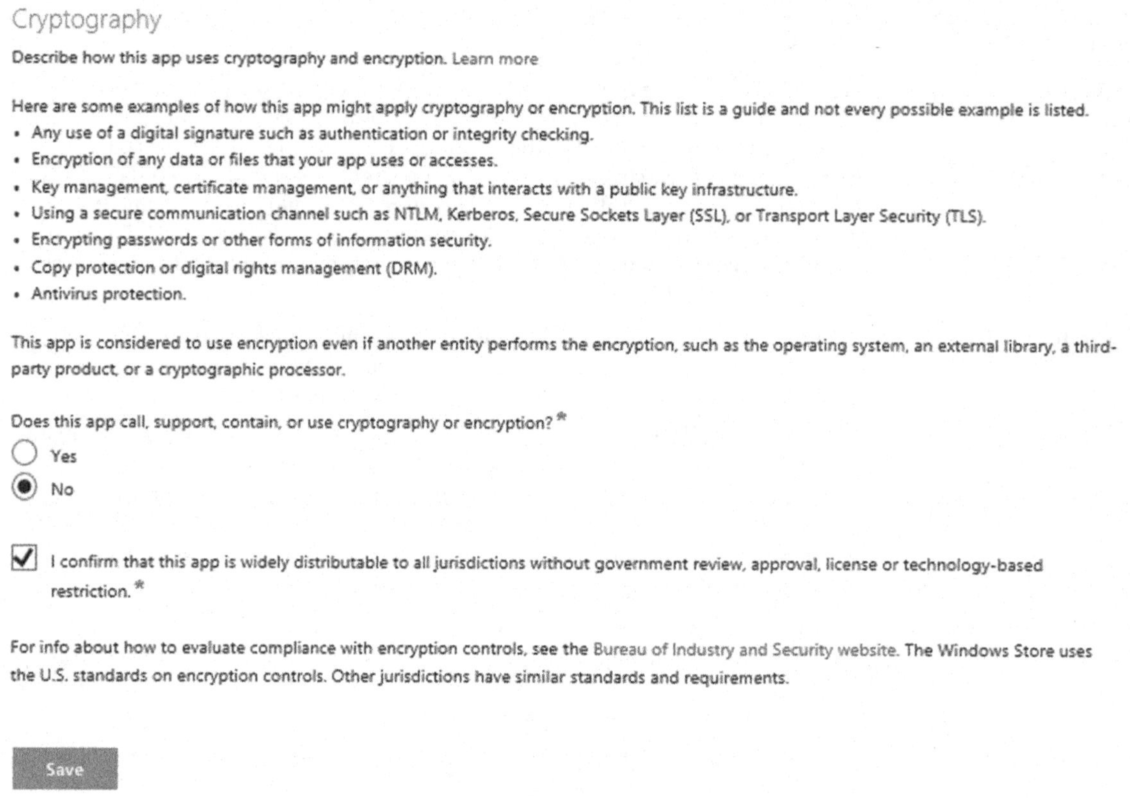

Cryptography

Describe how this app uses cryptography and encryption. Learn more

Here are some examples of how this app might apply cryptography or encryption. This list is a guide and not every possible example is listed.

- Any use of a digital signature such as authentication or integrity checking.
- Encryption of any data or files that your app uses or accesses.
- Key management, certificate management, or anything that interacts with a public key infrastructure.
- Using a secure communication channel such as NTLM, Kerberos, Secure Sockets Layer (SSL), or Transport Layer Security (TLS).
- Encrypting passwords or other forms of information security.
- Copy protection or digital rights management (DRM).
- Antivirus protection.

This app is considered to use encryption even if another entity performs the encryption, such as the operating system, an external library, a third-party product, or a cryptographic processor.

Does this app call, support, contain, or use cryptography or encryption? *

○ Yes

◉ No

☑ I confirm that this app is widely distributable to all jurisdictions without government review, approval, license or technology-based restriction. *

For info about how to evaluate compliance with encryption controls, see the Bureau of Industry and Security website. The Windows Store uses the U.S. standards on encryption controls. Other jurisdictions have similar standards and requirements.

    Save

Figure 10-13. *Cryptography screen*

If the app's encryption extends beyond these common cases, you must obtain, enter, and save an export commodity classification number from the US Department of Commerce. (Information on this process can be found at http://export.gov/logistics/eg_main_018803.asp.)

Uploading Your App

You've reached the step at which you're actually ready to upload your package. First you need to recover your package in Visual Studio. Open your app package's folder to find the file system to which it was saved. You can find the file using a File dialog, or you can drag and drop the APPX upload file for your current version into the drop zone on the Packages page (see Figure 10-14). To ensure that all the needed files and resources are included in the package, the system performs a validation, which completes with an error or a success message.

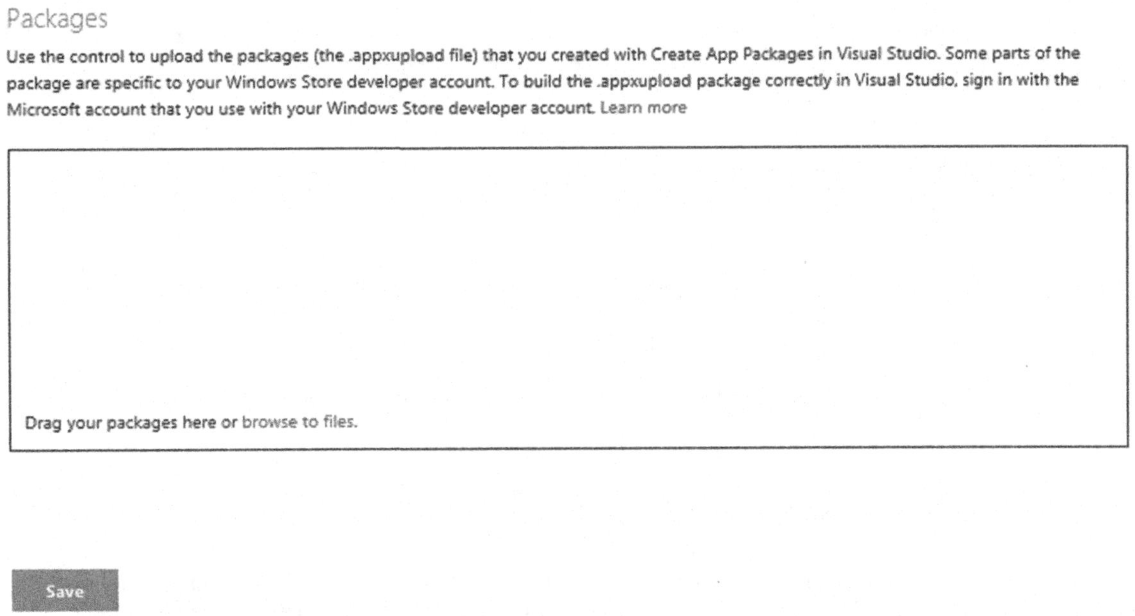

Packages

Use the control to upload the packages (the .appxupload file) that you created with Create App Packages in Visual Studio. Some parts of the package are specific to your Windows Store developer account. To build the .appxupload package correctly in Visual Studio, sign in with the Microsoft account that you use with your Windows Store developer account. Learn more

Drag your packages here or browse to files.

Save

Figure 10-14. *Packages screen*

Description

Now for the fun part. Take a little pride in your hard work by entering a description of your app on the Description page. You're also prompted to enter the app's features, keywords, and screenshots, accompanied by brief descriptions. This is the same information that will be visible to potential users as well as approvers, so the content should be accurate, concise, and compelling. Figure 10-15 shows the top part of the Description page, where you provide the description and application features.

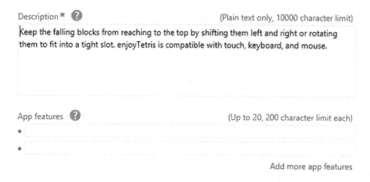

Figure 10-15. *Top part of the Description page*

All apps must provide at least one, and as many as eight, screenshots. You may choose to use the Windows 8 Simulator, which will also store the images in your `Pictures` library folder, by opening your app in Visual Studio and using the Capture Screenshots item. Figure 10-16 shows this section of the Description page.

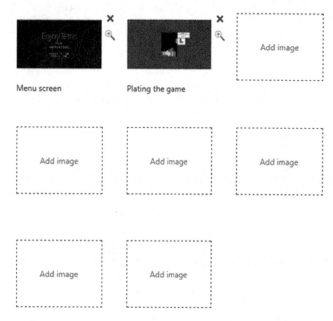

Figure 10-16. *The screenshots section of the Description page*

The next part of the Description page allows you to provide search keywords as well as extra information like the app's license terms, copyright information, and required or recommended hardware. If at some point you go back and edit your app submission (for instance, if you have a new version), you're required to include a separate description of the update. The hardware field is where you specify whether your app requires the existence of sensors or devices in order to operate. Figure 10-17 shows this section of the Description page.

Required

Description of update * ②   (1500 character limit)

Example: "In this update, we added features and fixed bugs."

Recommended hardware ②   (Up to 11, 200 character limit each)

•

•

Add recommended hardware bullet points

Keywords ②   (45 character limit)

tetris   games

arcade   touch

Copyright and trademark info * ②   (200 character limit)

Copyright © 2012, Xochi LLC

Additional license terms ②   (10000 character limit)

Example: "You can't reverse-engineer this software."

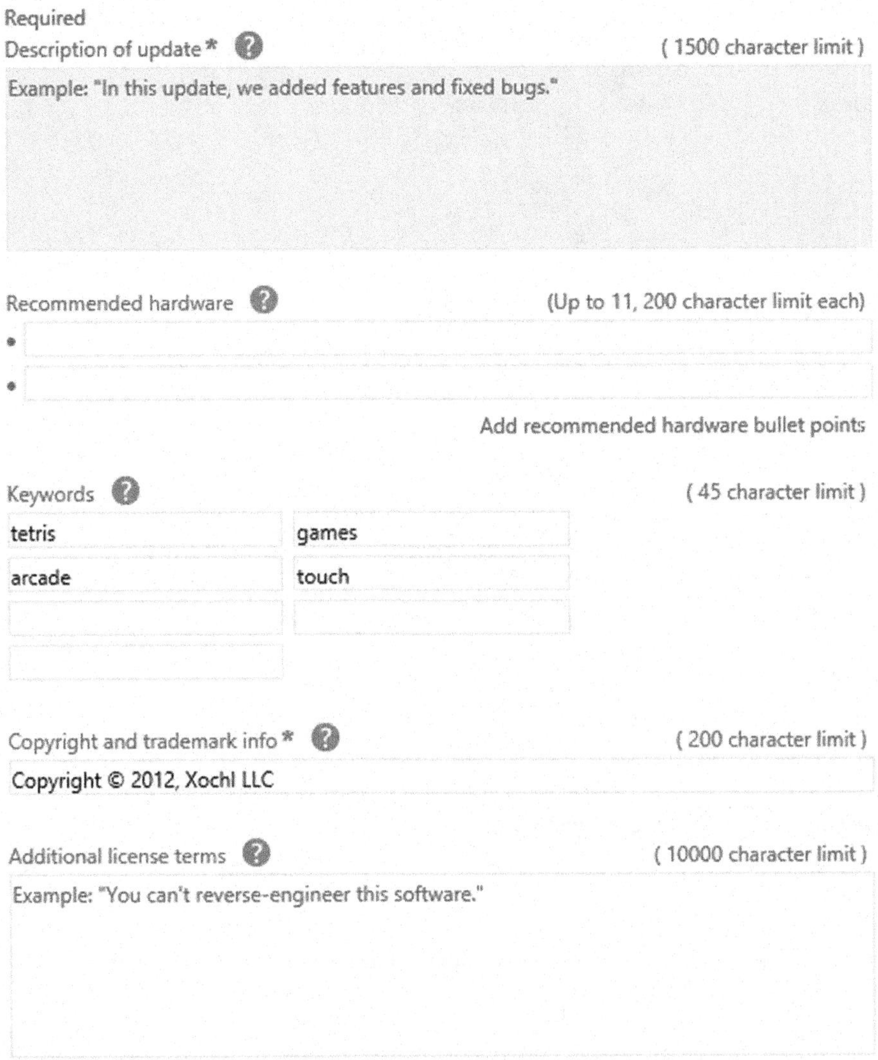

Figure 10-17. Extra description information on the Description page

Finally, you're allowed to upload promotional images for your app. These include any images to be used for the purposes of marketing in the App Store. You can enter the website associated with your app or company, if you have one. You can also provide all those final yet important details, including a support contact address and URL and the link to your online privacy statement. See Figure 10-18.

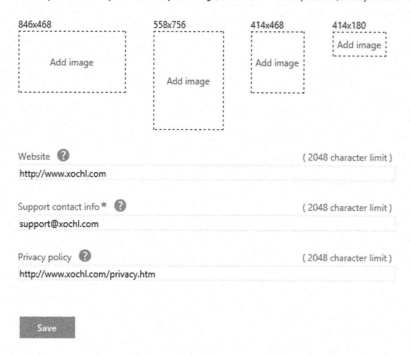

Figure 10-18. *The Promotional Images section of the Description page*

Notes to Testers

The next and final screen, shown in Figure 10-19, lets you to enter any other information you choose to make available to the testers. Note that this is the place to enter login test credentials.

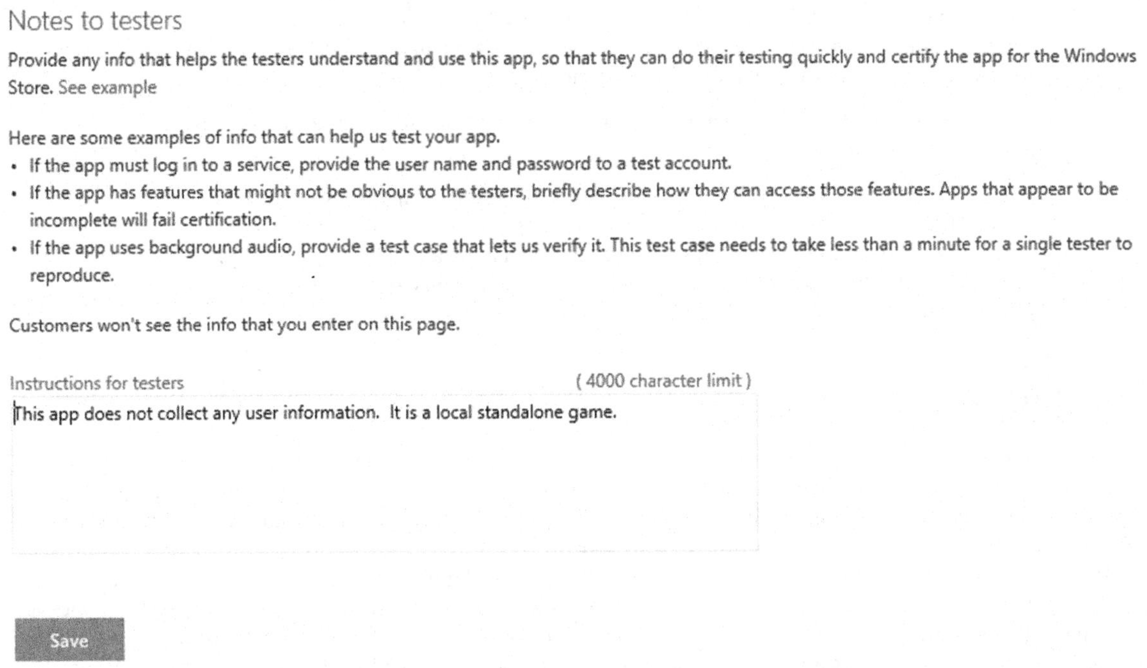

Notes to testers

Provide any info that helps the testers understand and use this app, so that they can do their testing quickly and certify the app for the Windows Store. See example

Here are some examples of info that can help us test your app.

- If the app must log in to a service, provide the user name and password to a test account.
- If the app has features that might not be obvious to the testers, briefly describe how they can access those features. Apps that appear to be incomplete will fail certification.
- If the app uses background audio, provide a test case that lets us verify it. This test case needs to take less than a minute for a single tester to reproduce.

Customers won't see the info that you enter on this page.

Instructions for testers   (4000 character limit)

This app does not collect any user information. It is a local standalone game.

Save

Figure 10-19. *Notes to Testers screen*

Getting Your App Certified

Now comes the easiest—or hardest, depending on how you look at it—part: monitoring your dashboard as you wait for certification, and subsequent publication, of your app. Following submission, you'll receive a confirmation e-mail from the Windows Store team so you know it wasn't all just a dream. This e-mail also provides the link to your dashboard for tracking the app's progression through the approval process.

This process entails six steps and gives you an estimated wait time of six days. If at any point a test results in a fail, you're be notified through your dashboard and via e-mail and are allowed to resubmit when you've addressed the error:

1. The submitted app is run through a series of automated tests.

2. The app proceeds to security testing. (Everyone appreciates downloading secure apps to their Windows 8 devices, after all.)

3. The app is put through a technical compliance test, which, if you had no problems running the WACK tool, should be smooth sailing, because Microsoft is running the WACK tool on its own servers. This completes the automated testing of the app.

4. Your humble creation is sent to an actual tester (what a fun job!) for compatibility testing. Your dashboard provides an estimate in terms of days, but because this is the most subjective stage of the approvals, there can be some variance in this estimation. Once it passes this step, your app is ready to be published.

5. The app receives digital signage and proceeds to the Windows Store servers and on to release in the Windows Store!

6. But, ugh, there is still a potential for post-publication failure during what's called the Manual Content Compliance test. In this environment, your app is tested for bugs, security, and appropriateness. You'll receive an e-mail if the app fails this final step, directing you to the report detailing the fail reasons and actions to resolve in the Dev Center.

Updating Your App

Hopefully, your app will do so well that, as technology advances, so will the need for updated app features. Rest assured, dear reader, you will receive feedback from your faithful users—perhaps more than you bargained for! This user feedback can provide valuable insight into usability issues, what works and doesn't work for your users, and what may be lacking in the current version of your app.

When development is complete on your updated version, you will find that the Store update process is a pared-down version of the initial submission process. The Windows Store requires submission of a new app package, and app updates go through the same six-step verification process. You can run the WACK tool again for your own local test. Fortunately, submitting and gaining approval for an updated app version should prove simpler as far as adhering to style guidelines, a reduced risk of bugs, and other potential issues.

Here's a quick checklist of things to do and remember:

- Click the Update button to initiate a new update on the app page.

- Before submitting a new version 2.0, remember to create the new version number in the Create App Package Wizard.

- Grab your updated app package, and head back to the dashboard.

- Before submitting for certification, I recommend providing a brief description of the changes or added features. The update page looks similar to the submission page for a new app, except that most of the information is already provided.

- If you need to update any of the information about your app, from its features or licensing terms to screenshots or in-app purchase offers, you can revisit the relevant sections and update the information accordingly. Otherwise you can head right to the Upload Package step and upload the latest version of your app. Once the upload is complete, go to the Details step to complete the Description of Update field, which is required.

Summary

A big congratulations! You made it not only through the book, but through the final fulfilling step of getting your Windows 8 app into the Windows App Store. From reading this chapter, you know that the steps in the process are straightforward and simple; yet you probably can also ascertain that this may be a tense experience that may result in a lot of debugging or error fixes. But once you've made it to this step, don't give up or get frustrated. If anything, take a break from your code and revisit it with fresh eyes. Now, here's a brief review of the key points covered in this chapter:

- Reserving a name for your app. This name is reserved for a year, during which you can get your app published under this name. After that, the name is redistributed into the pool.

- Submitting your app and the tools you use in the Windows Store submission process, including the Create App Package Wizard, the Dev Center, and your developer dashboard.

- A certification tool called the Windows App Certification Kit (WACK) tool, which you can use to test your app.

- The certification process, including automated testing, human testing, and Manual Content Compliance testing.

- Creating updates to your app by release new versions. This is an important aspect of keeping your app relevant, keeping your users satisfied, and maintaining an app that is at the forefront of technological advancement.

Index